Presented to:

_____

From:

_____

Message:

_____
_____
_____

Amazing Stories for Young Believers

Originally published under the title *Living Great for God*

Copyright © 2018 by Christian Art Kids,
an imprint of Christian Art Publishers
PO Box 1599, Vereeniging, 1930, RSA

359 Longview Drive,
Bloomingdale, IL, 60108, USA

First edition 2018

Cover designed by Christian Art Kids

Scripture quotations are taken from the *Holy Bible*, New International Version®
NIV®. Copyright © 1973, 1978, 1984, 2011 by International Bible Society.
Used by permission of Biblica, Inc.® All rights reserved worldwide.

Set in 11 on 14 pt Myriad Pro
by Christian Art Kids

Printed in China

ISBN 978-1-4321-2885-2

21 22 23 24 25 26 27 28 29 30 – 16 15 14 13 12 11 10 9 8 7

Printed in Shenzhen, China
DECEMBER 2021
Print Run: PUR402070

AMAZING STORIES FOR YOUNG believers

DAVE STREHLER

Dedicated to my
two eldest grandchildren
Levi & Keira.
May this book be a blessing to you
as you grow in your faith
and love for the Lord.

Introduction

Have you thought of what you'd like to be one day? Maybe you've dreamed of being someone great – someone who serves the living God with honor.

As you read this book, you will notice that the Bible characters God used were just ordinary people until He touched their lives in a special way. Some are remembered for their obedience and faith – while others may be remembered more for the wrong choices they made. None of these men and women were perfect, yet God was able to work through each person in a different way to do what He had planned. As you read about their faithfulness (and failures), you can learn valuable lessons from their lives and apply it to your own.

God has a special plan for your life too! You don't have to be perfect for God to use you and you don't even have to wait until you're older. If you allow God to use you in small ways, He will prepare you and use you for great things!

This book was written to help you understand the Bible. So read it with your Bible – and not instead of it! Ask God every day to help you understand and live out the exciting truths of His Word.

God bless you as you spend time with Him!

~ Dave Strehler

January

ADAM

In the beginning

It was the sixth day of creation. Adam the first man on earth, found himself surrounded by a beautiful garden called Eden. Up above, the sun shone with a warm glow. Around him were all kinds of trees and flowers and shrubs. There were many kinds of animals too, and all of them were tame. There were birds, furry animals, climbing animals and creeping insects. God brought all the creatures He had created to Adam, and whatever name Adam decided on, that was its name.

Meanwhile, the Lord noticed that Adam had no one like himself to talk to. Although Adam was made in the image of God and could talk to God, Adam was human and had no one to be his close friend and helper.

What makes me so special?

Isn't it wonderful to realize that of all the thousands of creatures God created, only Adam was made in His image? God placed a spirit inside Adam so that he could talk to God, be creative (like thinking up all sorts of names), love, and feel the need to be loved.

When God made you He also placed a spirit inside you – a part of you that will live for ever and ever. "He has made everything beautiful in its time. He has also set eternity in the hearts of men" (Ecclesiastes 3:11). You are part of God's beautiful creation. God took as much care to form you as He did when He created Adam (Psalm 139:13).

God has made you with a special purpose: to know Him and to bring Him pleasure. Whenever you pray, your spirit reaches out to the Lord, which makes Him very happy. Other creatures cannot do that because *they* don't have a spirit. That's what makes you so special!

VERSE FOR TODAY

In the beginning God created the heavens and the earth.
GENESIS 1:1

Genesis 2:9, 15-17

ADAM

The one in the middle

There were many trees in the Garden of Eden and Adam had lots of delicious fruit to choose from. He was allowed to eat and grow whatever he wanted. Of all the many fruit trees, there was only one – right in the middle of the garden – from which God told him not to eat.

The tree in the middle of the garden would allow Adam to know the difference between good and evil, and that meant he would be able to sin. The Lord told Adam that if he ate of the fruit, he would die.

Why can't I have everything I want?

Imagine being left alone in a room of colorful boxes filled with every imaginable treat. You are allowed to enjoy anything from the many boxes, except one box – a black box in the middle of the room – that you may not open.

Would you ignore the black box and be happy to enjoy the things in the colorful boxes? Or would you move closer and closer to the black box, lift the lid slightly and take a peep?

The world is filled with many good things for us to enjoy and fun things to do. Yet sometimes we become bored and unhappy with the good things God allows us to have. Do you sometimes feel like being naughty just to see what will happen? Of the thousands of good words you know, do you sometimes find yourself saying a bad word?

God knows that there are things that will harm us, and things we may do that will hurt others. He cares about us, and so He clearly shows us in the Bible what we should and shouldn't do.

VERSE FOR TODAY

Every good and perfect gift is from above, coming down from the Father of the heavenly lights, who does not change like shifting shadows.

JAMES 1:17

ADAM

Someone like me

Although the day had not yet ended, Adam suddenly became sleepy. Could it be that he was exhausted from thinking of different names for all the creatures? No, God was putting him to sleep! In fact, God made Adam sleep so well that he didn't feel God taking out one of his ribs and closing him up again.

Then God formed a woman from the rib and brought her to Adam. When he woke up from his deep sleep, he couldn't believe his eyes! "At last, someone who is like me!" he exclaimed.

Now Adam had a companion – a very special person to talk to and be with all day long.

Does God know when I am lonely?

If you have ever been lonely, you will know what Adam must have felt like before God made Eve to be his friend and wife.

The beginning of a new year often brings changes. You may have recently moved to another town, started in a new school, or moved to a class without your best friends. It is often a time of loneliness; a time of being afraid and unsure of what to expect.

Remember that God will always be there for you. He will never leave your side! Although you cannot see God, you can talk to him just like Adam did.

If you long to have a special friend, ask God to help you meet someone who will enjoy the same things you do – someone who will be a loyal companion. God knows and understands when you are lonely because He made you to need a friend and be a friend.

VERSE FOR TODAY

The Lord God said, "It is not good for the man to be alone.
I will make a helper suitable for him."
Genesis 2:18

ADAM

The first sin

The serpent was the most cunning of the creatures that God had made. One day, the serpent came to the woman God had given to Adam and asked, "Has God really said you are not allowed to eat from any tree in the garden?"

The woman quickly pointed out that there was only one tree from which they were not allowed to eat. If they did, they would die.

"That's not true!" the serpent replied. "You won't die if you eat of it. God doesn't want you to take from it because then you will also know everything."

When the woman saw how good the fruit looked, and thought about how wise it would make her, she took some of the fruit and ate it. Then she gave Adam some to eat.

What is the difference between temptation and sin?

While the serpent was speaking to the woman, he was tempting her to do what God told them not to do. Temptations usually come through our senses, especially what we see and hear. The devil uses our senses to put bad thoughts in our minds and bad desires in our hearts. While we are being temped, we have not done wrong. The temptation is not sin! However, temptation can lead to sin when we actually do what the devil is tempting us to do.

The woman was close enough to the tree to see how beautiful it was. Remember that it is best to stay away from places where you could easily be tempted.

VERSE FOR TODAY

But each one is tempted when, by his own evil desire, he is dragged away and enticed. Then, after desire has conceived, it gives birth to sin ...
JAMES 1:14-15

ADAM

The cover-up

When Adam and Eve had eaten of the fruit God had forbidden them to eat, they realized they were naked, so they sewed fig leaves together to make clothes for themselves.

That evening, when they heard God walking in the garden, they were afraid and hid among the trees. But God called, "Where are you, Adam?"

Adam replied, "I was afraid when I heard You, so I hid because I am naked."

How can I get rid of my feelings of guilt?

When you've done something wrong, you'll do anything not to be found out. You hope that somehow your guilt will just fade away. You try to cover up your sin by telling lies or pretending that nothing happened. But you're afraid all the time that someone will find out. The horrible feeling of guilt makes you feel sick as it chews away at your peace and joy. It's no fun to feel this way.

The good news is that there is a way out. You can have peace in your heart again!

There is only one way to get rid of the sin in your heart and the guilt that it brings; that is to admit that you have done wrong and ask God to forgive you. You also need to apologize to the person you wronged, and if possible, make things right. It takes courage, but it makes your character stronger and helps your friendship with others to be built on a solid foundation.

No one is perfect. We all do wrong and sin against God. But we can live a peaceful, happy life by confessing our sin the minute we slip up!

VERSE FOR TODAY

You know my folly, O God; my guilt is not hidden from you.
PSALM 69:5

ADAM

It wasn't my idea

After Adam and Eve had disobeyed God, they tried to hide. But God found Adam and asked him if he had eaten of the fruit He had told him not to eat.

Adam answered, "The woman You put here with me gave me the fruit to eat."

The Lord asked the woman, "Why did you do this?"

She replied, "The serpent tricked me, and I ate it."

What should I do when others say it is okay to do wrong?

Have any of your friends ever said, "Just do it! No one will ever find out." Deep down, you don't have a good feeling about what they are daring you to do. Then, just to convince you, they add, "Everyone is doing it!"

You start wondering if it really is wrong. It doesn't seem that bad, and no one will find out anyway.

Adam was in a situation like this. Just one bite of the forbidden fruit seemed reasonable. He had seen Eve eat the fruit, and she seemed okay – she did not die as God said they would if they ate of it.

So Adam took a bite. Immediately his purity and innocence was ruined; and to spit the fruit out wouldn't make things right again. Sin had entered Adam's heart and broken the close friendship he had with God.

You don't need to learn the hard way and end up with regrets! Always say no to the things God and your parents have forbidden. Next time someone tells you to do wrong, say that it is sin and stay away from people who want you to disobey.

VERSE FOR TODAY

There is a way that seems right to a man, but in the end it leads to death.
PROVERBS 14:12

ADAM

Genesis 3:14-23

Expelled!

JANUARY 7

Sin had entered the heart of man, and God had to deal with it. God said to the serpent, "From now on you will crawl on your belly and eat dust for as long as you live."

Then God said to the woman, "You will have trouble and pain when you give birth."

To Adam, He said, "Because you listened to your wife and ate of the fruit, the ground will be cursed. You will have to work hard every day to get enough food, and weeds will come up from the ground."

Then God made proper clothes for Adam and Eve out of animal skins and sent them out of the garden.

Can God take away the trouble caused by sin?

Once we have sinned, some things change and will never be the same as they were before we sinned.

If you have said something nasty about a friend, that friend may not want to visit anymore even though you said sorry. Breaking the rules in a game could get the whole team disqualified. Disobeying a safety rule could cause you to get hurt. The consequences of your sin affect you, and others.

Although God forgives all your sin no matter what you have done, the problem and sadness that sin brings cannot simply be wiped away. Even so, God who is kind and loving will also help you as He helped Adam and Eve when He made clothes for them after they sinned.

VERSE FOR TODAY

If we confess our sins, he is faithful and just and will forgive us our sins and purify us from all unrighteousness.
1 John 1:9

CAIN

A right way and a wrong way

Adam and Eve had two sons, Cain and Abel. When they grew up, Abel became a shepherd and Cain was a farmer.

One day, Cain brought some of his harvest and gave it as an offering to the Lord.

Abel too, brought an offering: the first-born lamb of one of his sheep.

The Lord was pleased with Abel's offering, but He was not happy with Cain's offering. Cain was furious!

Then the Lord said to Cain, "Why are you so angry. If you had done the right thing you would be happy. Be careful, sin is stalking at the door."

Is God pleased with any kind of worship?

Some people think that we can worship God in any way we want. Although God has given us the freedom to show our adoration in different ways, false acts of worship that only look impressive on the outside are an insult to God.

We should always show honor and respect when we worship God. Think of how you would act if you were allowed to go right into the throne room of a king. God is the King of kings, and before we go in to worship Him, we should prepare ourselves by making sure that we have a right attitude, and that our hearts are clean.

Think of three different ways to worship God that will please Him. Here are some verses that may help: Psalm 100:2, Luke 2:37, and Matthew 2:11.

VERSE FOR TODAY

God is spirit, and his worshipers must worship in spirit and in truth.

JOHN 4:24

CAIN

Sin – a growing problem

Cain was jealous because God had accepted Abel's offering, but not his. God had told him to do what is right, but instead, he allowed anger to grow in his heart.

"Let's go to the fields," he said to his brother Abel.

When they were far away, Cain turned on his brother and killed him.

How can I get rid of my feelings of anger and jealousy?

God warned Cain of the jealousy that had crept into his heart. But, instead of doing what is right, his angry heart made him think of a way to get rid of his brother.

Feelings of anger and jealousy don't just go away on their own. When something happens that makes us feel jealous or angry, we must stop those selfish feelings and thoughts right away.

Ask God to make your heart clean and to give you His peace.

Go to the person with whom you are angry and talk about the way you feel. If you've been hurt, tell the person that you forgive him.

If you are jealous of someone, make a point of being kind to that person. Also, be grateful for what you have – even the little things.

Remember that you first need to take action (do what is right) before your feelings will start to change.

By following Jesus' example of love, you will find it a lot easier to get along with others. Jesus did not tell us to like everybody (that would be impossible); He told us to love others!

VERSE FOR TODAY

Dear children, let us not love with words
or tongue but with actions and in truth.
1 John 3:18

NOAH

Sin makes God very sad

More and more people were being born, and all sorts of evil and violence spread wherever people settled.

When the Lord saw how wicked people had become and how evil their thoughts were, He was sorry He had made them.

However, there was one good man and his family who believed in God. His name was Noah. The Lord was pleased with Noah.

God decided to put an end to all the evil by wiping out the whole human race.

Why do so few believe in God?

Do you sometimes wonder why there is so much violence and hatred in the world? Why does God allow wars, crime, and abuse?

God grieves to see the beautiful world He created messed up by the people He created. His heart breaks to see those who cannot defend themselves being hurt. Yet, just as God gave Adam a choice between doing right and disobeying, God has given every person that same choice.

Since Adam sinned in the Garden of Eden, every person in the world has been born in sin. Because we are sinful, we do not have a natural longing to do right and follow God's ways.

Yet the Lord patiently works in our lives, wanting to change our sinful hearts and make us pure. Even though God touches the heart of every person, some people want to carry on doing evil, and they don't allow God to change their stubborn hearts (John 3:19).

VERSE FOR TODAY

[Jesus said] "Here I am! I stand at the door and knock. If anyone hears my voice and opens the door, I will come in and eat with him, and he with me."
REVELATION 3:20

NOAH

Genesis 6:13-22

Obey God despite the odds

JANUARY 11

God said to Noah, "I will put an end to the whole human race because the world is full of their violent deeds.

Build a boat for yourself, for I am going to send a flood that will cover the whole earth.

The boat must have a roof over the top. It must have three decks with rooms, and a door on the side. Then, cover the inside and outside with tar."

So Noah did exactly as the Lord had told him to do.

Why doesn't God just make wicked people vanish?

Noah was given a huge task. He had to build a boat that would take many, many years to complete.

What thoughts would have gone through your mind if God had told you to build an ark? Would you perhaps have thought it rather unfair that you had to do such hard work just because others were so sinful? Was there not an easier way to get rid of sin and wickedness?

God made the universe with certain physical laws – for example, the Law of Gravity. Everything on earth gets pulled toward the center of the earth; and that is how we keep from falling off.

Although God has the power to work outside of the natural laws He put in place, He often shows His power by using natural laws in a supernatural way. God does not rush into decisions or take shortcuts to carry out His will. He often chooses to show His power through people, and patiently waits for His perfect will to take place.

VERSE FOR TODAY
"For my thoughts are not your thoughts,
neither are your ways my ways," declares the Lord.
ISAIAH 55:8

NOAH

Two by two

When Noah had finished building the ark, God said to him, "Go into the boat with your whole family. Take pairs of every clean animal, and pairs of every kind of unclean animal. Also take pairs of every kind of bird. Do this so that every kind of animal and bird will be kept alive when the flood is over."

Noah did everything the Lord told him to do.

He and his family went into the boat, and with them, every kind of animal you can think of – one male and one female of every living creature.

Then God shut the door!

Do animals obey God?

God, the Creator of the universe, has power over all He has made. God holds the whole of creation together. He makes sure that the sun rises and sets, that rain falls on dry ground, and that every creature – from the biggest to the smallest – has its place in His creation.

Because God created animals, He has the power to make them do whatever He wants them to. However, animals cannot choose to obey or disobey God like we can. They are not aware of God the way we are because they do not have a spirit. God does not speak to animals the way He speaks to us. When animals do what God wants them to, they do it without having to think about it.

Can you think of the time that God used birds to feed His servant in the desert? (1 Kings 17:4)

VERSE FOR TODAY

They were terrified and asked each other, "Who is this?
Even the wind and the waves obey him!"
MARK 4:41

NOAH

Genesis 7:11-24

Rain, rain and more rain

JANUARY 13

When God shut and sealed the door of the ark, it started to rain! It rained and rained, and the water streams under the earth burst open too. Slowly, but steadily, the water rose, and soon the big boat started to float. Within days the water covered the tallest trees, and some days later, the water had covered the highest mountain.

Are floods and earthquakes the judgment of God?

In the time of Noah, the people's wickedness was getting worse and worse. God decided to use a flood to give goodness a chance to rule on the earth again. At that time, only Noah was good – and he was already old. What do you think would have happened if Noah died and only the wicked were left to rule on earth?

After the flood, the people slowly increased again, and they moved to different parts of the world. Some believed in God, but many did not. Today, the Church of Jesus is unstoppable! Jesus Himself said, "I will build My church, and even the gates of hell won't be able to stand against it." God is allowing goodness and evil to 'grow' side by side like good plants and weeds that grow next to each other (Matthew 13:24-30).

Floods and other natural disasters happening in the world today are not the same as God's judgment in Noah's time. Most times, disasters also affect those who believe in God.

Next time you hear of a flood or an earthquake or a hurricane, pray that those going through a difficult time will turn to God and be helped in their time of trouble.

VERSE FOR TODAY
We know that the whole creation has been groaning as in the pains of childbirth right up to the present time.
ROMANS 8:22

Genesis 8:1-5, 15-19

NOAH

Blue skies!

While Noah and his family and all the animals were floating around in the ark, God kept His eye on them. He sent a wind to blow across the earth, and the level of the water slowly started going down. God stopped the springs from gushing out water and He stopped the rain.

After many months, the water had gone down so much that the boat came to rest on a mountain. Some time later, God said to Noah, "Come out of the ark and bring all the creatures out with you."

So Noah, his family and all the animals stepped out onto dry ground.

If the world is as bad now as it was in Noah's time, why doesn't God punish the wicked now?

God used the flood to make everything new. For a while, the evil that had brought such misery to the world was gone. It seemed as though the flood had washed the earth clean of sin. Yet, there was a problem: the hearts of people were still sinful, and soon evil started to spread again.

Even with all the sin in the world today, God is still making things new. He is not using floods to get rid of sin from the earth, but the blood of Jesus to get rid of sin from the hearts of those who believe. God says, "I will give you a new heart and put a new spirit in you" (Ezekiel 36:26).

God is merciful and patient – He does not want anyone to die in sin. God is holding back His judgment of evil for as long as possible so that many people can be saved (2 Peter 3:9).

VERSE FOR TODAY
As it was in the days of Noah, so it will be at the coming of the Son of Man.
MATTHEW 24:37

NOAH

Genesis 9:8-17

God's promise

God blessed Noah and his sons. He said to them, "Be fruitful and have many children."

Then God said to Noah, "I am making a promise that I will keep forever; to you, your children and those who will come after them and to every living creature. I will never again send a flood that will destroy all life on the earth.

As a sign of My promise, I am putting a rainbow in the clouds. Whenever I cover the sky with clouds and the rainbow appears in the clouds, I will remember My promise to you."

Why are there rainbows?

Rainbows had not existed before the time of the flood.

After the flood, God promised that He would never again wipe out the whole of creation. He placed a rainbow in the sky as a sign to the whole world of the promise He made to Noah. The rainbow helps us remember God's mercy and faithfulness.

Whenever you see a rainbow it should also remind you of the many other promises God has made. All God's promises can be found in the Bible! Some special promises come with instructions from God and depend on your obedience. God will do what He promised if you do what He asks.

Our God who is unchanging and all-powerful, can and will keep every promise He has made.

Find a promise for every color of the rainbow, then draw a rainbow and write a promise in each color.

VERSE FOR TODAY

The Lord is faithful to all his promises and loving toward all he has made.
PSALM 145:13

ABRAM

Get up and go

When Abram was 75 years old, the Lord said to him, "Leave you country and your relatives and go to a land that I will show you.

I will give you children and grandchildren who will become a great nation.

I will bless you, and you will become great. You will be a blessing, and through you I will bless all the nations."

Then Abram, his wife Sarai, and his nephew Lot, took all they had and set out for the land of Canaan.

Why does God sometimes get us to move far away?

Abram was living a comfortable life. He was married, he had servants … and the weather was great!

However, God had a much bigger plan for Abram, and to put that plan in to action, He needed Abram to get up and move to the land of Canaan. God could see into the future to a time when there would be so many people born from Abram's children, it would be as hard to count them as it would be to count the grains of sand on the beach, or the stars in the sky. You could say that God had a dream for Abram: that through him all the people of the earth would be blessed.

Abram obeyed God. He left the place where he had lived for so long and started his journey to a distant land.

God may need you in the place you are now and move you somewhere else in the future. Who knows where and how God wants to bless you and make you a blessing to others?

VERSE FOR TODAY
"For I know the plans I have for you," declares the LORD, "plans to prosper you and not to harm you, plans to give you hope and a future."
JEREMIAH 29:11

ABRAM

A bad plan

After a long journey, Abram, Sarai and Lot arrived in the land of Canaan.

While Abram was in Canaan, there was a famine in the land. Because there was hardly any food, Abram decided to go to the land of Egypt, to live there.

When he got there, he was afraid that the Egyptians would kill him and take his wife away. So he said to her, "Say you are my sister so that I will be treated well."

When Pharaoh (the king of Egypt) saw how beautiful she was, he treated Abram well and took Sarai into his palace.

But the Lord brought a serious disease on Pharaoh because he had taken Abram's wife.

Is it okay to tell a lie in certain situations?

In a tricky situation, doing things our way usually leads to trouble. When we put our trust in our own plans instead of putting our trust in God, we usually mess things up.

Abram was afraid for his life. He thought that if he pretended that Sarai was just his sister the Egyptians would not kill him. His plan seemed to work at first, and Pharaoh gave him sheep, cattle and camels. But in exchange, he wanted Sarai.

Abram's plan had gone wrong! But God stepped in and brought a disease on Pharaoh. Only then did Pharaoh find out that Sarai was actually Abram's wife and he immediately gave her back to Abram.

Do you think God had a better plan lined up so that Abram would not have had to deceive Pharaoh?

VERSE FOR TODAY

Dear friends, if our hearts do not condemn us, we have confidence before God and receive from him anything we ask.

1 JOHN 3:21

Genesis 13:1-12

ABRAM

You choose!

After a time, Abram went back to the land of Canaan with his wife and his nephew Lot.

God had blessed Abram with many sheep, goats and cattle. Lot also had some flocks and herds. They had so many animals that there wasn't enough land for all of them and Lot's shepherds started to quarrel with Abram's shepherds.

Abram said to Lot, "Our men should not be fighting among each other. We must separate."

Then Abram let Lot choose the land that he wanted. When Lot saw the fertile valley of Jordan, he chose to move there, while Abram stayed in Canaan.

Should one always let others choose first?

If you were given two slices of cake to share with a friend, would you let your friend choose a slice first, or would you take the biggest and hand the other to your friend?

Abram could have decided which part of the land he wanted. But instead, he trusted God to bless him, no matter which part of the land Lot would choose.

If you have something to share, you have the right to give what you want and keep what you want. Remember though, that the Lord loves a giving heart because He Himself is generous – He loves to pour out His blessing on us.

Even though we seem to lose out by letting someone else choose the best, we will always end up with a far greater reward from God.

VERSE FOR TODAY

"But seek first his kingdom and his righteousness,
and all these things will be given to you as well."
MATTHEW 6:33

ABRAM

The winner takes nothing

Lot went to settle in the valley near the city of Sodom where wicked people lived.

One day, the king of Sodom joined kings from other cities to fight against an enemy. The kings of Sodom and Gomorrah lost the battle, and the enemy took Lot with all his possessions. One of the men escaped and went to tell Abram what had happened. When Abram heard about Lot, he took his men to fight the enemy and defeated them.

After Abram got back, the king of Sodom together with Melchizedek, who was a king and a priest, brought Abram gifts. Melchizedek blessed Abram and praised God for their victory.

Then Abram gave Melchizedek a tenth of the loot he had brought back. He also gave back all the belongings that the enemy had taken from the king of Sodom.

Should I give back something I have found or rescued?

Have you ever found something valuable? Have you ever climbed high up to get someone's tangled kite out of a tree, or reached down in to a gutter to rescue a little kitten? Because of your daring mission you may feel that you deserve to keep what you found.

Abram had risked his life and the life of his men to rescue Lot and bring back the people and possessions of Sodom. Abram had every right to keep all the goods, and in fact, the king of Sodom said he could keep the loot.

However, Abram felt that it was not right to keep the things he had brought back because they weren't his in the first place. Abram set a good example for us to follow.

VERSE FOR TODAY

If you see your brother's ox or sheep straying,
do not ignore it but be sure to take it back to him.
DEUTERONOMY 22:1

ABRAM

Listening to the right advice

After living in Canaan for ten years, Abram's wife still had no children. It seemed as though she could never have any, so she said to Abram, "Why don't you let my servant have a baby instead. Then the baby will be like my own."

Abram agreed, and let Hagar have a baby. While she was pregnant, Hagar became proud and looked down on Sarai because she couldn't have a baby of her own.

Then Sarai complained to Abram, saying, "It is your fault that Hagar looks down on me."

Abram replied, "She is your slave. Do whatever you want with her." Then Sarai became so mean and nasty toward Hagar that she ran away.

Should I listen to the advice of others?

Often, life is not as simple as we'd like it to be. Sooner or later we come across tough problems that need to be solved. Sometimes the solution is obvious, other times it is not and we are faced with a difficult decision.

Perhaps we may ask for advice, trusting that others can tell us what the best option is. Unfortunately, some people's ideas come from things that have happened in their own lives. They only see the way a plan would work for them and not how it will affect you in the future – or how it will affect others.

It is great to know that we can turn to God for wisdom and guidance. He not only sees into the future, but also leads us in the way that is best for us.

VERSE FOR TODAY

"I will instruct you and teach you in the way you should go;
I will counsel you and watch over you."

PSALM 32:8

ABRAM

Abandoned, but not forgotten

Sarai's servant Hagar was alone out in the desert. She felt rejected and abandoned.

While she was at a spring, the angel of the Lord came to her and asked, "Where have you come from and where are you going?"

Hagar answered, "I am running away from my mistress."

Then the angel said, "Go back to her. The Lord has heard your cry. I will give you so many descendants that you will not be able to count them. You will have a son, and you will call him Ishmael."

Then Hagar called the Lord who had spoken to her "A God Who Sees."

Does God see and care when I feel unwanted?

Have you been to a party where no one seems to notice you or talk to you? Everyone there seem to look right through you. Maybe you don't even get invited to parties and life is very lonely.

Abram and Sarai had rejected Hagar, and maybe she wondered whether Abram's God had also forgotten her. She had no family to go to and no one to give her food. Yet God saw Hagar's tears and He understood the pain in her heart!

God sees the pain of loneliness in every sad heart. In Isaiah 53:3, the prophet wrote that Jesus was despised and rejected by men; a man of sorrows who knew what it is like to suffer. Jesus, more than anyone else, knows what it feels like to be rejected. He wants to come to you and be your best friend, forever.

VERSE FOR TODAY

"I will be with you; I will never leave you nor forsake you."
JOSHUA 1:5

ABRAHAM

God's way, in God's time

When Abram was ninety-nine years old, the Lord spoke to him again. He reminded Abram of His promise to give him many descendants, The Lord said, "Your name will no longer be Abram, but Abraham, because I am making you the father of many nations. You must no longer call your wife Sarai; from now on her name is Sarah."

Later, the Lord again spoke to Abraham in the middle of the day. Abraham looked up and saw three men standing there. He invited them to stay and brought them water to wash their feet. Then he hurried to the tent and said to Sarah, "Quick, bake some bread for our guests!"

Then, as Abraham served his visitor their meal, one of them said, "A year from now Sarah will have a son."

Should I remind God of His promises?

Years had passed since God told Abraham that he would be the father of many nations. Maybe Abraham wondered whether God had forgotten His promise. Abraham had already tried to make God's promise work out in his own way by letting Hagar have a son. But somehow it wasn't the same. It wasn't the special way he expected God's promise to happen. But God had not forgotten! In His time, God brought about a miracle by letting Abraham and Sarah have a son in their old age.

God does not need to be reminded of His promises. Yet by reminding Him, we are actually reminding ourselves and showing God that we are waiting patiently and trusting Him to do what He promised.

VERSE FOR TODAY

O Lord God, do not reject your anointed one.
Remember the great love promised to David your servant.
2 Chronicles 6:42

ABRAHAM

A city in flames

Abraham's nephew Lot had moved into the wicked city of Sodom.

God told Abraham that He was going to destroy the whole city. Abraham pleaded with God saying, "Are you really going to destroy the innocent with the guilty? If there are fifty innocent people, won't you spare the city to save the innocent?"

The Lord replied, "I will spare the city."

Then Abraham carried on speaking to the Lord. "What if there are forty-five, forty, thirty, twenty? What if there are ten? Would you destroy them with the rest?

The Lord replied, "I will not destroy the city for the sake of ten good people."

Can God's people keep the world from becoming worse?

Did you know, long ago when a sailing ship went out to sea, the sailors had no way to keep their food frozen, so they used salt to preserve their food.

Abraham knew that God is a just God, and because He is completely fair, He would not destroy a wicked city if there were good people living in it. And so Abraham pleaded with God to spare the city if He could find just a few good people living in it – but there were not even ten.

Where there is goodness there is life. If there had been some goodness in Sodom, God would have spared the city. Jesus said that we are the salt of the earth. We are keeping schools and cities from becoming completely rotten with sin, and because of us God is holding back His judgment.

VERSE FOR TODAY
"You are the salt of the earth."
MATTHEW 5:13

ABRAHAM

Isaac and the offering

At the very time God had promised, He let Sarah have a baby, and Abraham named him Isaac. God's promise to Abraham had come true even though he and Sarah were very old.

When Isaac was a young boy, the Lord said to Abraham, "Take your son, Isaac, and sacrifice him on a mountain I will show you."

Without questioning God, Abraham took Isaac and left with his servants early the next morning. On the third day, Abraham saw the place in the distance and told his servants to stay while he and Isaac went on ahead.

Abraham and Isaac reached the place that God showed him. Then Abraham built an altar and put wood on it. He tied up Isaac and laid him on the altar. But the angel of the Lord called from heaven, "Abraham, do not harm the boy. Now I know that you fear God."

Why does God ask us to do difficult things?

If God can see our hearts, surely He already knows how much we love and trust Him. God does know all things, yet He sometimes puts our faith and commitment to the test (Deuteronomy 8:2).

This test is not like a test you do at school where you need to get a certain score to pass. Even if you mess up altogether, God loves you just as much and you still have eternal life by believing in Him (John 5:24).

God's tests actually strengthen our "faith muscles" and help us realize how much we really need Him. Usually it is in these times of testing that we grow the most in our spiritual lives.

Because of Abraham's trust in God and his obedience, he is listed in the Bible as one of the great people of faith – see Hebrews 11:17.

VERSE FOR TODAY

Test me, O Lord, and try me, examine my heart and my mind.
PSALM 26:2

ABRAHAM

Genesis 22:13-19

God provides!

Abraham was about to sacrifice his son Isaac on the altar when the voice of the Lord stopped him. God said, "Do not harm the boy. Now I know that you fear God because you have not kept back your only son."

Just then Abraham looked up and saw a ram caught in a bush by its horns. He took the ram and sacrificed it to the Lord on the altar he had made.

Abraham called that place "The Lord Will Provide." Then he and his son returned to the waiting servants.

What is a sacrifice?

A sacrifice is a costly gift – something that is precious and means a lot to the one making the sacrifice; as it did to the woman who poured expensive perfume on Jesus (Mark 14:3). A sacrifice could also be something one cannot see, like giving up a privilege or right. You could sacrifice your time by spending a whole afternoon looking after a younger brother or sister.

Even though Abraham had been asked to do a very difficult thing, his love for God and complete trust in Him made Abraham willing to show total obedience.

In Old Testament times, an animal was killed and put on a pile of large stones, called an altar. The sacrificed animal would then be burned.

A sacrifice for sin is a very important sacrifice, and later on you will see how Jesus became a sacrifice for our sin. Just as Abraham was willing to sacrifice Isaac, so God sent His Son, Jesus, to earth to be a sacrifice for us. But unlike with Isaac, God did not spare Jesus, but sacrificed Him to die for our sins.

VERSE FOR TODAY

This is love: not that we loved God, but that he loved us
and sent his Son as an atoning sacrifice for our sins.
1 John 4:10

ISAAC

An act of kindness

When the time had come for Isaac to get married, Abraham said to his servant, "Go to the land where I was born and find a wife for my son."

Abraham's servant knew that the task he'd been given was too big for him to do by himself. When he finally reached the country where Abraham had been born, he prayed to God saying, "When a woman comes to draw water here at the well – and I ask her to give me a drink – may the one You have chosen, offer to give my camels water as well."

Before he had even finished praying, a beautiful woman called Rebekah came along, so he asked her for a drink. She lowered her jar and said, "Here sir, drink – and I will also give your camels to drink." She went back to draw more water until all the camels had had enough to drink. Then the servant knew that this woman was the one God had chosen.

Should I be kind to a stranger?

The Bible encourages us to be kind to others. Every kind and helpful action shows the love of Jesus working in our hearts.

Unfortunately, some people take advantage of the kindness they receive from others. Some bad people may use a child's kindness as a trap to get something else they want.

God sees your willing heart. If you would like to help a person you don't know, ask your parents to show you the best way to help the person. In this way you can still do good to those who need help, but in a way that is safe and keeps you free to serve God joyfully through your kind and helpful deeds.

VERSE FOR TODAY

Therefore, as we have opportunity, let us do good to all people, especially to those who belong to the family of believers.
GALATIANS 6:10

ISAAC

A wife for Isaac

God had given Abraham's servant the special sign he had asked for. He knew that the woman who was giving his camels water was the wife God had chosen for Isaac.

The servant gave Rebekah jewelry and asked if he could stay for the night. So Rebekah ran home to tell everyone what had happened. Her brother Laban was almost as excited as Rebekah and invited Abraham's servant to stay. The servant wanted to settle the matter straight away.

When Rebekah's father Bethuel heard the whole story, both he and Laban said, "This whole matter is up to the Lord; it is not for us to decide. Here, take Rebekah to be the wife of your master's son."

Will someone else decide whom I marry?

There are many traditions that make one group of people different from another. You may have heard someone talk about their culture – the way they do things.

In Abraham's time, it was a father's duty to find a wife for his son. The father of the daughter would then decide if he would let his daughter get married to the other man's son.

In this way, a father would try to make sure that his son or his daughter would be happily married.

Although your parents may not choose a life-partner for you, it is always good to listen to their advice when the time comes. And don't forget that you have a heavenly Father who will help you make the best choice of all.

VERSE FOR TODAY
Commit to the Lord whatever you do, and your plans will succeed.
Proverbs 16:3

ISAAC

A father's blessing

Isaac and Rebekah got married and had two sons, Jacob and Esau. As time passed, Isaac became old and blind. It was the custom for a father to speak a blessing on his eldest son. This is called a birthright. So Isaac called Esau and asked him to go out and hunt for a wild animal and cook it for him.

When Isaac's wife, Rebekah, heard this, she thought of a plan to trick Isaac into blessing Jacob instead, because Jacob was her favorite son.

While Esau was out hunting, Rebekah prepared a pot of goat meat. Then she gave Jacob the goatskin to cover his arms because Esau's arms were hairy, while Jacob's arms were smooth.

As Jacob served the food to his father, Isaac asked, "Esau, is it really you, my son? Come here so that I can touch you." Jacob held out his arm covered with the hairy goatskin. When Isaac felt it, he thought it was Esau standing there and spoke his blessing, but he was blessing Jacob.

What does it mean to be blessed?

Do you think that Jacob did a bad thing? What Jacob did was not right because he lied to his father and took the special blessing that was meant for Esau.

But what is a blessing? One hears the words "bless you" so often that it doesn't seem all that special anyway.

When a father or mother honors the Lord, God's special favor is on all their children. This blessing from God doesn't necessarily mean that a child will grow up to live a long and healthy life or become rich, but rather that God will draw the child close to Himself. God will answer the prayers of a parent and bless every son and daughter, not just the eldest son.

VERSE FOR TODAY

But from everlasting to everlasting the Lord's love is with those who fear him, and his righteousness with their children's children.
Psalm 103:17

JACOB

Genesis 28:5, 10-15

What a dream!

Esau hated his brother Jacob for having taken his father's blessing from him. Meanwhile, when his mother Rebekah found out that Esau was planning to kill Jacob, she thought of a plan. She suggested that Jacob should go to the country where his grandfather lived, to find a wife for himself there. And so Jacob left.

On his way to Haran, as the sun was setting, Jacob found a place to camp for the night. While he slept, he dreamed that he saw a stairway reaching up from earth to heaven. Angels were going up and down on it.

Then the Lord said to him, "I will give you the land on which you are sleeping. I will be with you and will protect you wherever you go."

Does God still speak to us through dreams?

Do you wish that all your dreams would come true? You may have had a dream that seemed so real, that you were quite disappointed to wake up and find that it was only a dream.

For Jacob, his dream did come true. God actually spoke to him in the dream and told him what would happen in the future.

God can and does still speak to people through dreams, although it is not the usual way that God speaks to us.

We have a more sure way to hear from God, and that is by reading the Bible. You can go back to a verse or passage from the Bible as many times as you like to see what God is telling you. Unlike a dream, with God's Word, you don't even need to figure out the meaning. With the help of others and the Holy Spirit who lives in you, God will let you know about His plan for your life.

VERSE FOR TODAY

Your young men will see visions and your old men will dream dreams.
ACTS 2:17

Genesis 29:9-20

JACOB

Seven short years

After many days, Jacob was near Haran; the place where he would look for a wife from his own people.

As he talked to some shepherds at a well, Laban's daughter Rachel arrived with her flock of sheep. Jacob wasted no time. He rolled away the heavy stone that covered the well so her flock could drink.

When Rachel found out that Jacob was a relative of theirs, she ran home to tell her father about him, and Jacob stayed with them for a month. Then Rachel's father Laban said to Jacob, "I don't expect you to work for nothing just because we are related. How much do you want to be paid?"

Jacob replied, "I will work for you for seven years if I may marry your daughter Rachel."

Laban agreed and Jacob worked for him for seven years, even though it seemed like only a few days because he loved Rachel so much.

Why must I go to school for so many years?

For Jacob, it took seven years of hard work to get what he wanted (in fact, it took twice as long). You will probably spend even more years studying and working hard at school to get what you want some day.

Things that are worthwhile and lasting take time. Even creation took time. God could have brought everything into being in a split-second. But it took time and effort to make it perfect. In fact, God put so much into creating everything just right that He rested from his work on the seventh day.

Work hard and you will be rewarded for your effort. The work might be really difficult or it might be easy. Whatever the task, always give it your best.

VERSE FOR TODAY
The plans of the diligent lead to profit as surely as haste leads to poverty.
PROVERBS 21:5

JACOB

A deal is a deal

After seven years of working for Rachel's father, Jacob said to Laban, "The time is up; let me marry your daughter now."

So Laban gave a wedding feast and invited everyone. But that night after the feast, instead of giving Rachel in marriage, Laban gave his older daughter Leah to Jacob. (Jacob didn't know that it was Leah because her face was covered.)

The next day, Jacob went to Laban and said, "You tricked me!"

Laban replied, "It is our custom to give the older daughter to be married first. If you work for another seven years, I will give you Rachel as well."

Jacob agreed to the new deal. And so, after the bridal week was over, Rachel became Jacob's other wife, and he worked for Laban another seven years.

How should I react when I am tricked?

Have you ever made a deal with someone only to find out that you've been tricked? What should you do?

Maybe you are angry because you feel used and humiliated. Don't react in anger or take revenge. Don't let bitterness (hateful thoughts) make your life miserable.

Sometimes the problem can be sorted out by explaining it to an adult. They may be able to make a wise decision like a judge does when two people have a disagreement about something.

If there is nothing that can be done to change the situation, accept what has happened and trust the Lord to make things right.

VERSE FOR TODAY

Do not take revenge, my friends, but leave room for God's wrath, for it is written: "It is mine to avenge; I will repay," says the Lord.
ROMANS 12:19

February

JACOB

Genesis 31:3, 17-18, 33:1-11

Making things right

Jacob had worked for Laban for many years and eventually owned his own sheep and goats. His uncle Laban became jealous of him because God had blessed him with so many animals. Then God told Jacob to go back home to the place he had left as a young man.

So Jacob took his two wives and his children, and everything he owned, and left Laban to go back to his father in the land of Canaan. The problem was that Jacob had to face his brother Esau whom he had tricked, and he remembered that Esau wanted to kill him.

When he got to the country of Edom, he sent servants ahead with many gifts for Esau. Meanwhile, Esau was coming toward him with four hundred of his men, and Jacob was afraid. But he knew he would have to face Esau; and when he finally did, he bowed down in front of him to show how sorry he was for what he had done. Then Jacob gave Esau large herds of camels and other animals, and the two brothers made peace with each other.

Is it enough to say sorry?

Maybe you have been trying to avoid someone because of something that has come between you. It is time to go make things right.

Saying "I am sorry" are three short words, but they are sometimes the hardest words to say. However, even these three words won't always make things right again – especially if they are said in an uncaring way.

To show that you are truly sorry, think about the words you use and how you say them. For example, you could say; "I am really sorry for what I said to you," or "I am sorry that I hurt you – please forgive me."

Like Jacob, think of a way to show kindness to the person you wronged.

VERSE FOR TODAY

But Zacchaeus stood up and said to the Lord, "Look, Lord! Here and now I give half of my possessions to the poor, and if I have cheated anybody out of anything, I will pay back four times the amount."
Luke 19:8

JOSEPH

Talk about way-out

Joseph was the second youngest of Jacob's twelve sons. The family moved back to Canaan where Joseph looked after sheep and goats.

Jacob loved Joseph more than any of his other sons and gave him a special, way-out coat. It was obvious who the favorite in the family was and that made his brothers very jealous. What made Joseph's brothers hate him even more is that Joseph told his father what they were up to.

One night, Joseph dreamed that while he and his brothers were tying up sheaves of wheat in the field, his sheaf stood up straight, while his brothers' sheaves made a circle around his and bowed down to it. Then Joseph had another dream in which he saw the sun, the moon, and eleven stars bow down to him.

When Joseph told his brothers the dreams they were furious and asked, "Do you think you are going to be king and rule over us?" And they hated Joseph even more.

What's wrong with being the favorite?

How do you feel when a few people are treated better than the rest, getting favors they don't deserve?

Maybe *you* are someone's favorite, and if so, there is usually a good reason why people like you. There is nothing wrong with being liked! But problems come when someone does special favors for one child, or spends more time with one than with the others because they like that child more.

You cannot change someone's feelings toward you, but you can be sensitive about how it makes others feel. So, if you are favored, try to step back from getting too much attention.

VERSE FOR TODAY

That is why Scripture says: "God opposes
the proud but gives grace to the humble."
JAMES 4:6

JOSEPH

Genesis 37:14-24

The pit(s)

FEBRUARY 3

One day, Joseph's brothers were out in the fields looking after their father's flock. Their father, Jacob, asked Joseph to go out and see how they were doing.

When Joseph's brothers saw him coming, they said to each other, "Here comes the dreamer. Let's kill him and throw his body into one of the dry wells. We can say that a wild animal got hold of him and killed him."

When Reuben, one of the brothers, heard them plotting to kill Joseph, he said, "No, let's not kill him. Just throw him into this well, but don't hurt him."

So Joseph's brothers ripped off his coat and threw him into a deep pit.

Can bad people hurt God's children?

The Lord is our Shepherd: He watches over us night and day! (Psalm 23)

Jesus said, "My sheep listen to My voice. I give them eternal life, and they shall never perish; no one can snatch them out of My hand" (John 10:27-29). Isn't it comforting to know that God holds us in His mighty hand?

God's enemy, the devil, will try everything he can to hurt and harm those who belong to Him. Although God has allowed the devil some power, he can never upset or spoil God's purpose for our lives. Even when the devil uses bad people to hurt us, he cannot change God's perfect plan for us. We may seem powerless for a while, but God cares about us. He knows what we are going through and He will rescue us.

It may have seemed as if Joseph's brothers did something that not even God could stop. Yet, we will soon find out how God had placed a hedge of protection around Joseph, even as He has placed one around you!

VERSE FOR TODAY
"The LORD will keep you from all harm — he will watch over your life."
PSALM 121:7

JOSEPH

Sold as a slave

While Joseph's brothers were having lunch, they saw some travelers in the distance on their way to Egypt.

Then Judah, one of Joseph's brothers had an idea. "How about selling Joseph to those traders," he said. "Then we won't have to kill him. After all, he is our brother."

All the others agreed, so they pulled Joseph out of the well and sold him to the traders for twenty pieces of silver.

Joseph was taken to Egypt where he was sold as a slave to Potiphar, one of the king's officers.

What am I worth?

When you think of what a person is worth, twenty pieces of silver doesn't sound like much. What do you think you are worth?

People often judge a person's worth by who they are, what they can do, or what they own. Those who are popular, talented, and rich often have bodyguards to protect them. They make front-page news and are fussed over by those who seek their favor.

Do you know that you have been bought by Someone for a lot more than twenty pieces of silver? The price that was paid for you is far more than all the silver and gold in the whole world! You were bought with the precious blood of Jesus because you are worth that much to Him.

VERSE FOR TODAY

"For you know that it was not with perishable things such as silver or gold that you were redeemed … but with the precious blood of Christ, a lamb without blemish or defect."
1 PETER 1:18-19

JOSEPH

Genesis 39:1-6

Serving with excellence

The Lord was with Joseph and made him successful in Potiphar's house where he served as a slave. Joseph's new master noticed that the Lord was with him.

Potiphar was so pleased with Joseph that he put him in charge of the whole house and everything he owned.

Potiphar had never had it so easy. Joseph took care of everything and God blessed Potiphar's whole household and his fields.

Why should I do my best if I get nothing extra for it?

Have you ever wondered what motivates a person to work hard for someone else? Some people work hard because they want to make a lot of money. Some work hard to be known as an expert, and some do their best to get to the top in their place of business. But why would someone do their best when doing a job well doesn't bring in extra money or lead to some reward?

In one of Paul's letters, he gives us the best reason to have a good attitude toward working and serving: Serve wholeheartedly, as if you were serving the Lord, not men, because you know that the Lord will reward everyone for whatever good he does (Ephesians 6:6-8).

God created us with a need to work. One of the first things He told Adam was that he should look after the garden and work in it. Hard work honors the Lord. That means, whatever task you do, when you do the best you can, you are pleasing the Lord. And as a bonus, you will feel good about a job well done.

VERSE FOR TODAY

"Whatever you do, work at it with all your heart,
as working for the Lord, not for men."
COLOSSIANS 3:23

JOSEPH

The set-up

While Joseph took care of things in Potiphar's household, everything went well. As he went about his daily chores, Potiphar's wife noticed how handsome Joseph was. She liked him, and it wasn't long before she invited him to her bedroom. Joseph knew trouble when he saw it – and this was trouble! So Joseph refused to do what she wanted.

Then one day, when Potiphar was away, his wife again said to Joseph, "Come to my bedroom with me." She grabbed him by his robe. Joseph pulled and squirmed until he was free and ran away, leaving her clutching the robe.

Potiphar's wife kept the robe, and when her husband got back, she showed him Joseph's robe, saying, "This slave you brought into our house came into my room and said bad things to me, and when I screamed he ran away."

Potiphar believed her and was so furious that he had Joseph arrested and put in the king's prison.

What should I do when I'm wrongly blamed?

Being treated unfairly or accused for something you didn't do can make you feel very angry. Talk to someone about those feelings and ask God to give you peace by helping you forgive the person who wronged you.

If someone has got you into trouble and you need to explain what happened, stick to the facts (James 5:12).

Let God deal with it! Don't threaten the person or try to get even with the one who accused you wrongly.

Remember, bad people lied about Jesus too (see Mark 14:53-56).

VERSE FOR TODAY
"Blessed are you when people insult you, ... and falsely
say all kinds of evil against you because of me."
MATTHEW 5:11

JOSEPH

Making the best of it

Joseph found himself being punished in the king's prison for something he hadn't done.

But instead of grumbling and complaining, Joseph carried on being cheerful and helpful. The jailer soon noticed Joseph because he was so different from everyone else. In fact, the jailer was so impressed with him that he put him in charge of the other prisoners. He also made him responsible for everything that needed to be done in the prison. God blessed Joseph and helped him do everything well.

Does it help to complain?

Grumble, groan, mumble, moan. Does it really help? How else will people know that you're not happy with the way things are? Here are a few facts about being grumpy:

- Complaining doesn't change things – people change things.
- Grumbling upsets other people – it makes *them* feel unhappy!
- When you put on a miserable look, you will start to feel miserable.

Does that mean you should always look happy – even when you're not? Should you just accept whatever happens? No! For something to change you need to take action. So, if something isn't right: think about the situation for a while. Then ask yourself: Who could help me do something about it? What can I do? How would my idea affect others?

Go speak to someone who can help. Tell the person what happened and how you feel about it. Suggest how the problem could be sorted out.

Like Joseph, be patient and keep doing what is right and good. Remember, God sees and knows everything, and He will help you.

VERSE FOR TODAY
Do everything without complaining or arguing.
PHILIPPIANS 2:14

Genesis 41:1-7, 16-36

JOSEPH

The right words

Joseph had been in prison for a long time when the king of Egypt had a dream. The king dreamed he was standing at the Nile River when he saw seven thin cows eat up seven fat cows; but the thin cows stayed thin.

When the king woke up, he remembered the dream and called his wise men and magicians, hoping that they could explain the dream to him. But no one could!

One of the king's servants, who had been in prison with Joseph, remembered that Joseph had told him the meaning of his dream. He told the king about Joseph. So the king sent for him.

Joseph said to the king, "I cannot tell you the meaning of your dream, but God can. This is what it means. There will be seven years of plenty followed by seven years of famine. You must store up food during the seven good years so that you will have enough during the seven years of famine."

FEBRUARY 8

Will God give me the right words to say?

Do you think Joseph was nervous when he stood in front of the king? What if he couldn't figure out the king's dream either? Anxious thoughts of staying in prison for life or being killed could have distracted him.

But Joseph remembered how – through a dream – God had showed him what would happen in his life. He told the king that God alone could give him the meaning of his dream. And God did!

If you honor God as Joseph did, He will also give you the right words to say as you trust Him to guide your thoughts.

VERSE FOR TODAY

"Do not worry about how you will defend yourselves or what you will say, for the Holy Spirit will teach you at that time what you should say."
LUKE 12:11-12

JOSEPH

Genesis 41:37-46

What a big task

FEBRUARY 9

When Joseph told the king what his dream meant and what he should do, the king said, "We will never find a better man than Joseph – who has God's spirit in him – to take charge of the great task of collecting and storing grain during the seven years of plenty."

Then the king said to Joseph, "It is obvious that you have greater wisdom than anyone else, so I am putting you in charge of my country, Egypt." Then the king gave Joseph his very own ring and put a fine linen robe on him.

Why would God want to use me?

God sees those who are obedient to Him and love Him. "For the eyes of the Lord range throughout the earth to strengthen those whose hearts are fully committed to Him" (2 Chronicles 16:9).

God is looking for those who will serve Him in a humble way, not boasting in their abilities, but willing to do any task – and do it well. Joseph had to learn to do little tasks well before he was given more responsibility. Whether he found himself in prison, or being the second in charge of Egypt, he listened to God and always did his best.

God has given you special abilities, talents and spiritual gifts so that He can use you in a special way. In addition, you may have had experiences that make you unique. The things you are good at, and even those you are not so good at, help to make you all the more useful. Remember, God can use anyone who is available and has a pure heart.

VERSE FOR TODAY
"But God chose the foolish things of the world to shame the wise;
God chose the weak things of the world to shame the strong."
1 Corinthians 1:27

JOSEPH

Saving and spending

When the seven years of plenty had passed, the storehouses in Egypt were full. Then, just as God had said, seven years of famine followed. Joseph opened the storehouses and started selling grain to the Egyptian people. Things were getting so bad that even people from distant countries came to buy food.

Joseph's father Jacob heard that there was food in Egypt and sent his sons to buy grain there. Only his youngest son, Benjamin, stayed behind because Jacob was afraid something bad might happen to him.

Should I spend my pocket money or save it?

Whether your parents give you pocket money, or whether you do chores to earn money, what you do with the money is up to you.

It is probably best to keep a balance between spending money and saving it. By keeping money for a while (saving), you can make sure you have money when you need it. If you spend all of it straight away on buying things you don't really need, you may not have enough when you want to buy something special. By learning to save now, even if it is only a small amount, you will be starting a good habit.

If you want to use money wisely, don't rush into buying things. Rather wait a while and pray that you make a good decision.

Jesus tells us not to store up treasures on earth (Matthew 6:19-20). This means that we should be careful not to heap up treasure – whether money or things – here on earth where they won't last, but rather store up lasting treasure in heaven.

VERSE FOR TODAY

"Ants are creatures of little strength,
yet they store up their food in the summer."
PROVERBS 30:25

JOSEPH

Genesis 42:5-11, 19-25

Now it's my turn

FEBRUARY 11

Jacob's ten sons finally arrived at the storehouse in Egypt where Joseph was selling grain. Food was scarce everywhere because of the great famine.

Joseph recognized his brothers who had sold him as a slave many years before, but his brothers didn't recognize him. Joseph asked them about their father and he also found out about Benjamin, his youngest brother who was not with them. He told them to go back and fetch Benjamin, and had Simeon put in prison until the others returned with him. Then he filled their bags with grain and sent them on their way.

While on their way back, one of them discovered that the money they had brought to buy grain had been put back in the top of their sacks.

How should I treat someone who has hurt me?

Has someone hurt you recently and now you keep thinking of a way to get even? Our sense of fairness makes us think that we need to even the score and show the other person what it feels like to be hurt.

But there is a far better way to handle the situation, and the Bible tells us how: "Do not take revenge, my friends, but leave room for God's wrath, for it is written: 'It is Mine to avenge; I will repay,' says the Lord" (Romans 12:19).

Things had changed for Joseph. He had the power to get back at his brothers for what they did to him. But instead he chose to show kindness.

What would you have done if you were Joseph? Imagine if the person who hurt you was standing before you pleading for mercy. Now think of the many wrong things you have done.

Just as God has forgiven you, forgive the person who hurt you.

VERSE FOR TODAY

(Jesus said) "But I tell you: Love your enemies
and pray for those who persecute you ..."
MATTHEW 5:44

JOSEPH

From bad to worse

When Jacob heard that Simeon was still in Egypt and that the governor in charge of selling food wanted to see Benjamin, his youngest son, he was very upset. He said to his other sons, "Joseph is dead, Simeon is in Egypt, and now you want to take Benjamin from me as well."

As the famine continued, Jacob began to realize that the only way their family would survive would be to send his sons back to Egypt to buy food, this time with Benjamin.

All this time, Jacob and his sons did not know that Joseph was alive and well, and that *he* was the one in charge of the food supply in Egypt.

How can I help people in famine-stricken countries?

How would you feel if you were in charge of all the food in Egypt? Would you feel powerful and important, or would you feel happy to be serving others? Maybe you have seen pictures of starving children. How do those pictures make you feel? You may feel upset that children your age are suffering and no one seems to care.

You could do something to help needy people! Even though your part may seem small, God sees your heart and can turn something small into something much bigger:

Pray for God's mercy on their country, and if they need rain for their crops, that God would send them rain.

Try to find out more about poor countries. Start a scrapbook with pictures and information about countries in need.

Ask God to show you how you can help.

VERSE FOR TODAY

"I tell you the truth, whatever you did for one of the least of these brothers of mine, you did for me."
MATTHEW 25:40

JOSEPH

Genesis 45:16-20, 46:5-6

Together again

FEBRUARY 13

When the king of Egypt heard about Joseph's brothers, and that his father was still in Canaan, he said, "Let your brothers go back to Canaan and fetch your father and everything they own and let them stay here in Egypt."

So Joseph sent his brothers back to Canaan with wagons to fetch their wives and children, and their father Jacob.

From that time on, Jacob and all his sons, their wives and their children, stayed together in Egypt where they had more than enough food and land.

Do family break-ups always have a happy ending?

Jacob and all his sons were together again. How happy he must have been to have everyone safely together after what his family had been through over the years. Jacob had honored God, and God had kept His promise to bless him.

Perhaps you know of a family that is not together anymore. Death, divorce, and living far from one another can scatter a family like pieces of a broken-up puzzle.

God loves families and will always bless the family that honors Him. Whether family members are in one place or scattered all over the world, God can bless them wherever they are.

Although God can bring families together that have been broken through divorce, He does not interfere with the decisions of a mother and father. He will not make people do something they don't want to, nor can He force people to love each other. There may not always be a happy ending for families here on earth, but a time is coming when all who believe will be one big family in heaven, living together forever!

VERSE FOR TODAY

"I will not leave you as orphans; I will come to you."
JOHN 14:18

MOSES

Blessings as God planned

As the years went by, Joseph and his brothers eventually died in Egypt. However, their children and grandchildren continued to live there and their descendants, the Israelites, became a strong nation.

A new king had come to power in Egypt and he did not even know about Joseph. The king became worried and said, "These Israelites are becoming a threat to us."

So the Egyptians made them slaves. Yet, even though they tried to make the lives of the Israelites miserable, they only grew stronger and more in number.

Does God's blessing mean a life without difficulty?

God had made a promise to Abraham – to bless him and make his descendants a great nation. He had made the same promise to Abraham's son Isaac, and to Isaac's son Jacob. Now, Jacob's twelve sons had become such a great nation that the Egyptians became worried. And so the Egyptians forced them to be slaves so that they would never be able to rise up and conquer them. It doesn't seem fair, does it? Surely God's special favor includes His protection. Had God stopped blessing them? No, it was God's blessing that made the Egyptians worried in the first place.

However, God's promise to them was not complete. He had promised them a certain country to live in, and they were not in that country yet. If things had continued to go well in Egypt, they would have had no reason to leave.

Although you may only see a part of what God has promised, He may be using the struggles in your life to prepare the way for something better!

FEBRUARY 14

VERSE FOR TODAY

"All these people were still living by faith when they died.
They did not receive the things promised; they only
saw them and welcomed them from a distance."
HEBREWS 11:13

MOSES

Exodus 2:1-10

A baby on the river

When Pharaoh realized that his plan to stop the Israelites from becoming powerful was failing, he ordered every Hebrew boy to be killed.

A man and his wife who belonged to the tribe of Levi had a baby son. The mother was able to hide him for three months, but when she could not hide him any longer, she got a basket and coated it with tar. Then she hid the baby in a basket among the reeds on the bank of the River Nile.

When Pharaoh's daughter went down to the river to wash, she noticed the basket in the reeds and sent one of her slaves to get it. To her surprise she found the baby boy inside! His sister, who was standing nearby, quickly went up to the princess and asked if she should get one of the Hebrew women to look after him. Pharaoh's daughter replied, "Yes go." So she went to fetch her mother who nursed him. When the boy grew older she took him back to Pharaoh's daughter who named him Moses.

Did God know what I would be like before I was born?

Find the answer in Psalm 139:15-16: "My frame was not hidden from You when I was made in the secret place … Your eyes saw my unformed body."

Isn't it wonderful that God could see you before you were even born? He could see you grow inside your mother and He formed you exactly the way He wanted you to be. God gave you your personality; He knew what your strong points would be and what you would struggle with.

God wanted Moses to be a great leader and so He carefully worked in his life. God gave him strong leadership skills, and some weaknesses that would make Moses humbly depend on Him (Numbers 12:3).

No one is perfect. God loves you just the way you are.

VERSE FOR TODAY
"Before I formed you in the womb I knew you,
before you were born I set you apart …"
JEREMIAH 1:5

MOSES

A false start

When Moses had grown up, he went to see his own people the Hebrews, who were working very hard. There he saw an Egyptian beating a Hebrew slave – one of his own people! Looking around, Moses saw no one watching. Then he killed the Egyptian and hid his body in the sand.

The next day he went out to watch the Hebrews again. This time he saw two of his own people fighting. He said to the one, "Why are you beating your fellow Hebrew?"

The man replied, "Who made you ruler over us? Are you going to kill me like you killed that Egyptian yesterday?"

Moses was afraid because he realized that someone else knew what he had done. When Pharaoh got to hear about what had happened, he tried to kill Moses. But Moses ran away and went to live in the land of Midian.

Should we defend someone who is being bullied?

God had planned for Moses to be the leader who would free His people from slavery. The Lord made sure that Moses got the best training and education in Egypt.

One day, Moses decided that he was ready to start leading God's people, but he messed up because he went about it the wrong way. God had not finished preparing him. Moses still needed to learn to be completely obedient and to wait for God to lead him.

It is always good to protect the weak from being teased and hurt. However, to do what Moses did is not the best way to stop a bully. It is always better to ask God for wisdom first. To help someone who is being bullied, start by staying close to him or her and be a loyal friend!

VERSE FOR TODAY
"Speak up and judge fairly; defend the rights of the poor and needy."
PROVERBS 31:9

MOSES

Who is your master?

Moses had fled from Pharaoh and was sitting at a well when the seven daughters of Jethro came along to draw water for their flock. Other shepherds also arrived and drove the girls away. Moses came to their rescue. When the girls' father heard about Moses, he invited him to stay and help look after the flock.

Many years passed. During that time, the king of Egypt died. However, for the Israelites who were still slaves in Egypt, life didn't get any better. But God heard their cries for help and remembered the promise He had made to Abraham, Isaac and Jacob.

Can a slave ever be set free?

Moses, like his fellow Israelites, was a descendant of Jacob. Moses became a servant; his people worked as slaves.

Unlike a servant, a slave does not have a choice about who his master is, and he can never set himself free. His master owns him and forces him to work, giving him little or nothing in return. A slave has no rights and is treated very harshly. The only way a slave can ever be free is if someone pays for his freedom.

We are descendants of Adam, and because he sinned, we are born as slaves of the devil. He is a cruel master who only pays with pain, sadness and suffering because he has nothing else to offer.

The good news is that Jesus can set us free from being a slave of the devil. When Jesus died for us, He paid the price to buy us back. If you have asked Jesus to be your new Master, you are free from the devil's control. You now belong to God and are part of His family.

VERSE FOR TODAY

Jesus replied, "I tell you the truth, everyone who sins is a slave to sin. Now a slave has no permanent place in the family, but a son belongs to it forever. So if the Son sets you free, you will be free indeed"
JOHN 8:34-36.

A burning bush

One day, Moses was looking after Jethro's sheep far away in the desert. Near a mountain called Sinai, he saw a bush burning. "This is strange," he thought. "The bush isn't burning up!" So he went closer to have a look.

As Moses got closer, the Lord called to him, "Moses! Moses!"

"Yes, here I am," Moses replied.

"Do not come any closer," God said. "Take off your sandals because the ground you are standing on is holy."

Moses was afraid to look at God, so he covered his face.

What does *holy* mean?

When Moses heard the voice in the desert, he knew that it was God speaking to him. God does not often speak directly to people, and Moses was very afraid because his heart was sinful.

Only God is holy. That is why it is difficult for us as sinful people to understand the full meaning of holiness.

To be holy means to be without sin, completely pure and good. But holiness is much more than just being without sin. Holiness is also having a love so great that it cannot be measured, mercy that never ends, and faithfulness that never fails. In fact, holiness is all that God is.

God wants us to be like Him, and even though we will never be perfect here on earth, we can follow the example of Jesus by living like He did.

VERSE FOR TODAY

"But just as he who called you is holy, so be holy in all you do ..."
1 PETER 1:15

FEBRUARY 18

MOSES

"I AM"

The Lord continued to speak to Moses from the burning bush in the desert. "I have seen the misery of My people in Egypt and have heard their cries," He said. "I am sending you to Pharaoh to bring My people out of Egypt."

Moses replied. "Who am I that I should go to Pharaoh?"

"I will be with you," God said to him.

Moses realized that the Israelites might not be happy with him as their leader. So he said, "If I go to the Israelites and they ask who sent me, what will I say?"

Then God said to Moses, "I AM WHO I AM. You must tell them that I AM has sent you."

Can God be in the past, the present, and the future?

Do you look forward to the end of a long school day or to the end of the week? Do you sometimes think back to some fun things you did with your friends, or wonder what you will be when you grow up?

Everything in life has a beginning and an end, whether it is a day or a lifetime. We measure the time between the beginning and end of something in minutes or hours, in days or in years. It is hard for us to understand what it would be like not to have time.

God uses the name "I AM" to help us understand that He is in the past, the present and the future. God doesn't just see into the future, or travel back in time. He is in the past right now, He is here at this very moment and He is in the future at this instant – all at the same time! He just is; that is why He calls Himself I AM.

VERSE FOR TODAY

"Jesus Christ is the same yesterday and today and forever."
HEBREWS 13:8

MOSES

Making excuses

After the Lord told Moses that He must free the Israelite people from slavery, Moses said, "O Lord, I do not speak well. I have never been able to speak well and nothing has changed since You started speaking to me."

The Lord became angry with Moses. "What about your brother Aaron? He can speak well. He is on his way to meet you and will be glad when he sees you. You can tell him what to say, and I will help you both.

Take this stick with you, for with it you will do miracles."

How can I serve God with my weakness?

Moses was no longer as sure of himself as he had been when he lived in Pharaoh's palace. For the past forty years he had just been a shepherd looking after sheep and goats in the desert. By this time he probably felt rather unimportant and of little use. He told God that he wouldn't be able to speak to Pharaoh because he wasn't good at speaking.

Are *you* afraid that God may ask you to do something big like He asked Moses to do? Maybe you have felt the Lord telling you to speak to someone who is older than you about Jesus. God doesn't expect you to do it in your own strength. In fact, He prefers using people who are unsure of their own ability because they rely on Him for everything: for strength, for wisdom, and for courage.

The Lord shows His power best through those who are weak! He has given you all you need to do the tasks He has for you! All God needs is for you to be ready to obey.

VERSE FOR TODAY
"I can do everything through him who gives me strength."
PHILIPPIANS 4:13

MOSES

Exodus 4:18, 27-31

Two can do it

FEBRUARY 21

Moses went back home to his father-in-law Jethro and told him that he was returning to Egypt. Then he took his wife and his sons – and the special stick God had told him to take – and started on his journey.

Meanwhile, the Lord had told Aaron to meet Moses in the desert. So Aaron met him at the holy mountain. There, Moses told his brother everything the Lord had said.

Together, Moses and Aaron went to the leaders of the Israelites and told them that the Lord would free them from the Egyptians. After that, Moses did miracles as a sign of God's power, and the people believed them.

Should I trust God to help me do a task on my own, or should I ask others for help?

God may tell you to do something He knows you can't do in your own strength. If He has promised to help you do a job on your own, He wants you to trust Him and not rely on others to make your task easier. However, sometimes God does want us to work with those whose strengths can help our weaknesses.

Whenever we do something for God, we need to be humble; either by relying on God to use us in spite of our weakness, or by working together with others who can do certain things better than we can.

Remember though, if we always rely on others to help us, we cannot grow in faith the way God wants us to. We need to learn to depend on God, and practice working side by side with others.

VERSE FOR TODAY

"The man who plants and the man who waters have one purpose, and each will be rewarded according to his own labor."
1 CORINTHIANS 3:8

Exodus 5:1-2, 11:1

MOSES

The king says no!

Moses and his brother Aaron went to tell Pharaoh that God said he must let the Israelites go free. But Pharaoh simply said, no! He refused to let God's children go and made them work even harder.

Then God sent many plagues to make the king realize who was in charge. He let the river turn to blood; He sent frogs, gnats, flies, sickness, hail, locusts and other terrible things. Every time the curses only harmed the Egyptians and not the Israelites. After each plague, God gave Pharaoh a chance to let the Israelites go, but he was stubborn and refused.

Finally, God said, "I will send one more plague. I will take the life of the oldest son in every family. Then Pharaoh will know that I am God, and he will let My people go."

Can a mighty king put a stop to God's plan?

Think of the most powerful king who ever ruled, or the greatest president who ever lived. With a single word or signature, powerful leaders can start or end a war.

Pharaoh, the ruler of Egypt, could decide who should live and who should die. With the wave of his hand he could have a man killed, or let him live. Even if God did get rid of the king of Egypt, his army would still be far more powerful than the defenseless Israelites who had been slaves for over four hundred years.

But Pharaoh forgot who was in control of his life; who controls the seasons, and who holds the whole universe in His hands. Foolishly he tried to challenge the One who makes the sun rise and set.

God decides when things will begin and end. He decides who will rule.

FEBRUARY 22

VERSE FOR TODAY
"He changes times and seasons; he sets up kings and deposes them."
DANIEL 2:21

MOSES

Blood on the doorpost

God told Moses: "Every Israelite family must choose a lamb or young goat that has no spot or fault. On the fourteenth day of the month, every family must kill the animal and put some of the blood on the doorposts and above the door. They must roast the meat and eat it together with bitter herbs and bread made without yeast. They must eat the meal quickly and be dressed and ready to leave at any time."

The Lord said, "On that night, I will go through the land of Egypt and take the life of the oldest son in every house except the houses where blood has been sprinkled on the doorposts and above the door."

What is the Passover?

The word *Passover* describes how the Lord passed over the houses where the blood of the lamb had been sprinkled on the doorframes. Everyone inside one of the houses where the blood had been sprinkled would be free from the curse of death.

From that night on, God's people remembered the Passover night by having a special Passover feast every year to honor the Lord.

God told His people how they should prepare the feast and what they should eat. The lamb would remind them of how the blood protected them as the Lord passed over the houses.

The bitter herbs would remind them of the bitterness and hardship they had faced as slaves. The bread made without yeast would remind them that there wasn't enough time to wait for the bread to rise as they made their escape from Egypt that night.

VERSE FOR TODAY

"This is a day you are to commemorate; for the generations to come you shall celebrate it as a festival to the LORD — a lasting ordinance."
EXODUS 12:14

MOSES

The great escape

On the night that God had told them about, the Israelite families put the blood of a goat or lamb on the doorposts and above the door.

At midnight, the oldest son in every family and the firstborn of every animal died, except in the houses where the angel of death saw the blood of the animal on the doorframe.

There was loud crying all over Egypt when the Egyptians found that the oldest son in every family had died. Even the king's son was dead! Then Pharaoh, the king of Egypt, let the Israelites go and the Egyptian people gave the Israelites jewelry and gold because they were afraid that God would punish them even more.

How can the blood of a lamb save someone's life?

You may have heard how one person's blood can help save the life of another by "pumping" blood from the one person into the body of the other.

Yet the blood of an animal is not the same as that of a person, and the blood was only sprinkled on the outside of the door! How could that keep someone inside the house from dying?

The Israelites believed God and they were obedient. They did not understand or question why they had to put blood around their doors. By *faith* they simply obeyed and were saved!

Looking back, we can see that this is a perfect picture of Jesus, the Lamb of God (John 1:29). He came to earth to die in our place and let His blood flow for us. When, by *faith*, you ask Jesus to cleanse your heart from every sin, you will be saved! (1 John 1:9).

VERSE FOR TODAY

"By faith he (Moses) kept the Passover and the sprinkling of blood, so that the destroyer of the firstborn would not touch the firstborn of Israel."
HEBREWS 11:28

MOSES

The Egyptians are coming

The Israelites were well on their way when they came to a place where the Red Sea stretched out in front of them. The problem was how they would get to the other side.

Suddenly someone noticed a cloud of dust in the distance. Pharaoh had changed his mind and was sending his army after them.

The Israelites started to panic. "What now, Moses?" they cried. "We should rather have stayed as slaves in Egypt. Now we are going to die out here in the desert." With the sea on the one side, mountains on the other and an army behind them, there seemed to be no way of escape!

Then Moses said, "Don't be afraid, you will see what the Lord will do today; the Lord will fight for us."

What must I do when I am cornered?

In a disaster such as a fire, a flood, or an earthquake, people are sometimes trapped under rubble, unable to escape the approaching flames or the rising water. Being trapped is very scary!

Can you imagine being cornered by a vicious, snarling dog! Maybe you have had a bad experience – a time when you were really scared. Maybe someone hurt you and you couldn't get away because the person was stronger than you.

If you are ever trapped and you can't get away from danger, call out to the Lord and He will rescue you and help you. Maybe you have had a bad experience that still makes you afraid and gives you bad dreams. Tell your mom or dad about your fears; then pray that God will take those thoughts away and give you His peace.

VERSE FOR TODAY
"Call upon me in the day of trouble;
I will deliver you, and you will honor me."
PSALM 50:15

MOSES

A wall of water

The Lord told Moses to stretch out his special stick toward the sea. Immediately, a strong wind started blowing from the east, and the sea divided, making a path right across from the one side to the other.

Meanwhile, the angel of the Lord went behind the Israelites and caused a pillar of cloud and fire to make it dark on the side where the Egyptians were, but give light to the Israelites. While the Egyptians were struggling to see where they were going, the Israelites were safely walking across the Red Sea on dry ground.

Will God make a path through water if I ask Him to?

A trickle of water from a dripping tap slowly twists and turns down a pathway like a little river. An ant stops just as the water passes in front of it. The ant cannot walk or swim across the flowing water. How easy would it be for you to help the ant get to the other side? Of course it would be easy for you to help the ant. You could lift the ant across, turn the tap off, or block the flow of water with your hand.

God can easily make a path through the sea. He can do whatever He chooses to do, but He will not just do anything and everything people ask Him to do. Even Jesus – who did amazing miracles like healing a blind man – did everything for a good reason. He knew that things like jumping off a tower and expecting angels to catch you are just foolishness (Luke 4:9-12).

If you are ever in trouble and pray to God for help, He will hear and answer you, but He may not answer in the way you expect. Sometimes God answers our prayers in very ordinary ways.

FEBRUARY 26

VERSE FOR TODAY
Jesus answered, "It says: `Do not put the Lord your God to the test.'"
LUKE 4:12

MOSES

Giving thanks

When all the Israelites had passed though the sea on dry ground, the Egyptians chased after them with their horses and chariots. But the Lord made the wheels of their chariots get stuck, and the Egyptians panicked.

Then the Lord said to Moses, "Hold your hand out over the sea, and the water will come back and drown the whole Egyptian army."

Moses obeyed the Lord, and the great walls of water on either side of the path came crashing down on the Egyptians and drowned every single one.

When God's people saw how He had saved them in such a wonderful way, they sang songs of praises and gave thanks.

What is the difference between thanking God and praising God?

When your mom or dad gives you something you have wanted for a long time, or when they have done something very special, you are thankful and you may give them a big hug.

When you tell your mom that she is the best cook in the whole world, you are praising her. Or you may tell a friend how you admire your dad's great strength because he can lift you off the ground with one arm.

You can thank God for a prayer He has answered, or for the things He does for you every day. You can praise the Lord by telling Him how great He is, or by telling others of His awesome power and unfailing love.

You can thank and praise God with words, with singing, or even by dancing like Miriam did.

VERSE FOR TODAY

"Enter his gates with thanksgiving and his courts with praise;
give thanks to him and praise his name."
PSALM 100:4

MOSES

Bitter water

After the Israelites had crossed the Red Sea, Moses led them into the desert of Shur. They had been walking for three days but had not found a drop of water.

They came to place called Marah, but the water there was so bitter that they could not drink it. Everyone started complaining. "What are we going to drink, Moses?" they asked.

So Moses prayed to the Lord, and the Lord showed him a piece of wood. He threw the wood into the bitter water and the water became fresh and sparkling.

How can a piece of wood change the taste of water?

Do you think that the piece of wood Moses threw into the water was special in some way; that it flavored the water or sucked up the bitter taste like a sponge? That piece of wood was probably like any other you'd find lying around in the desert. So what made the piece of wood so special? The wood was not special at all – it was God who made the bitter water fresh!

Problems like the Israelites had can remind us how much we need to rely on God. He wants us to ask Him for help and trust Him to do the impossible. Doing something that doesn't make sense shows that we are willing to trust God and obey Him, without first wanting to know the reason for having to do it.

God still makes bitter things sweet: He takes away our angry thoughts and bitter feelings and puts the sweetness of His peace in our hearts. The Holy Spirit is a well of living water that flows with love from each one who is born again (John 4:10-14).

VERSE FOR TODAY
"See to it that no one misses the grace of God and that no bitter root grows up to cause trouble ..."
HEBREWS 12:15

MOSES

Exodus 16:1-6, 13-15

Bread from Heaven

The Israelites had been in the desert for only a few weeks when they started complaining to Moses. "If only we had stayed in Egypt," they said. "It would have been better for us to have died there. Back in Egypt we had pots of meat and as much other food as we wanted."

Then the Lord said, "I will rain down bread from heaven for you. You are to go out every day and gather only enough for that day. Only on the sixth day you must gather twice as much as on the other days and keep it for the next day – the day of rest."

What is manna?

What do you think manna is? Not sure? Well, neither were the Israelites. That's where the name comes from: manna actually means, "what is it?" The first morning that God sent manna from heaven, people woke up to find white "stuff" lying on the ground. It was food sent from God to feed all the people. All they needed to do was gather it.

Many years later, when Jesus came to earth, He said, "I am the bread of life. He who comes to Me will never go hungry ..." (John 6:35).

What Jesus was saying is that we can only have eternal life by letting His eternal life become a part of us, just like the bread we eat.

When Jesus comes to live in us, He fills the emptiness inside. And when we are filled with His goodness, we lose our appetite for the pleasures that the devil offers us.

VERSE FOR TODAY

Jesus said, "Just as the living Father sent me and I live because of the Father, so the one who feeds on me will live because of me. This is the bread that came down from heaven ... he who feeds on this bread will live forever."
JOHN 6:57-58

March

MOSES

Exodus 17:1-7

Water from a rock?

The Israelites had grumbled against the Lord in a place called the Desert of Sin. They had also disobeyed the Lord by keeping some extra manna for the next day instead of trusting God to give them fresh food every day.

The people became thirsty because they had found no water. They said to Moses, "Why did you bring us out here into the desert to die of thirst?"

Then Moses prayed to the Lord and the Lord said to him, "Walk on ahead with some of the leaders and take your special stick with you. I will stand in front of you on a rock at Mount Sinai. When you strike the rock with your stick, water will come out for all the people to drink."

How can a rock give water?

If you had to squeeze a raw potato really really hard, you may get a few drops of water from it; but water from a rock? That sounds impossible! But with God, nothing is impossible!

God loves doing things in unusual and unexpected ways. We don't know how the water got into the big rock; whether God had been storing it up over a long time, like water that is stored under the ground, or if He created the water from nothing. God had done it before when He created the world, so why should it have been any harder for Him this time? Either way, Moses could have gone around striking rocks in the desert for years and not found a single drop of water. Yet God showed him exactly which rock to strike, and when he struck it, there was enough water for thousands of people and their animals.

Jesus, the Rock, gives us the life-giving water of the Holy Spirit. Everyone is invited to drink freely from Him (John 4:13-14).

MARCH 1

VERSE FOR TODAY

They drank from the spiritual rock that accompanied them, and that rock was Christ.
1 Corinthians 10:4

MOSES

Good advice

Jethro, Moses' father-in-law, heard about everything God had done for the people of Israel, so he came to see Moses. He watched Moses being kept busy from morning till night trying to settle all the quarrels and disagreements the people had.

"Why are you doing this on your own?" he asked Moses. "You will wear yourself out!"

"I have to help these people with their problems. They need to know God's rules and laws," Moses replied.

Then Jethro said, "Take some leaders you can trust and teach them God's rules. Let them rule over different groups of people." So Moses did what Jethro told him.

From then on, Moses only judged the very difficult matters. And Jethro returned to his own country.

How do great leaders get all their work done?

Have you ever wondered how a leader gets all his work done? Think of all the things that go on at your church. How can a pastor do everything and be everywhere at the same time? He can't! You may have noticed that many people help in different ways, like welcoming people, teaching children, or singing in a group. Others do things that no one sees, like sending out letters or cleaning the church.

Even Jesus had a group of disciples that helped Him in different ways. You can learn to be a good helper by doing things that will make life a little easier for your mom or dad.

MARCH 2

VERSE FOR TODAY

When morning came, he [Jesus] called his disciples to him and chose twelve of them, whom he also designated apostles.
LUKE 6:13

MOSES

Exodus 19:1, 9-12, 16-20

Mount Sinai

In the third month of their journey through the desert, the Israelites set up camp at the foot of Mount Sinai while Moses went up the mountain to meet with God.

The Lord said to Moses, "Go tell the people that I will come down in a thick cloud. Tell them to wash their clothes and purify themselves for worship. I will come down to where they can all see Me. Mark a boundary around the mountain that no person or animal may cross."

On the day that the Lord said He would come, there was thunder and lightning on the mountain, and a loud trumpet was heard. The whole mountain was covered with smoke. God spoke to Moses and told him to come up and meet with Him. So Moses went up and disappeared into the thick smoke.

MARCH 3

Can people really meet with God?

God is so big that the whole mountain was covered with His glory. The people were not allowed to come near the mountain. If they even put a foot across the line that Moses had marked off, they would die. Everyone had to get ready to meet God by doing certain things and also by not doing certain things.

When we go to church to meet with God, it can also be an awesome experience for us if we prepare our hearts properly. If we are casual about meeting with God and there is sin in our lives, our hearts cannot come near to Him. But when our hearts are clean and we are ready to worship Him with gladness, we can sense His closeness and become aware of His glory. We can come right into God's presence (Hebrews 4:14-16).

VERSE FOR TODAY

Let us then approach the throne of grace with confidence, so that we may receive mercy and find grace to help us in our time of need.
HEBREWS 4:16

MOSES

God's rules

After Moses had gone back down the mountain to tell everyone what God had told him, God again called Moses to come up the mountain.

God said, "I will give you two stone tablets on which I have written commandments and directions for the people to follow."

So Moses went up Mount Sinai, which was still covered by a cloud, and stayed on the mountain for forty days.

What is a commandment?

A commandment is an instruction from God. He has given us ten very important rules for life – rules to protect our relationship with Him, and rules that protect our relationships with others.

This is what God's ten rules mean:

1. You must only worship the true God.
2. Do not let anything take God's place in your heart.
3. Do not use the Lord's name thoughtlessly or as a swear word.
4. Keep the Lord's Day just for Him and let it be a day of rest.
5. Respect and obey your parents.
6. Do not take someone else's life.
7. Be loyal to the person you are married to.
8. Do not take something that does not belong to you.
9. Do not say anything untrue about someone else.
10. Do not long for the things others have.

These rules weren't given to us to make life difficult. God gave us the Ten Commandments to keep our lives peaceful, safe and happy. By keeping the commandments we honor God and respect others.

VERSE FOR TODAY

I seek you with all my heart; do not let me stray from your commands.
PSALM 119:10

MOSES

Exodus 25:1-9

The Tabernacle (Holy Tent)

MARCH 5

Moses stayed on the mountain for forty days and forty nights, and the Lord told him many important things. The Israelites camping at the bottom of Mount Sinai had seen a dazzling light come down on the mountain. Now it was covered with cloud.

The Lord said to Moses, "The people must make a sacred Tent for Me so that I can come and live among them. Let them make an offering to Me and I will receive whatever anyone wishes to give."

Then the Lord told Moses what the people could bring as an offering and explained to him exactly how the Tent should be built.

Can God fit into a tent?

God wanted to be close to His people as they wandered through the desert. He wanted to meet with His people just as He had met with Adam in the Garden of Eden before he sinned. The sin in Adam became like a wall between him and God.

Because of sin, people would never be able to go in and out of the Tent to meet God face to face. A special curtain in the Tent separated the people from God. Only the High Priest could go into the very Holy Place behind the curtain once a year to ask for forgiveness for everyone.

If God is bigger than the whole universe, how could He get down into a tent to be close to His people? (1 Kings 8:27). Just as an artist does not become part of his painting, so God does not have to get inside His own creation in a physical way. He can be everywhere and in a certain place at the same time! What is even more amazing is that God, through the Holy Spirit, comes to live inside every person who believes in Jesus!

VERSE FOR TODAY

For this is what the high and lofty One says – he who lives forever, whose name is holy: "I live in a high and holy place, but also with him who is contrite and lowly in spirit ..."
ISAIAH 57:15

MOSES

The Covenant Box

Inside the Holy Tent, where God would meet with the people of Israel, there was to be a holy box.

The Lord told Moses exactly how big it should be and what it should look like. It was to be made of acacia wood and covered with gold on the inside and the outside. It was to have rings on the sides where the poles for carrying it could be placed.

Moses was told to put the stone tablets – on which the commandments were written – inside the Covenant Box.

How can I remember all God's rules?

Do you sometimes have trouble remembering things? God knows how easily we forget rules and instructions, especially a whole long list of them. That is why God wrote the commandments on stone tablets that would last a long, long time. God told Moses to keep them safely inside the Covenant Box.

However, now the people wouldn't be able to read the commandments to make sure they were following them. So Moses told the parents to teach the commandments to their children. He also told them to write the commandments on their doorposts; to wear them on their foreheads, and to tie them around their arms (Deuteronomy 6:4-9).

An even better way of remembering God's rules (and doing them), is to write the commandments in your heart. That means, if your heart wants to please the Lord, the Ten Commandments actually become one rule: Love the Lord with all your heart and love others as you love yourself (Matthew 22:37-40). Now that is a lot easier to remember!

MARCH 6

VERSE FOR TODAY

I have hidden your word in my heart that I might not sin against you.
PSALM 119:11

MOSES

The altar

The Lord told Moses about all the other things that must be inside the Holy Tent and in the courtyard that surrounded it.

God said, "Make a square altar out of acacia wood and put rings on the sides for the poles that will be used to carry the altar. You must also make shovels, bowls, hooks, and pans out of bronze."

Moses did what the Lord told him to do and had the altar made exactly as the Lord had said.

Do we still have altars today?

An altar was used for all the offerings that were made to the Lord (see Leviticus 1-5). It was made of wood or big stones, and a fire would be made on top of it. Different kinds of offerings could be made on it, and it was the only place where people could offer an animal to God for their sin. The animal would be killed and laid on the altar as a sign that the sin had been paid for by death and blood. This sign was pointing to Jesus who would come to earth to lay down His life, once and for all, and die for every sin in the world.

Because the blood of Jesus washes every sin from our hearts (1 John 1:7), we no longer need to sacrifice animals for the forgiveness of our sins, and so we don't need an altar (see Hebrews 10:1-7).

Once we are forgiven, the good we do and say become our sacrifice – a sacrifice of praise that God will accept because Jesus has made us pure (Hebrews 13:15-16).

MARCH 7

VERSE FOR TODAY

You also, like living stones, are being built into a spiritual house to be a holy priesthood, offering spiritual sacrifices acceptable to God through Jesus Christ.

1 PETER 2:5

MOSES

The golden calf

Moses had been up on Mount Sinai for a long time and the people in the camp below were becoming impatient. They said to Aaron, "We don't know what has happened to Moses, so make a god that will lead us."

So Aaron told the people to take off the golden earrings they had received from the Egyptians and he melted the gold. Then he formed it into the shape of a calf.

As Moses was coming down from the mountain he saw the people worshiping the calf. He was so furious that he smashed the stone tablets the Lord had given him. When he got to the camp, he melted the golden calf, ground the gold into a fine powder and mixed it with the drinking water.

What is idolatry?

Isn't this one of the silliest things you've ever heard? These people made a statue of a calf and actually believed that it had led them out of Egypt! Although they had made the calf themselves, they respected it as though it had become greater than them. The calf became their idol.

Idolatry means worshiping or believing in things instead of in God. Do you remember the second commandment? Look up Exodus 20:2-5 and read it again.

Even though you probably don't have idols in your room and you don't bow down to things in nature, there is a danger of other things creeping into your heart; things that become so important that you let them take God's place. When your thoughts are filled with a particular thing all the time, it means that it is taking up God's space in your heart.

MARCH 8

VERSE FOR TODAY
You shall have no other gods before me.
Exodus 20:3

MOSES

Shining for the Lord

Moses went up the mountain again; this time with a new set of stone tablets for God to write on. Moses had smashed the first set of commandments in anger when he saw the Israelites worshiping the golden calf.

When he got back, his face was shining because he had been speaking with the Lord. When the people saw the face of Moses shining, they were afraid to go near him. Moses didn't know that his face was shining and he called them closer. First, Aaron and the leaders went to him, then the others gathered around, and Moses gave them the laws the Lord had given him on the mountain.

How can I shine for Jesus?

If you have a glow-in-the-dark sticker or a watch with glowing hands, you would probably have noticed that when you hold it next to the light and then turn the light off, it shines brightly. After a while, it loses its glow, and by morning it is rather dim.

Moses had been with God for such a long time that his face started shining. Every time he met with God, his face shone so brightly that he had to cover it with a cloth.

We know that God is so pure and holy that we cannot look at Him and live (Exodus 33:20). So, whenever God spoke to someone, He would shield them so they would not see His face.

The more time we spend reading the Bible and praying, the more we allow God's light to shine in our hearts (2 Corinthians 4:6). The more time we spend with the Lord, the more brightly we will shine for Him – not like an ordinary light, but with the beauty and purity of God.

VERSE FOR TODAY

"In the same way, let your light shine before men, that they may see your good deeds and praise your Father in heaven."
MATTHEW 5:16

MOSES

Craftsmen needed

Moses said to the people of Israel, "This is what the Lord has commanded: All the skilled workers are to come and make the Tent of the Lord, the Covenant Box, the table, the lampstand, the two altars and all the fittings."

Then God chose a man from the tribe of Judah and gave him the skill, ability and understanding to do every kind of work. The Lord also gave him a helper from the tribe of Dan to teach their crafts to others. So Bezalel, and his helper, Oholiab, got the list of instructions from Moses and started working.

How can I use my talents for God?

God has given each of us talents and abilities to do certain things well. Even if others have the same talent you have, your talent is special because you are unique – with different strengths and weaknesses, likes and dislikes. The way you were brought up, the help and encouragement you've received and even the hardships in your life, can help to develop your abilities in a certain way.

If you are wondering whether God could actually use your abilities, remember that He made you the way He wanted you to be. He put everything inside you that you will ever need to please Him. God does not wait until you are perfect. He wants to use you right now – just the way you are.

And, in case you thought you don't have a talent; whatever you're good at is your God-given talent. Use your abilities for His glory. Humbly honor God when you are praised and look for ways to help and encourage others.

VERSE FOR TODAY
For we are God's workmanship, created in Christ Jesus to do good works, which God prepared in advance for us to do.
EPHESIANS 2:10

MOSES

More than enough

Now that Moses was back, and the Israelites had seen God's awesome power, they realized that it had been a bad idea to make the golden calf.

God was giving them another chance to show their love for Him by letting them bring gifts that would be used to build the Tabernacle. The Tabernacle would be a special place where God would meet with them – right in their camp!

The people were so excited that they brought piles and piles of stuff: there was a pile for gold, a pile for silver, a pile for fine linen. Eventually there was so much that Moses had to tell everyone to stop bringing things. (The full list of things people brought is in Exodus 25:1-7).

Can I also give something to God's work?

God loves a cheerful giver (2 Corinthians 9:7). God loves it when we give gladly without feeling that we have to give in order to stay in His "good books."

Remember how the wise men traveled a long way to take beautiful gifts to Jesus the King of kings (Matthew 2:11). They did not just send a few gifts with someone traveling that way. They wanted to take the gifts themselves. When we give to God, we should become part of the gift by giving of ourselves, our time, and perhaps even some of our hard-earned pocket money.

God can use whatever we give when we give with a heart of joy. By giving to God, we worship Him. We show Him our love by the gifts we bring. Remember, Jesus sees even the smallest love-gift you give.

MARCH 11

VERSE FOR TODAY

But a poor widow came and put in two very small copper coins, worth only a fraction of a penny. Calling his disciples to him, Jesus said, "I tell you the truth, this poor widow has put more into the treasury than all the others."
MARK 12:42-43

MOSES

The Lord lives with His people

At the beginning of the second year after the Israelites left Egypt, the Tent of the Lord was ready. The stone tablets were put in the Covenant Box, the table and the lampstand were put in the Tent and the curtain that kept the people from the holy presence of God was hung across the front of the Tent.

When everything was in place, a cloud covered the Tent and the dazzling light of God's presence filled it.

Why is there no cloud in church?

In a way, the Holy Tent was like a church building today. It was a special place where God and ordinary people would meet in a close way. It was a place where people could come to worship God, ask for forgiveness at the altar, and bring an offering of thanks to God. It reminded people that the Lord is always close to us and that He is very real!

Through Jesus, God is in every place where even a few people gather together in His Name (Matthew 18:20). A church is a group of people who believe in God and have come together to worship Him.

You may be wondering why we don't see the bright light of God's presence in church, or a cloud covering the church building. Before Jesus left the earth to go back to His Father in heaven, He told His disciples that He would send the Holy Spirit to help them, to comfort them and to guide them. Forty days later the Holy Spirit came down and filled every believer.

When a person becomes a believer (a follower of Jesus), the Holy Spirit fills him or her. In other words, God lives inside every believer and we are now His Holy Tent.

MARCH 12

VERSE FOR TODAY

Your body is a temple of the Holy Spirit,
who is in you, whom you have received from God.
1 CORINTHIANS 6:19

MOSES

Numbers 9:15-23

The pillar of cloud and fire

The cloud that covered the Tent of the Lord was a sign to the Israelites that the Lord was with them. At night, the cloud was like a fire above the Tent.

The Israelites did not carry on walking when the cloud stopped over the Tent. But when the cloud lifted and moved, the Israelites would follow it. And wherever the cloud stopped, the Israelites would set up their camp.

Sometimes the cloud would stay over the Tent for only a day or two and sometimes it stayed for a whole year or even longer.

How does the Lord guide us?

The cloud of God's presence showed the Israelites when to walk, when to stop and where to go. The dark cloud guided them during the day and the fiery cloud guided them at night.

The Israelites had a cloud to guide them, but how can you know the way God wants you to go when you need to make an important decision and you don't know what to do?

When you ask Jesus to save you, and you follow Him, the Holy Spirit lives inside you. Through the Holy Spirit, God guides you in a very special way. He puts good thoughts in your mind. He also lets your heart feel peaceful when you obey Him, or uneasy when you're going the wrong way.

Yet relying only on feelings can be confusing. That is why God has given us the Bible as a light to guide us when the way gets dark.

MARCH 13

VERSE FOR TODAY

Trust in the Lord with all your heart and lean not on your own understanding; in all your ways acknowledge him, and he will make your paths straight.
PROVERBS 3:5-6

MOSES

The spies

The Israelites were very close to Canaan – the land God had promised them.

The Lord said to Moses, "Choose a leader from each of the twelve tribes and send them as spies into the land of Canaan." So Moses sent out twelve spies and told them to find out what the country was like, how many people lived there, and how strong they were.

After forty days, the spies came back carrying large bunches of grapes and other fruit. They told Moses that there were cities with high walls and very big people living there. Of the twelve spies, only Joshua and Caleb trusted God and said that they had nothing to fear because God was on their side. The other ten said that they would never be able to conquer the ungodly people who lived in the Promised Land.

If God can see everywhere, why does He need spies?

God did not need spies in order to get information about the people or the land He had created. God knew exactly how many grains of sand were in the Promised Land and how many hairs were on the head of each person living there. If God did not need to find out more about the land and the people, why did He tell Moses to send spies to go find out about them? Do you think that Moses needed to know what they were up against?

God wanted to see whether the Israelites believed that He was able to give them what He had promised. From what the spies had said, the Israelites realized that they would not be able to simply walk in and take over. Would they trust God enough to face the challenge of conquering the land? Joshua and Caleb passed the test of faith by trusting God; the other spies failed and caused the whole nation to doubt God.

VERSE FOR TODAY

Remember how the LORD your God led you all the way in
the desert these forty years, to humble you and to
test you in order to know what was in your heart.
DEUTERONOMY 8:2

MOSES

Moses gets it wrong again

Moses was just as disappointed as Joshua and Caleb that God was sending the Israelites back into the desert instead of letting them go into the Promised Land. The Israelites would have to spend forty years in the desert as punishment for their unbelief!

What made things worse for Moses was that the people were always complaining. This time they were in the Desert of Zin. "Why have you brought us out into this miserable place where there is no water and where nothing will grow," they moaned.

Then Moses and Aaron went to the Holy Tent where God told Moses to speak to a certain rock and water would come from it. So Moses took his stick and had everybody gather around the rock. "Listen," he said, "must we get water out of this rock for you?" Then Moses struck the rock with his stick and water gushed out. But the Lord was not pleased with Moses because he did not obey and honor Him by speaking to the rock.

How can I control my temper?

We all have bad days; days when everything goes wrong, when we are disappointed, when others annoy us and when we are very tired. Our sinful nature can easily take advantage of our weakness. We feel like shouting at everyone and throwing things around. When you feel that way, allow the Holy Spirit to control you instead of your feelings.

Don't let angry feelings pile up inside. Find good ways to let angry feelings come out in a controlled way – for example, by telling someone why you feel angry, or by using your emotional energy through exercise.

Ask the Lord to give you peace and help you feel calm inside.

VERSE FOR TODAY

My dear brothers, take note of this: Everyone should be
quick to listen, slow to speak and slow to become angry.
JAMES 1:19

MOSES

The bronze snake

The Israelites would have to stay in the desert until all those who had complained and grumbled against the Lord had died. Only their children would be allowed to go into the Promised Land (Numbers 14:31-32).

Yet, even while they were on their way from Mount Hor to the area of Edom, the people started complaining again. So God put poisonous snakes among the people and many Israelites were bitten and died.

The people realized that they had sinned against the Lord and asked Moses to pray for them. Then God said to Moses "Make a snake and put it on a pole; anyone who is bitten can look at it and live."

So Moses made a bronze snake and lifted it up on a pole. And all those who obeyed God and looked up at the snake were healed.

Why did God make snakes?

Are you scared of snakes? Imagine creeping into a tent on a dark night and putting your hand on something soft and slithery.

Snakes, like other dangerous animals, are all a part of God's creation. Before Adam and Eve sinned, there was no danger and no death. Eve wasn't even afraid of a snake! Sin changed that. The day Adam and Eve sinned, God cursed the snake and said, "I will make you and the woman hate each other. Her children will crush your head, and you will bite their heel" (Genesis 3:14-15). For the Israelites, the snake had again become a sign of death – the punishment for disobedience and rebellion.

Only Jesus could come and make things right again.

Many years later Jesus did come, and He was lifted up on a cross to die and to bring healing to all those who look to Him.

VERSE FOR TODAY

Just as Moses lifted up the snake in the desert, so the Son of Man must be lifted up, that everyone who believes in him may have eternal life.

John 3:14-15

BALAAM

Numbers 22:21-31

God uses a donkey

The Israelites eventually moved to the valley of Moab. When the king of Moab heard how God had helped them defeat the Amorite army, he was terrified. So he sent messengers to fetch Balaam to curse the Israelite nation.

At first, God told Balaam not to go with them. Later, when the king sent more messengers, the Lord told Balaam to go with them but to only do what He told him to. The next day Balaam left with them. On the way, the angel of the Lord stood in front of the donkey that Balaam was riding on. When the donkey ran into the field, Balaam lost his temper and beat it. But the angel moved on ahead and stood in a place where the path narrowed. The donkey saw the angel and lay down, so Balaam beat it again.

This time, the Lord made the donkey speak to Balaam. "What have I done to you and why are you beating me?" the donkey said. Then the Lord let Balaam see the angel standing in the road with his sword. So Balaam fell with his face to the ground.

MARCH 17

Can a donkey really speak?

Balaam did not listen to God – perhaps he would listen to his donkey! Balaam's selfish heart was leading him, not his desire to do what God wanted. We know this because God was very angry when Balaam left with the messengers.

Although a donkey cannot speak, God used it to speak to Balaam. God warned Balaam before his stubborn heart got him into big trouble.

Learn to listen patiently and carefully to what God is saying so that the voice of His Spirit in your heart is not drowned out by other voices.

VERSE FOR TODAY

"I tell you," Jesus replied, "If they keep quiet, the stones will cry out."
LUKE 19:40

BALAAM

Bless you!

The angel of the Lord stopped Balaam while he was on his way to the king of Moab. He said to Balaam, "Go with the men, but say only what I tell you to say." So Balaam went with them to meet King Balak.

When Balaam got there, he told the king that he could only say what God told him to say.

The next morning, the king took Balaam to a place where he could see the people of Israel. Balaam went alone to the top of a hill where the Lord told him what to say. Then Balaam went back down to the king.

"Put a curse on the Israelites now!" the king demanded. But instead, Balaam started to speak words of blessing on God's people!

Can the words we say really bless someone?

You may have heard someone say, "bless you," and wondered if those words really mean anything, or if it's just a nice thing to say. Words can be very powerful and can even change someone's life. When we say "bless you" (and mean it), we are asking God to bless that person. Only He can send real blessing into someone's life.

God's blessing is His special favor and kindness. It is also His protection and a feeling of closeness to Him. God loves to bless people because He is good and kind (Psalm 145:9).

Just as bad, unkind words can hurt people, so words of blessing can be encouraging and can heal sad and lonely hearts. You can go around spreading as many blessings as you want because God's supply of blessings never runs out!

MARCH 18

VERSE FOR TODAY

Praise be to the God and Father of our Lord Jesus Christ, who has blessed us in the heavenly realms with every spiritual blessing in Christ.
EPHESIANS 1:3

MOSES

Moses hands over to Joshua

Moses was now one hundred and twenty years old. He called everyone together and said to them, "Love the Lord your God; obey Him and be faithful to Him and you will live long in the land He has promised to give you." Moses also told the Israelites that he would no longer be their leader. Joshua would become the one to lead them into the Promised Land.

Then Moses went to the top of a high mountain where God showed him the land He had chosen for His people. Yet, Moses himself was not allowed to enter into the Promised Land because he had disobeyed God by striking the rock instead of speaking to it. Moses died in the land of Moab and the Lord buried him there.

Does God know when I will die?

God knows exactly how many days each of us will live here on earth. Does it seem a bit scary to know that there is a certain day on which you will die and there is nothing that can change that?

On the other hand, isn't it comforting to know that nothing can take your life before that time – that you are completely safe in God's hands! It is also comforting that God Himself will be there to take us to be with Him, right into His presence where we will be safe and happy forever.

For those who believe in Jesus and have been saved from sin, death is not the end! If you read Matthew 17:1-3, you will see that Moses was actually talking to Jesus hundreds of years later, when Jesus was on earth. Moses did not have his human body anymore. He had received a different kind of body; one that never gets old and will never die (2 Corinthians 5:1).

MARCH 19

VERSE FOR TODAY

All the days ordained for me were written
in your book before one of them came to be.
PSALM 139:16

JOSHUA

Honoring the new leader

After Moses had died, the Lord spoke to Joshua. "Get the people ready to cross the Jordan River into the Promised Land. I have given to you and all My people the whole land."

While Moses was their leader, two of the tribes had said that they would rather settle on the east side of the Jordan River than cross into the Promised Land (Numbers 32:15-25). Moses said that if they helped the other tribes conquer the enemy in Canaan, they could return to their homes on the east side of the river.

So Joshua said to the two tribes, "Remember the promise you made to Moses to help the other tribes conquer the Promised Land. If you do what you said you would, the Lord will give you the land you want."

Then they said to Joshua, "We will do everything you have told us, and go wherever you send us."

For how long must I keep a promise?

If you want someone to be sure that you will do what you said you would, simply tell the person that you will do it. If you are known as a person who can be trusted, that is enough. Always be someone who can be trusted and counted on to keep your word.

If you do make a promise, be sure that you are able to do what you promised. If your promise depends on good weather, someone else's help, or Mom's permission – don't promise! You should rather say, I will do my best, or, as soon as I can, or, if I am allowed to.

Always keep a promise because a kept promise shows your honor; a broken promise becomes a lie.

MARCH 20

VERSE FOR TODAY
"Simply let your 'Yes' be 'Yes,' and your 'No,' 'No.'"
MATTHEW 5:37

RAHAB

Two spies risk their lives

The first city that the Israelites would have to conquer in the land of Canaan was the city of Jericho. Joshua sent spies to secretly explore the land and the city of Jericho.

The two spies managed to get right inside the city without being noticed. There, they found a woman who was willing to let them stay for the night. Somehow the king found out that the spies were staying with Rahab and sent his soldiers to arrest them.

Meanwhile, Rahab had hidden the spies under a pile of flax stalks. When the soldiers knocked on Rahab's door asking about the men, she told them that some men had been there earlier, but that they had left the city before sunset. Then the king's men rushed out to go track them down.

Can I be a spy for God one day?

MARCH 21

Have you ever spied on someone? It can be a lot of fun to watch people going about their work not knowing that someone is watching them.

God may not need you to be a spy for Him, but He does have an equally daring assignment for you: to go right into the enemy's territory and tell others about Him. The people out there are not the enemy though: God's enemy cannot be seen.

His enemy is the devil, who goes around spreading all sorts of evil. He sows doubts in the minds of people and scatters despair in their hearts. Everywhere he goes he leaves misery and sadness. But you can bring hope to those who don't know Jesus by telling them about His love for them. Jesus will forgive their sins and give them hope. He will be their best friend, forever!

VERSE FOR TODAY

And God is able to make all grace abound to you, so that in all things at all times, having all that you need, you will abound in every good work.
2 Corinthians 9:8

RAHAB

The great escape

The king of Jericho had his men looking all over the countryside for the Israelite spies who were still hiding under the pile of drying linen plants on the roof of Rahab's house.

Rahab went up and said to them, "We have heard how your God dried up the Red Sea and let you conquer the kings east of the Jordan River. Now be as kind to me and my family as I have been to you. When you attack the city, promise me that you will not let us be killed."

The spies said to her, "When we invade your land, tie this red cord to the window and you will not be harmed."

Then Rahab, whose house was built into the wall surrounding the city, helped the spies escape by letting them down the outside of the wall with a long rope.

Is believing in God all I must do to be saved?

It took a lot of courage for Rahab to hide the spies in her house. She was willing to risk her life because she had heard about the great things God had done for the Israelites. She believed that their God is the only true God.

Rahab not only believed – she acted. She showed that her faith was real. By tying the red ribbon to her window, she showed that she believed her life would be spared (see Hebrews 11:31).

Although Rahab believed in God, it was the red cord that saved her. Even though we believe in God, it is the blood of Jesus that saves us. Merely believing that God exists will not save us just as Rahab's belief alone would not have saved her. She had to tie the red cord where it could be seen.

There is only one way to be saved – by asking Jesus to forgive us.

MARCH 22

VERSE FOR TODAY

For it is with your heart that you believe and are justified, and it is with your mouth that you confess and are saved.

ROMANS 10:10

JOSHUA

Crossing the river

After hiding in the countryside for three days, the men that had spied on the city of Jericho returned to Joshua.

Then the Lord said to Joshua, "Tell the priests to carry the Covenant Box and walk toward the river, and when they reach it, they must not stop."

The priests did what the Lord said, and when they stepped into the Jordan River, the water stopped flowing and everyone walked across on dry ground.

Then the Lord said, "Choose a man from each tribe to carry a big stone from the middle of the river to where you camp tonight." So the twelve men carried the stones and made them into a pile. "This pile of stones will remind the people of what happened here today," Joshua said.

How can I remember all the great things God has done for me?

MARCH 23

Has God answered a prayer of yours in an unusual way? Has He shown you His faithfulness at a time when you really needed Him to help you?

If we don't remember the times when God has done amazing things in our lives, we may become like the Israelites who forgot how God had made a way for them through the Red Sea when Pharaoh's army was right behind them. God opened a way for the Israelites again, only this time they made a big pile of stones that would remind them of His faithfulness.

One way in which you can remember God's answers to your prayers and the promises He has given you, is to write down what happened and the date on which it happened. You could also add verses from the Bible. Write them in a journal or in the back of your Bible.

VERSE FOR TODAY
Devote yourselves to prayer, being watchful and thankful.
COLOSSIANS 4:2

JOSHUA

The strong walls of Jericho

At last the Israelites were in the Promised Land! But their troubles were not over yet. They had to face the people living there and conquer them. The gates of Jericho were kept shut and guarded, and the wall around the city was very high. Then God said to Joshua, "I am giving you Jericho with its king and all its fierce soldiers."

The Lord told Joshua exactly what to do. On the first day, the people walked around the city once. The priest carrying the Covenant Box followed the priest blowing the trumpets. They marched around the city once every day for six days. On the seventh day, they marched around the city seven times. On the seventh time around, Joshua ordered the people to shout and the priests to blow their trumpets – and the wall collapsed! Then the Israelites went up into the city and took it.

Can God make my "big wall" come down?

Do you have a problem in your life that seems to be like a huge wall? Maybe it is there all the time – wherever you go; whatever you do, the same wall blocks your way.

Life is not a smooth highway. There will always be ups and downs, bumps in the road, and unexpected turns. Jesus did not promise us an easy, trouble-free life (Luke 9:23).

Although problems help us to grow stronger in our faith, some may be so big that we cannot climb over them or get around them. They don't seem to go away, no matter what we do. Only God can break down the walls in your life that are keeping you from doing your best and growing in your relationship with Him. Ask Him to break them down.

MARCH 24

VERSE FOR TODAY
Jesus said, "In this world you will have trouble.
But take heart! I have overcome the world."
JOHN 16:33

JOSHUA

Joshua 7:1-7, 20-21

Sin in the camp

The city of Jericho lay in ruins! Joshua had told the people of Israel not to take anything from the city: they were not to keep a single thing for themselves. However, one man disobeyed the Lord's instruction. He secretly took a beautiful coat, some silver and a bar of gold, and buried them in his tent.

Joshua did not know that Achan had taken the treasures and hidden them. He sent some soldiers to the nearby city of Ai to attack it. Yet even though it was only a small city, the Israelite army was defeated and chased back. The Israelites lost their courage and were afraid.

When Joshua prayed and asked the Lord why He had let them be defeated, God told him that Israel had sinned.

MARCH 25

Why are others punished for one person's disobedience?

Has your whole class ever been punished for making a noise when you weren't even talking to anyone? It seems unfair that everyone has to suffer just because one or two break the rules and don't care.

God had given the Israelites a strict order not to take anything from the city. To Achan, it seemed such a waste to leave the gold and silver behind, and besides, if he didn't take it, someone else was bound to take it. Yet his disobedience cost him his life and the lives of many Israelites who were killed in battle. It is unfair that the innocent suffer because of others; but remember, the devil who encourages disobedience never plays fair.

Because God is completely holy and fair, He cannot overlook sin. He also cannot bless His people when there is unforgiven sin in their lives.

VERSE FOR TODAY
Search me, O God, and know my heart ... See if there is any offensive way in me, and lead me in the way everlasting.
PSALM 139:23-24

JOSHUA

Victory!

Achan, whose sin had caused the Israelite army to be defeated, was punished by death. Now that the sin of disobedience had been dealt with, God could bless the Israelites again.

God said to Joshua, "Don't be afraid or discouraged, I will give you victory over the king of Ai."

The next day, Joshua sent his best fighting men behind the city where they could not be seen. The rest of the army went toward the gates as if they were going to attack. When the king's men came out to fight them, the Israelite army started running away as they had done the first time. All the men of Ai chased after them and left the city gates wide open. Then the Israelites, who had been hiding, ran into the city and set it on fire. Now, the men of Ai could not run back to the safety of their city.

So Joshua's men turned around to attack them from the front, while the other soldiers came and attacked from behind, and the men of Ai were defeated.

How can I have victory over temptations around me?

When you are on God's side, you are on the winning side! The devil will never be able to win against God. Jesus conquered the devil, once and for all, when He died on the cross for all our past sins and the wrong things we still do. Yet, it is up to you to win over daily temptations.

Here are a few things to help you be a winner:

Pray every morning for God's help and for His protection from evil (Matthew 6:13). Don't go to places where you will be tempted more easily. Fill your mind with good things (Philippians 4:8).

MARCH 26

VERSE FOR TODAY
Submit yourselves, then, to God. Resist the devil, and he will flee from you.
JAMES 4:7

JOSHUA

Joshua is tricked

The victories of Israel became known all over the land. When the people of Gibeon heard how Joshua had conquered Jericho and Ai, they decided to fool him. They sent men dressed in worn-out clothes and with moldy bread to meet with Joshua. The men said to Joshua, "See, we have come from a distant land to make peace with you. We are at your service."

Then Joshua's men said, "Why should we make a treaty with you? Maybe you live nearby."

"Look at our bread," they replied. "When we left home, this bread was freshly baked. Even our clothes and sandals are worn out from the long journey."

So Joshua made a peace treaty with them – without asking the Lord. Three days later Joshua found out that the men lived nearby, but the Israelites could do nothing to them.

How do I know whom to trust?

It is in the nature of a young child to trust others because that is the way God has made us. From birth, we learn to trust our parents. Later, we trust our family, and eventually we start trusting teachers and other adults.

If you have been brought up around good people, it may come as a surprise that not everyone can be trusted. Even ordinary people with a friendly smile may have a heart that cannot be trusted. Joshua should have prayed and asked God what to do.

Let your parents know about the people you talk to. And before you make any deals or plans with someone you don't know well, ask your parents what they think – and above all, ask God!

MARCH 27

VERSE FOR TODAY
The LORD is good, a refuge in times of trouble.
He cares for those who trust in him.
NAHUM 1:7

JOSHUA

The day the sun stood still

When the other kings in the land heard that the people of Gibeon had made peace with the Israelites, they joined forces to attack them. So the people of Gibeon sent a message to Joshua, "Please don't abandon us; come help us at once!"

So Joshua and his army made a surprise attack on the Amorite army, and while they were running away, the Lord made large hailstones fall on them. While all the fighting was going on, Joshua spoke to the Lord so that others could hear: "Sun, stand still over Gibeon," he said.

Then the Lord made the sun stand still in the middle of the sky and it did not go down for a whole day. Never before, and never since, has there been a day like that, when God listened to the command of a person.

Does the sun go around the earth?

You have probably heard about our Solar System and the path the planets take around the sun. The planet closest to the sun is very hot, while the one farthest away is very, very cold! God has put the earth at just the right distance from the sun so that we can enjoy the outdoors without frying or freezing.

If the planets are going around the sun, how could God have made the sun stand still? As far as Joshua was concerned, the sun stopped moving across the sky – that is all that mattered.

On the other hand, the thought of God stopping the earth from spinning for a day is just as awesome! Exactly how God did what He did doesn't really matter. The fact that He actually stopped the sun from moving across the sky is so amazing that no one can explain it. Isn't that great!

MARCH 28

VERSE FOR TODAY
The Mighty One, God, the Lord, speaks and summons the earth from the rising of the sun to the place where it sets.
PSALM 50:1

JOSHUA

The promised reward

At last, the Israelites conquered the land the Lord had promised them. The people settled in their new homes and villages and the Lord gave them peace. Not one of their enemies had been able to stand against them because the Lord had given them victory.

Then Joshua called the tribes that wanted to settle on the far side of the Jordan River but had helped the rest of Israel fight their battles.

He said to them, "You have done everything Moses ordered you to do and have obeyed my commands. You have not deserted your fellow-Israelites. Now, go back to your land on the east side of the Jordan, and make sure you obey the commandments of the Lord. Always be faithful to Him. You are going home with many clothes, lots of animals, silver and gold. When you get back, share them with the others." So the men from the two tribes went home.

Will I ever get a reward from God?

Have you ever wished you would get a prize for doing well at school or perhaps earn a big trophy for a sports achievement? How disappointed we feel when we have worked and trained as hard as everyone else, but we go home with nothing to show.

Always remember: rewards for achievements on earth do not last forever. However, Jesus said that even if we give a cup of cold water to someone, we will be rewarded (Mark 9:41).

Each time you do good for Jesus, your reward (which you can't see yet) is getting bigger and bigger in heaven – where it is being kept safe until you get there one day (Matthew 6:19-20).

VERSE FOR TODAY

Everyone who competes in the games goes into
strict training. They do it to get a crown that will not last;
but we do it to get a crown that will last forever.
1 CORINTHIANS 9:25

Judges 2:1-8, 3:5-6

JOSHUA

Mixing with the wrong people

Not long after the Israelites had settled in the Promised Land, they became friendly with the wicked people they were supposed to have driven from the land. The Israelites did not tear down the idols and altars of the heathen people as God had told them to. So God said to them, "I will no longer drive out the people living in your land. They will be like thorns in your sides."

Joshua died at the age of one hundred and ten, and the next generation forgot what the Lord had done for Israel. They settled among the heathen tribes, married with them and worshiped their gods.

Is it okay to have friends who don't believe in God?

One of the greatest gifts God has given us is the gift of friendship. It is wonderful to have close friends with whom you can have fun and share your dreams. And isn't it comforting to have someone who understands you and encourages you when life gets tough?

Jesus had a group of close friends with whom He spent most of His time. The night before He faced death on a cross, He went to a garden to pray with them. The human part of Jesus longed for the support of those closest to Him.

Yet, Jesus did not only have His twelve close friends. He also made friends with sinners – bad people who probably didn't even know how to pray. Jesus wanted them to know about God's love too, and they would only see the love of the Father by seeing how much He loved them.

God also wants us to reach out to those who don't know Him, but He doesn't want us to get caught up in the wrong things they do. Always make sure that your closest friends know what you believe.

MARCH 30

VERSE FOR TODAY
A righteous man is cautious in friendship,
but the way of the wicked leads them astray.
PROVERBS 12:26

GIDEON

Judges 6:1, 11-14

God chooses a brave man

The Israelites had forgotten all that God had done for them: how He had brought them out of slavery in Egypt.

Life had settled down, and the people now lived comfortably and peacefully in the land God had promised them. They no longer trusted and depended on God, and they even started worshiping the gods of the heathen people living in the land! The Lord did not want them to become like the other nations. He wanted His chosen people to be separate and devoted to Him. So God allowed the people of Midian to rule over the Israelites.

One day, the angel of the Lord came to Gideon while he was secretly threshing wheat (Gideon was afraid the Midianites would find him). The angel said to him, "The Lord is with you, brave and mighty man. Go with your great strength and rescue Israel from the Midianites!"

Does God only choose special people to do important tasks?

Don't you hate it when teams are being chosen from a whole bunch of kids, and the leaders start choosing the strongest, fastest or cleverest kids? Some kids wait and wait, hoping that they will be the next to be chosen, but the longer they wait, the more embarrassing it becomes.

Isn't it great to know that God doesn't choose us that way: God looks at our hearts. Even Gideon couldn't believe that the Lord actually wanted to use him, and he asked, "How can I rescue Israel? My family is the weakest in the tribe and I am the least important in my family."

Then the Lord replied, "You can do it because I will help you!"

God is looking for those who will be brave for Him!

MARCH 31

VERSE FOR TODAY

The LORD does not look at the things man looks at. Man looks at the outward appearance, but the LORD looks at the heart.
1 SAMUEL 16:7

April

GIDEON

A daring act

The Lord's angel had told Gideon that God would use him to rescue the Israelites from their enemies. That evening, the angel told him to take two bulls and go destroy his father's altar to the heathen god, Baal. The Lord also told him to build an altar on the exact same spot and burn the second bull on it, using the wood from the Asherah pole, which was also an idol.

That night, while everybody was sleeping, he and ten of his servants took the two bulls and tore down the altar. In the morning, when the people of the town got up and found that their altar had been torn down, they asked one another, "Who did this?" When they found out that Gideon had done it, they said to his father Joash, "Bring Gideon here so we can put him to death."

But Joash said, "Are you trying to defend Baal? It is his altar that was torn down; let Baal defend himself!"

How can I openly honor God?

People usually talk and write about the things that fill their minds. David wrote many beautiful songs and poems about the Lord because he thought about God all the time (Psalm 63:6).

Those who watch and listen to horrible things, fill their minds (and hearts) with wrong things. The evil that pollutes their minds starts spilling out in different ways that can be seen and heard by those around them.

If someone in your school has scribbled bad words on a desk or a wall, or has written something bad about the Lord, you could ask your teacher if you may scrape it off or blot it out with a marker pen. God will honor your bold step when you, like Gideon, do the right thing.

APRIL 1

VERSE FOR TODAY
"Blessed are the pure in heart, for they will see God."
MATTHEW 5:8

Just checking

Gideon wanted to make very sure that God wanted him to rescue the Israelites from their enemies. He said to the Lord, "I will put a sheep skin on the ground outside tonight. In the morning, if there is only dew on the fleece and not on the ground, I will know that You are going to use me to rescue Israel."

When Gideon got up the next morning, the fleece was so wet that he filled a bowl with the water he squeezed from it even though the ground around the fleece was dry. Then Gideon said to God, "Don't be angry with me. Please just let me ask one more thing. This time, let the fleece be dry and the ground wet." The next morning when Gideon woke up, the fleece was completely dry, yet the ground around the fleece was wet!

Is it wrong to ask God for a sign?

In most cases, you won't need a special sign to show you whether or not to do something. You don't need the Lord to give you a sign to be kind to someone or to listen to your parents. These are things the Bible says are good and right. The Bible also tells us that we should not test the Lord or expect Him to answer a silly request (Luke 4:12).

Some people ask for a special sign from God because of their unbelief (Mark 8:11-12), and some because they don't want to do what God has already told them to do.

Gideon may have put the lives of many Israelites in danger if he had not made sure that he understood God's message clearly. God will also show you what to do if you earnestly ask Him to lead you.

APRIL 2

VERSE FOR TODAY
If any of you lacks wisdom, he should ask God.
JAMES 1:5

GIDEON

Judges 7:1-8

Too many!

Now that God had given Gideon a clear sign that He would give him victory over the Midianites, Gideon and his men got up early the next day and camped next to a little river.

The Lord said to Gideon, "You have too many men. Your men might boast that they won the battle all by themselves. Let those who are afraid go back home." After thousands had gone back home, the Lord said to Gideon, "You still have too many men. Take the men down to the river and I will show you who to choose."

Then the Lord showed Gideon that the men who scooped up the water with their hands and lapped it should go with him, while those who got down on their knees to drink were to go back home. So Gideon was left with only three hundred men.

How can fewer be better?

How would you feel if your coach decided to halve the number of players just before the team runs onto the field? You would surely hear comments from both sides about the crushing defeat that would take place. Probably you'd wonder if the coach even cared that you would be facing one of the strongest teams out there.

Yet, how would you feel afterwards if your half-sized team beat the strongest team so badly that the scorekeeper couldn't keep up? Wouldn't you be proud to have a coach who knows what he is doing?

Our Lord gets all the glory when the odds are against us – when victory seems impossible. Let us never boast in our own strength but in the strength of the Lord our God (1 Corinthians 1:28-29).

APRIL 3

VERSE FOR TODAY
It is not by sword or spear that the LORD saves; for the battle is the LORD's.
1 SAMUEL 17:47

GIDEON

A silly dream comes true

The Lord had told Gideon to send back most of the men in the Israelite army. He was left with only three hundred men. That night the Lord told Gideon to get up and attack the Midianite camp. Then He said, "If you are afraid to attack, go down to the camp with your servant and you will hear what they are saying."

So Gideon and his servant Purah went down to the edge of the camp. There they heard a man telling someone else about a dream he'd had. "I dreamed that a loaf of barley bread rolled into our camp and flattened a tent."

The other person replied, "It is the sword of the Israelite, Gideon."

When Gideon heard about the man's dream and what the other person said, he worshiped and praised God.

Does being afraid mean that I don't trust God?

God made us with a natural fear that keeps us from doing dangerous things and taking unnecessary risks. If we were scared of nothing at all, we would walk across a road without looking, jump off buildings and tease crocodiles!

Fear is only good when it keeps us from doing daring things that could harm us. Fear is not good when it keeps us from enjoying life; when it keeps us from being the best we can be; and when it keeps us from doing what God has planned for us to do.

The Lord called Gideon a brave man even though he was afraid (Judges 6:12). Being brave is when we trust God enough to step out in faith and obey Him, even when our fear tells us that the situation is not safe.

APRIL 4

VERSE FOR TODAY

When I am afraid, I will trust in you. In God, whose word I praise, in God I trust; I will not be afraid. What can mortal man do to me?
PSALM 56:3-4

GIDEON

Judges 7:15-22

Confusion and panic!

When Gideon got back from spying on the enemy camp, he divided his three hundred men into three groups. He gave each man a trumpet and an empty jar with a flaming torch inside. He told his men, "When I get to the edge of the camp, do exactly what I do."

Just before midnight, Gideon and his men got to the edge of the enemy camp. All at once, they blew their trumpets and smashed their jars. They held their torches high and shouted, "A sword for the Lord and for Gideon."

The enemy troops panicked. In the confusion they started attacking each other and fled. So Gideon sent a message to the tribe of Ephraim to stop the Midianites from crossing the Jordan River.

Does the devil know what God is planning?

No one knows what God has got planned or how He will do things. Only God is all-knowing and eternal. He doesn't have to wait for His plan to kick into action in order to see how things will work out. He already lives in the future! That means, even though God makes a decision now, He can already see His plan happening.

As believers, we have the Spirit of Jesus living in us. Because we are God's children, He lets us know as much as we need to know about His plan (1 Corinthians 2:16). God shows His children things that His enemy knows nothing about. God had worked out a plan; Gideon was told about the plan; and guess what – the enemy knew nothing!

The devil doesn't have a clue about God's plans. So when the devil tries to mess up what God is doing, God just goes ahead and uses the devil's little schemes for His own glory!

APRIL 5

VERSE FOR TODAY

In the same way no one knows the thoughts of God except the Spirit of God.
1 CORINTHIANS 2:11

GIDEON

Feeling left out

When all the fighting was over and the two Midianite chiefs had been killed, the people from the tribe of Ephraim complained to Gideon. "Why didn't you call us to help you fight the Midianites?" they asked.

So Gideon said to them, "The little I did was nothing compared to what you have done. With God's help you killed the Midianite chiefs! What have I done to compare with that?" When they heard what Gideon said, they were not so angry anymore.

In the end the Midianites were completely defeated and were no longer a threat. The Lord sent peace in the land for as long as Gideon lived.

What should I do about someone who feels left out?

Have you ever been told that you could only invite a certain number of friends to a party? If you were to meet one of the friends who wasn't invited and she feels hurt, what would you say?

Maybe you are the captain of a team and have to decide who gets to play in a match. How would you explain to your friend why you didn't choose him or her?

You could say, "You aren't quite good enough," or "There wasn't enough space for everyone." However, deep down you know that you would not be happy with an answer like that. On the other hand, trying to avoid your friend in the hope that the problem will go away will only make your friendship cool off.

Gideon realized that a tribe had been left out of the action, but he let them share the feeling of victory by making them feel important.

Can you think of some ways to encourage a friend who feels left out?

VERSE FOR TODAY

Each of you should look not only to your own interests,
but also to the interests of others.
PHILIPPIANS 2:4

SAMSON

Judges 13:1-5, 24-25

An unexpected messenger

Gideon had died and the Israelites had started sinning against the Lord again. So the Lord let the Philistines rule over them for forty years.

One day, the Lord's angel appeared to a woman who had not been able to have children, and said, "You will soon be pregnant and have a son. After he is born, you must never cut his hair because he will be dedicated to God."

When the angel had gone, the woman told her husband Manoah about the message from God. Manoah prayed to God and said, "Please let the man of God You sent come back and tell us how to raise the boy." So God answered Manoah's prayer and sent the angel again.

When the boy was born, his mother named him Samson, and the Lord blessed him and made him strong.

Why was Samson not meant to cut his hair?

During the time of Moses, if someone wanted to give himself to God in a special way, he had to follow God's instructions (Numbers 6:1-8). Any person could take a Nazirite vow to fully dedicate himself to God for a certain time. During that time, he was not allowed to eat grapes or drink wine, nor was he allowed to cut his hair (which was a sign of his dedication to God).

If you would like to give your life to God for Him to use in a special way, you don't need an outward sign to show others about your dedication to God. People will see your faithfulness to the Lord by the way you live.

If you want to do something to remember a promise you've made to the Lord, you could write it on a decorated card and keep it in your Bible.

APRIL 7

VERSE FOR TODAY
You are to be holy to me because I, the Lord, am holy, and I have set you apart from the nations to be my own.
LEVITICUS 20:26

Judges 14:1-4

SAMSON

Samson gets his way

When Samson had grown up, he went to a place called Timnah where he met a Philistine woman he liked. He went back home and said to his father and mother, "I have met a woman in Timnah and I want you to get her for me."

His parents asked him, "Why do you go to those heathen Philistines to look for a wife? Can't you find a girl from your own people?"

"She is the one I want," Samson said, "get her for me!"

Why do parents "always" say no?

At times, it may seem as though the only answer you get from your parents when you ask for something, is "NO!" Has the thought ever struck you that you may be asking for the wrong things?

Samson wanted to date a girl from the Philistine people who did not believe in God. His parents knew that this was not a good idea and tried to reason with him. "Surely there are many pretty girls here among God's people," they said.

But Samson was stubborn and wanted his own way. However, Samson didn't know that before long he would find out that the Philistines were not friendly people and that he couldn't even trust this Philistine girl.

In spite of how it seems at times, your parents want you to have what is best. But not only that, they want to keep you from things that are not good. They want to keep you safe and unharmed in every way. So whenever your parents say no, remember that they are either protecting you or helping you to control your many wishes.

APRIL 8

VERSE FOR TODAY
Children, obey your parents in the Lord, for this is right.
EPHESIANS 6:1

SAMSON

Judges 14:5-9

Keeping secrets

Samson was on his way to Timnah with his father and mother to meet the Philistine women he wanted to marry. On their way, walking through the vineyards, Samson heard a young lion roaring. The power of the Lord came on Samson and made him very strong. He went after the lion and killed it with his bare hands, but He didn't tell his parents what he had done.

A few days later, when Samson went back to marry the Philistine woman, he went to look for the dead lion. A swarm of bees had made a hive inside the lion's body, so Samson scraped the honey out and gave some to his parents when he got back. But Samson didn't tell his parents where he got the honey.

Should I tell my parents everything?

Isn't it amazing how parents seem to find out things their children try to hide from them? For a while, children may be able to cover something up, but in the end, parents always seem to stumble across the evidence or start asking uncomfortable questions. When you try to cover up your sin, you'll end up feeling guilty, dirty, dishonest, and miserable. God knows you are not perfect; so when you do sin, He wants you to confess your sin straight away (1 John 1:9).

Samson was not supposed to go near anything that was dead – and he knew it; yet he was disobedient and kept it a secret. You don't need to carry around guilt, or live with secret failures! Tell your parents about your temptations and struggles so they can pray for you and encourage you.

APRIL 9

VERSE FOR TODAY
Nothing in all creation is hidden from God's sight. Everything is uncovered and laid bare before the eyes of him to whom we must give account.
HEBREWS 4:13

SAMSON

Samson throws a party

Samson was having a party, which was the thing to do after getting married. He and his father went to the woman's house where thirty young Philistine men joined them. Samson said to the men, "Let me ask you a riddle. I bet each of you a piece of fine linen and special clothes that you can't solve the riddle by the time the wedding feast is over." They all agreed, so Samson said, "Here is the riddle: Out of the eater came something to eat; out of the strong came something sweet."

Day after day the young men tried to work out the riddle. On the fourth day, they went to Samson's wife and told her to trick Samson into telling her the riddle. At first, Samson wouldn't tell her, but after she had nagged and cried about it for days, he told her. She secretly went to tell the Philistines the meaning of the riddle, and Samson lost the bet.

Is it wrong to take a bet?

Why do people take bets? Is it because they are convinced they are right; is it because they enjoy proving someone wrong; or is it to get something for nothing out of the deal? These reasons (and probably some others) seem pretty selfish and are likely to cause quarrels and disappointment.

Solving a riddle can be a lot of fun and it is good when it is just a friendly brainteaser. In Samson's case, this was more than a friendly brainteaser – it was a show of power and pride. (Samson didn't even have the linen and clothes he promised as a reward.) With any bet, someone is always the loser! Don't take a bet in order to prove yourself better than someone else or to get something from the other person.

APRIL 10

VERSE FOR TODAY

Don't have anything to do with foolish and stupid arguments,
because you know they produce quarrels.
2 TIMOTHY 2:23

SAMSON

Judges 15:1-5

Mean, nasty and cruel!

Samson's wife had tricked him into telling her the meaning of his riddle. He was furious when he found out that she had told the Philistines what it meant.

So Samson went back to his parents' home, leaving his wife behind. Later, when he went back to look for her, her father told Samson that he had given her to someone else to marry. Samson was very angry and said, "This time I am not going to be responsible for what I do to the Philistines."

Then He went out and caught three hundred foxes and tied them in pairs by their tails. He put flaming torches in the knots and let them loose in the Philistine's cornfields. As the foxes ran, they burned all the corn in the fields, as well as the corn that had already been harvested.

Why did God allow Samson to use His strength in the wrong way?

How would you feel if you were given a wonderful present, then as you started using it, the person who gave you the present took it back because you didn't use it properly?

God has given you the gift of strength to do things. He has given you the gift of a mind to make decisions. And because God doesn't want to control you like a puppet, He has also given you the gift of freedom.

God trusts us to make good decisions and to use our abilities in a way that is good. He will not usually take gifts away from those who use them to do bad things because He respects their freedom to make decisions. However, the day is coming when everyone will stand before God and tell Him exactly how those abilities were used.

APRIL 11

VERSE FOR TODAY
From everyone who has been given much, much will be demanded; and from the one who has been entrusted with much, much more will be asked.
Luke 12:48

SAMSON

With God's power

Samson had destroyed the cornfields of the Philistines and they were determined to take revenge. They set up camp near the Israelites and attacked them. When the Israelites asked them, "Why are you attacking us?" they replied, "We have come to take Samson prisoner."

So the Israelites went to look for Samson and when they found him they said, "Don't you know that the Philistines are our rulers? Why did you burn their cornfields? We have come to tie you up and hand you over to them."

So Samson allowed himself to be tied up. As they got close to the Philistines, God's strength came on Samson and he broke the ropes. Then he found and old jawbone of and donkey and killed a thousand Philistines with it.

How strong are we without God?

Your mom has probably told you many times that you should eat all your food if you want to be healthy and strong. She is right! Our bodies do need good food, exercise and rest.

Do you sometimes wonder what made Samson so much stronger than anyone else? Is it because he ate all his vegetables or spent hours doing bodybuilding? Although Samson was probably well-built and strong, we read that his super-strength came from the Lord. Every time Samson had amazing strength, it was because the Spirit of the Lord had come upon Him (see Judges 14:6, 19, 15:14).

Yet, it is not only super-strength that comes from the Lord; our very lives depend on the strength He gives us, because He is the One who holds us in His hands.

APRIL 12

VERSE FOR TODAY

"I am the vine; you are the branches. If a man remains in me and I in him, he will bear much fruit; apart from me you can do nothing."

JOHN 15:5

SAMSON

The trap

Some time after Samson had killed the thousand Philistines, he fell in love with Delilah, another Philistine woman. A group of Philistine kings got together and offered her a big reward if she could find out the secret of Samson's strength. So Delilah nagged Samson to tell her the secret of his strength. Three times he told her what would make him weak, but each time she tried to make Samson weak, he broke loose without any effort.

Day after day she nagged him and said, "If you really love me you will tell me the truth." Finally, he got so tired of her nagging that he said, "I have been dedicated to God as a Nazirite, and if my hair were cut, I would be as weak as anyone else."

Later, while Samson was asleep, she cut off his hair. When she woke him up, he was truly as weak as anyone else and the Philistines captured him.

Can love make one blind?

Samson loved Delilah so much that he did not see how the Philistines were using her to find out the secret of his strength. Every time she would try to make him weak, the Philistines were right there to capture him. He was using his strength to tease the enemy, but sadly he didn't use his mind. He should have known better than to fall in love with one of the Philistine women. Selfish 'love' made him blind to the devil's trap.

God's kind of love also makes us blind, but in a good way. God's love makes us blind to the imperfections and faults in others (1 Corinthians 13:5), and His love helps us see the hidden traps of sin.

APRIL 13

VERSE FOR TODAY
Above all, love each other deeply,
because love covers over a multitude of sins.
1 Peter 4:8

SAMSON

One last time

The Philistines had finally found out where Samson's strength lay. They realized that he had been dedicated to God from the day he was born and that his hair was a sign of the Nazirite vow. Now Samson was their prisoner; blind and in chains, grinding grain in the prison. But his hair, which had been cut, started to grow again.

The Philistine kings got together to celebrate their victory over Samson, and said, "Let's get Samson here to entertain us." When they brought Samson out he asked the servant to put him between the pillars that support the temple.

Samson prayed to God and said, "Remember me, O God. Please make me strong just one more time." Then Samson put one hand on each pillar and pushed with all his might … and the whole temple came crashing down. Samson died with the people and killed more Philistines that day than he had during his whole life.

Can God still use me if I have really messed up?

If God stopped using everyone who made a mistake, sinned, or went the wrong way, there would be no one left to use. All of us have sinned and fallen short of God's glory (Romans 3:23). Even the apostle Paul said, "Not that I have already obtained all this, or have already been made perfect, but I press on to take hold of that for which Christ Jesus took hold of me" (Philippians 3:12).

Even though Samson had messed up, God was still able to use him. In the end, Samson turned to God because he knew where his strength came from.

APRIL 14

VERSE FOR TODAY

Therefore this is what the Lord says: "If you repent,
I will restore you that you may serve me."
JEREMIAH 15:19

RUTH

A peaceful home

During the time that Israel was ruled by judges there was a famine in the land. A man who was living in Bethlehem at that time moved to the land of Moab with his wife Naomi and their two sons.

While they were living there, Naomi's husband died and she was left alone with her two sons. Naomi's sons married women from Moab. One woman's name was Orpah and the other was Ruth. After about ten years both sons died and Naomi was left without a husband or sons.

Why do bad times come to ruin our good times?

Imagine if the world was as flat as a board: no canyons or cliffs, no valleys or mountains. What if it wasn't only flat, but everything on it was the same color: no happy reds and yellows, and no darker shades of blue and green.

Life is seldom uneventful for long. Our lives seem full of ups and downs. However, God doesn't just let us have good and bad times to keep us from getting bored; there is a purpose for everything that happens to us. God uses the ups and downs to help us grow in different ways. Struggles help our characters to grow strong; difficulties build our faith; and tough times help us become more like Jesus (Romans 8:28-29). Yet, more often than we realize, God sends us times of blessings so we can renew our strength, take courage and enjoy life!

Life was rather up and down for Naomi. First, it was the hardship of a famine and moving to a distant country. Then there were happy weddings and a peaceful home life. And then her husband and sons died. Life had also robbed Ruth and Orpah of their joy at a young age. Yet even as spring follows winter, and dawn follows the night, so seasons of hardship will pass.

APRIL 15

VERSE FOR TODAY
We know that suffering produces perseverance; perseverance, character; and character, hope.
ROMANS 5:3-4

RUTH

A tough decision

Some time after Naomi's husband and sons had died, she heard that the famine in her home country had ended. The Lord had given His people a good harvest. So she packed up her things and got ready to go back to her country with her two daughters-in-law. They started out together and as they were walking, Naomi turned to them and said, "Why don't you go back home and stay with your mothers? May the Lord make it possible for you to marry again and bless you both for what you have done for me."

So Orpah left to go back home, but Ruth said to Naomi, "Don't ask me to leave you. Wherever you go, I will go: wherever you live, I will live. Your people will be my people, and your God will be my God."

When Naomi saw that Ruth was determined to go with her she said nothing more and they carried on walking.

Whom should I follow when people have a different faith?

Who is right and who is wrong? How can I know whose god is the true God?

Ruth had grown up in Moab where they did not worship God as they did in Israel. Over the years she had watched Naomi's steady faith in God through good and bad times. Ruth saw how Naomi's faith had stayed strong and how God had been faithful to her. Now Ruth was ready to trust God with her life, as Naomi had.

You may know someone who believes in a different god, or who says he believes in the true God but doesn't believe that Jesus is the Son of God. You can know for sure that the God of the Bible is the living God who created the world and who hears your prayers (read Hebrews 11:6).

APRIL 16

VERSE FOR TODAY
For there is one God and one mediator between God and men, the man Christ Jesus.
1 TIMOTHY 2:5

RUTH

Ruth 1:22 2:1-10

Caring and being cared for

When Naomi and Ruth got to Bethlehem, the barley harvest was just starting. The women of the town recognized Naomi and welcomed her back.

One day Ruth said to Naomi, "Let me go to the fields to gather grain that has been dropped. I am sure someone will let me work with them."

So Ruth went to a field and walked behind the reapers, picking up grain. She didn't know that she was working in a field that belonged to Boaz, a rich relative of Naomi.

Boaz happened to arrive there some time later and when he saw Ruth he asked the workers about her. They told him that she had come from the land of Moab with Naomi and that she had worked in the field from early morning. Then Boaz went to talk to Ruth and told her not to gather grain from any other field except from his field.

Will God always provide for me?

Jesus said that we should not worry about our needs for tomorrow because our heavenly Father has taken care of them already (Matthew 6:31-34). So does that mean we should not plan ahead, save up, or work for a living? Not at all! God wants us to live responsibly by planning for the future and working hard. In fact, Paul had some strong words for a group of Christians who had stopped working and become lazy: he told them to get back to work (2 Thessalonians 3:11-12).

Ruth worked hard every day to gather enough grain for Naomi and herself. Yet Ruth knew that it was God who had provided the good harvest, the field, the kind reapers and a caring owner.

APRIL 17

VERSE FOR TODAY
"Look at the birds of the air; they do not sow or reap or store away in barns, and yet your heavenly Father feeds them. Are you not much more valuable than they?"
MATTHEW 6:26

RUTH

Loyalty is rewarded

Day after day, Ruth gathered grain from the field of Boaz (a relative of Naomi). One day, Naomi said to Ruth, "I must find a husband for you so that you can have your own home again. Boaz, in whose field you have been working, will be threshing barley tonight. Now, get dressed in your best clothes, put on some perfume, and go to where he is threshing; but don't let him see you. This evening, when he has finished eating, see where he lies down and when he is asleep, go lie at his feet."

Ruth did everything exactly as Naomi had told her to do. When Boaz woke up in the night, he said, "Who are you?"

Ruth answered, "It is Ruth, Sir. You are my relative. Please will you look after me and marry me?"

Then Boaz replied, "The Lord bless you! You are showing even greater loyalty by doing this than by what you have done for your mother-in-law."

What is true loyalty?

Loyalty is a quality that doesn't always seem that important to people. Often, a person's physical strength, power, influence, wealth, and cleverness impress people far more than their loyalty. Yet God sees things differently (see 1 Samuel 16:7).

Loyalty:
- ties love and faithfulness together.
- does not expect to be rewarded.
- wants only the best for the other person.
- is costly – it may cost a life.
- does not quit.

APRIL 18

VERSE FOR TODAY
Be devoted to one another in brotherly love.
Honor one another above yourselves.
ROMANS 12:10

RUTH

A branch of the tree

During the night, Ruth had gone to lie at the feet of Boaz and had asked him to marry her. Boaz loved Ruth very much and wanted to marry her, but there was a problem. Ruth had a relative who was closer to her than he was. So Boaz said to her, "Stay here for the night and in the morning we will find out whether he will look after you."

In the morning, Boaz sent Ruth home with a huge amount of barley. Boaz went to the meeting place in town where he waited for the other relative. When he came, Boaz said to him, "Naomi wants to sell her field, and you have the first option to buy it. However, if you buy the field, you must take Ruth too, so that her children will inherit the field." When the relative, who had children of his own, heard that, he said, "No, I don't want to buy it."

So Boaz was able to buy the field and marry Ruth. The Lord blessed her, and she had a son named Obed. Obed became the father of Jesse; and Jesse became the father of David – the greatest king of Israel.

What is a genealogy (family tree)?

Do you know who your grandfather is? Do you know who your grandfather's grandfather was? Every person has a family tree, which is a way of writing down the names of each person's parents, going back many generations.

Imagine that you are a twig joined to a thin branch, which is attached to a thicker branch that grows from the stem of a huge tree.

The genealogy (family tree) of Jesus is written in Matthew. In Matthew 1:5, you will see the name of Ruth. Isn't it great that someone who was hardly known during her lifetime became part of the family tree of Jesus?

APRIL 19

VERSE FOR TODAY
A shoot will come up from the stump of Jesse;
from his roots a Branch will bear fruit.
ISAIAH 11:1

SAMUEL

Brokenhearted

After the death of Samson, God raised up other judges to lead Israel.

There was a woman named Hannah who was very sad and upset because she couldn't have children. One day, after she and her husband had finished their meal, Hannah was really upset and went to the Tabernacle to pray. She sobbed as she prayed, "Lord Almighty, look at me and see my deep hurt. If You give me a son, I promise that I will dedicate him to You for the rest of his life."

Eli, the priest who had been watching her, thought she was drunk, but when he realized that she was talking to God about her deep hurt, he said, "May the God of Israel give you what you have asked Him for."

Does God understand my deepest hurts?

We cannot avoid disappointments or steer our lives around hurts along the way, but it helps when we have someone who understands what we are going through.

If there was ever someone who could have had an easy ride through life, it was Jesus. He had the power to calm a storm at sea and make enough food to feed thousands. He could heal any sickness, and even escape death (Luke 4:28-30). Yet Jesus chose to go without food for forty days and leave home even though He had nowhere to sleep. He was born in a smelly stable, and was buried in a tomb that did not belong to Him. Even though Jesus healed many others of their pain, He allowed Himself to be whipped and crucified. Jesus became a man so that He could feel the pain that you feel (Hebrews 4:15); and because He is God's Son, our Father in heaven can also feel your hurts.

APRIL 20

VERSE FOR TODAY
He heals the brokenhearted and binds up their wounds.
PSALM 147:3

SAMUEL

True to their word

A little while after Hannah had prayed to God for a son, she became pregnant and gave birth to a son whom she named Samuel.

Every year Hannah's family would go to offer sacrifices to the Lord at Shiloh. However that year, Hannah stayed behind with Samuel while her husband, Elkanah, went to offer their yearly sacrifice.

When Samuel was a bit older, Hannah and Elkanah took him to the house of the Lord at Shiloh. There they took Samuel to Eli the priest. Hannah said to Eli, "Do you remember me? I am the woman you saw praying to the Lord. I asked the Lord for a child and He has given me this boy. Now I am dedicating him to the Lord. As long as he lives, he will belong to the Lord."

What happens when parents dedicate their child to the Lord?

If you have been in a dedication service and watched parents dedicate their child to the Lord, you may have wondered what a dedication is all about. Perhaps you were dedicated as a baby, or even as an older child, and you wonder if your dedication changed things for you in any way.

When a mother and father dedicate their child, they choose to give their son or daughter back to God even though they raise their child themselves. By offering their child to God in front of others, parents are not likely to forget their promise to teach their child about the Lord. The others who are there can pray for the child and help the parents raise the child in such a way that he or she will gladly serve the Lord.

In this way, a child is surrounded by love and care from a young age.

APRIL 21

VERSE FOR TODAY

Then little children were brought to Jesus for him
to place his hands on them and pray for them.
MATTHEW 19:13

SAMUEL

A voice in the night

The boy Samuel served the Lord at the Temple by helping Eli. Eli was almost blind and slept in his own room while Samuel slept in the Temple near the Covenant Box. One night the Lord called Samuel. Samuel got up and went to Eli thinking that it was Eli who had called him.

But Eli said, "I didn't call you; go back to bed." A while later the Lord called Samuel again. Samuel didn't know it was the Lord and went to Eli again. Eli said to him, "I didn't call you; go back to bed." The Lord called Samuel a third time. This time, when Samuel went to Eli, Eli realized that it was the Lord and said, "Go back to bed, and if you hear the voice again say, 'Speak, Lord, your servant is listening.'" So Samuel went back to bed.

When the Lord called Samuel again, Samuel answered, "Speak, your servant is listening." And the Lord spoke to Samuel.

Can I really hear God speaking to me?

You may have heard people say that the Lord spoke to them, or that God has told them to do something. Does God really speak to people the way He spoke to Samuel that night? If not, how can we hear from God if we don't hear his voice?

Before Jesus came to earth, God used leaders like judges and prophets to give a message to His people. God would speak to them in a voice they could hear, through special dreams, or through an angel.

Then God sent His own Son Jesus to speak to us (Hebrews 1:1). Now we have the words and the example of Jesus, and we have the Holy Spirit who was sent to make the words of Jesus real in our hearts. This is the way God speaks to us now.

APRIL 22

VERSE FOR TODAY

Your ears will hear a voice behind you, saying, "This is the way; walk in it."
ISAIAH 30:21

SAMUEL

What a shame!

During the night, the Lord had told Samuel that He was going to do something terrible to the nation of Israel because of their disobedience.

Not long after that, the Philistines gathered for war against the Israelites and defeated them. When the survivors got back to camp the leaders of Israel said, "Why did the Lord let us be defeated? Let us fetch the Covenant Box and carry it into battle with us. Then the Lord will be right there with us and He will save us."

When the Covenant Box arrived, the Israelites shouted so loudly that the Philistines were afraid. But they fought even harder and defeated the Israelites again, this time killing thousands more and capturing the Covenant Box.

How do people dishonor the name of the Lord?

Have you ever felt embarrassed for God's kingdom when Christians do things that are shameful and wrong?

The Israelites had forsaken God. They did not rely on Him or ask Him about important decisions anymore. So when they were faced with the enemy, they fought in their own strength – and lost! God was wanting to show His glory through His people, as He had done in the past. Now the Israelites were doing their own thing. They had taken the holy Covenant Box – which was not supposed to be moved – and put it on the battlefield like a good luck charm.

God does not need to prove His power and glory to anyone. But we must be careful not to dishonor His holy Name by calling ourselves Christians and living in a way that is no different from how unbelievers live.

APRIL 23

VERSE FOR TODAY

Many will follow their shameful ways and
will bring the way of truth into disrepute.
2 PETER 2:2

SAMUEL

Trouble for the enemy

After the Philistines had captured the Covenant Box, they took it to the temple of their god Dagon. Early the next morning, the people of the city found the statue of Dagon lying in pieces, flat on its face. The Lord punished the people of the city by letting bumps grow on their bodies. When they saw what was happening, they said, "We are being punished by the God of the Israelites." And they took the Covenant Box to another city.

The Lord punished that city too, so the Philistines took the Covenant Box to another city. Wherever they took it, the people were punished.

Eventually, they put the Covenant Box on a wagon drawn by two cows. The cows headed straight for the town of Beth Shemesh in Israel from where it was taken to Kiriath Jearim. There it stayed for twenty years.

Can the enemy of God keep whatever he captures?

The Bible says that the devil has come to steal and destroy what belongs to God (John 10:10). He wants to take everything he can, and what he cannot steal, he will try to destroy. The devil hates anything that is pure and good!

God's enemy has stolen our innocence and left us with guilt. The devil robs us of joy and leaves us with sadness and pain. He takes peace from our hearts and leaves us with worry and fear.

But Jesus died on the cross to take away our guilt. He has given us His purity and made us acceptable to God (Ephesians 1:4). He gives us joy in place of sadness and puts His peace in our hearts. Paul said "I know whom I have believed, and am convinced that he is able to guard what I have entrusted to him for that day" (2 Timothy 1:12).

APRIL 24

VERSE FOR TODAY
"I give them eternal life, and they shall never perish;
no one can snatch them out of my hand."
JOHN 10:28

SAMUEL

Israel wants a king

When Samuel grew old, his sons became judges in Israel. But they were not good judges like Samuel was. They were dishonest. So the leaders of Israel met with Samuel and said, "You are getting old and your sons are not following your example. Choose a king to rule over us so that we can be like all the other countries."

So Samuel prayed and asked the Lord what he should do.

The Lord said to Samuel, "They have not only rejected you; they have rejected Me as their King and have turned away from Me to worship other gods. Let them have their way, but give them a strict warning about how an ordinary king will treat them."

What's wrong with having a king?

What could be wrong with a nation asking for a king to rule over them? Does God not like kings; does He not want someone to rule a country?

God is not against a nation having a ruler or king. The Bible even says that God sets up kings (Daniel 2:21), and in Hebrews 13:17 tells us that we should obey our rulers.

God was angry with Israel because they wanted a human king, while He was already their King. He had rescued them from slavery in Egypt, provided for them in the desert, and helped them conquer the heathen tribes in the Promised Land. He was better than any earthly king could ever be! He not only protected and provided for His people, He also loved them and cared for them. Now the Israelites were turning their backs on God and wanting a human king so they could be like the other nations.

Who is king of your heart? Let Jesus, the King of kings, rule in your heart.

APRIL 25

VERSE FOR TODAY
I will be their God, and they will be my people.
HEBREWS 8:10

Lost and found

There was a man named Kish who had a tall, handsome son named Saul. Some of his donkeys had wandered off, so Kish asked Saul and one of the servants to go look for the donkeys. For three days they walked all over the countryside looking for the donkeys. Eventually Saul said to his servant, "Let's go back home or my father may become more worried about us than about his donkeys."

His servant said, "Wait! There is a holy man in this town; maybe he can tell us where the donkeys are."

As Saul and his servant were going into the town, Samuel came walking toward them. Samuel said to Saul, "Don't worry, your donkeys have already been found."

What should I do when something is lost?

How terrible it feels when a pet you love disappears. It could be a puppy that has run away or a rabbit that got out. Or how would you feel if an important schoolbook went missing or something valuable got lost?

Saul did the right thing. First he went to look for his father's donkeys and then, when it was clear that they were nowhere to be found, he went to see Samuel, a man of God. Saul realized that God could see exactly where his donkeys were and could lead him straight there.

When something goes missing, you should pray to God. Remember, your prayer of faith is as valuable to God as an adult's prayer. After you have prayed, keep looking and trust God to lead you. If He gives you peace about it, then thank Him for hearing your prayer. Expect God to answer, and trust Him to work things out in the best way!

APRIL 26

VERSE FOR TODAY
"Rejoice with me; I have found my lost sheep.'"
LUKE 15:6

SAMUEL

God's second best

While Samuel the priest was speaking to Saul, God told him that Saul was the one He had chosen to be the king of Israel. So Samuel said to Saul, "The Lord has chosen you as ruler of Israel. You will rule His people and protect them from their enemies."

Then Samuel called the people together for a special meeting and said; "This is what the Lord says: 'I am the Lord your God who brought you out of Egypt. But you have pushed away your God who saves you out of all your troubles, and have asked for a king.'"

Then they brought Saul out to the people and Samuel said, "Here is the man God has chosen for you."

Can a bad decision ruin God's plan for me?

Israel wanted a king they could see. Their faith had become so weak that they no longer trusted in an unseen King. There was also another reason for wanting a king: they wanted to be like the other nations around them. The Israelites thought that a king would make their nation look strong.

God sometimes lets us have what we want if we insist on having our own way. When God sees that we are determined to do our own thing, He lets us learn from our mistakes.

Decisions always have consequences and, while God will forgive us for the bad choices we make, the results and effects of those choices don't go away. That is why it is so important to be careful when making a decision that could affect you (or others) for life. Important decisions should not be taken lightly or without asking God.

APRIL 27

VERSE FOR TODAY

Therefore this is what the Lord says: "If you repent,
I will restore you that you may serve me."
JEREMIAH 15:19

SAMUEL

The king looks good

After Samuel had introduced Saul as king to the people of Israel, he explained the rights and duties of a king and wrote a list of them in a book.

Not long afterwards, Saul heard that an enemy of Israel had threatened the town of Jabesh. When Saul heard this, the Spirit of the Lord took control of him. He was furious and gathered men from all over Israel to fight the enemy. Saul and his men went to attack the enemy at dawn, and by midday Saul's army had defeated them. Then the people of Israel said to Samuel, "Where are those who said that Saul should not be king. Let's get rid of them as well."

"No one must die," Samuel said, "for today is a day that the Lord rescued Israel!"

Does God also bless my bad decisions?

It seemed as though Israel's decision to have their very own king had not been such a bad idea after all. Saul had hardly begun his reign when the Israelite army went out and defeated an age-old enemy: Saul's first victory! Although Saul seemed to have gotten off to a good start, we are able to take a peep at what lay ahead. If you turn to 1 Samuel 16:1, you will see what God said about Saul.

God can and will do whatever He has planned to do – with or without our help. If we do things that displease the Lord, He finds other ways to carry out His plan. God may well decide to use a bad decision as part of His plan, but He may also choose to do something completely different. Either way, the person who decides to do things in his or her own way – and not God's way – loses out on the joy and blessings of being in the will of God.

APRIL 28

VERSE FOR TODAY

There is a way that seems right to a man, but in the end it leads to death.
PROVERBS 16:25

SAUL

Saul on a mission

The Philistines were back! They had gathered to fight the Israelites again and were in such a strong position that the Israelites hid in caves and behind rocks.

Meanwhile Saul was waiting for Samuel at a place called Gilgal. He had been waiting for seven days and was becoming impatient. Many of Saul's people started deserting him, so Saul decided to make a sacrifice to the Lord himself, instead of waiting for Samuel.

Just as Saul had finished his sacrifice, Samuel arrived and said, "What have you done?"

Saul replied, "The people were leaving me and you had not come. So I thought I could win the Lord's favor by offering a sacrifice to Him myself."

Samuel said, "That was a foolish thing to do. Because you have done this, your reign over the nation of Israel will end."

Why was God not pleased with Saul's sacrifice?

Saul must have thought to himself: "I will win this battle – no matter what! And, if Samuel doesn't come to offer a sacrifice to the Lord soon, I'll just have to bend the rules a bit and do it myself. I will do whatever it takes to get the Lord on my side so He can help me win this battle! And if I don't do it now, everybody will leave me … and there goes my popularity!"

Saul wanted to do something religious in order to get God to help him win. Saul was impatient and disobedient. He was relying on his own "good ideas" instead of trusting God to do things His way. Saul only wanted God's blessing so that he could win, and afterwards he would take all the glory for himself.

APRIL 29

VERSE FOR TODAY
To obey is better than sacrifice.
1 SAMUEL 15:22

SAUL

Faith and courage

One day, Jonathan, the son of King Saul, said to his helper, "Let's make our way across to the Philistine camp." Jonathan did not tell his father.

When Jonathan was near the Philistine camp, he said to his servant, "Let's cross over to the camp. Maybe the Lord will help us: If He does, we will have the victory even though it is only us against so many. This is what we will do: we will let the Philistines see us. If they tell us to wait while they come to us, we will stay here. But if they call us, we will go across to them because it will be a sign from the Lord that He will give us victory."

When the Philistines saw Jonathan, they said, "Look! Some Hebrews are coming out of their hiding places." And they called Jonathan, "Come here; we have something to tell you."

So Jonathan and the young man went across to the Philistines and attacked them. The Lord gave them victory.

Is a daring deed an act of bravery or foolishness?

Would you say Jonathan was brave or foolish? How can we know the difference? Below are some thoughts that may help:

Bravery: Did Jonathan do a courageous deed …
- in obedience to God?
- for God's glory and honor?
- to rescue people in danger?
  Foolishness: did Jonathan take a risk …
- for fun?
- to show off his power and skill?
- to get a reward?

APRIL 30

VERSE FOR TODAY
Be on your guard; stand firm in the faith; be men of courage; be strong.
1 CORINTHIANS 16:13

May

SAUL

What's that noise?

Saul fought against the enemies of Israel and won every battle. One day, Samuel said to Saul, "The Lord says that you must attack the Amalekites and completely destroy everything they own – don't leave a thing!"

So Saul went out and defeated the Amalekites, but he did not kill the best sheep and cattle or destroy things that were good. His army only destroyed what was worthless. Early the next morning, Samuel went to see Saul and asked, "What is all that mooing and bleating I hear?"

Saul explained, "My men kept the best sheep and cattle to sacrifice to the Lord, but we did destroy the weak and unwanted."

"Stop!" Samuel said, "I will tell you what the Lord said to me last night. He told you to destroy everything, but you disobeyed the Lord by keeping the best."

"I did obey the Lord," Saul replied. "We fought and killed the Amalekites."

"You did not obey the Lord's instructions fully," Samuel said, "and so He has rejected you as king of Israel."

Is it okay to obey most of God's commands?

Most kids in your grade would probably be happy to get eight out of ten questions right in a test. To pass a class test, you may not even need to score as high as that. What do you think God's pass mark for obedience would be? Would obeying just some of God's commands – or even most of them – be good enough?

When it comes to obeying God, we must do everything He says! Perhaps you have done something that didn't seem so bad but it bothers you. Ask the Lord to forgive you.

VERSE FOR TODAY
For whoever keeps the whole law and yet stumbles
at just one point is guilty of breaking all of it.
JAMES 2:10

DAVID

A young shepherd

Samuel was very sad that Saul had made such a mess of leading God's people. The Lord said to Samuel, "How long will you be sad for Saul? I have rejected him as king of Israel. Get some olive oil and go to Jesse who lives in Bethlehem, for I have chosen one of his sons as king."

When Samuel arrived at Jesse's house and saw his eldest son Eliab, he thought, surely this is the one God has chosen. But the Lord said to Samuel, "Do not look at how tall and handsome he is. I do not judge people by what they look like – I look at the heart."

One by one, each of Jesse's seven sons came to show themselves to Samuel; but the Lord turned each one down. "Do you have any more sons?" Samuel asked Jesse.

"I only have one more, but he is my youngest. He is a shepherd out in the field." So Samuel told Jesse to send for him.

When David came in, the Lord said to Samuel, "This is the one – anoint him." So Samuel took the olive oil and anointed David in front of all the others; and the Spirit of the Lord came on David and filled him.

What does anoint mean?

Whenever God chose someone to do a special task, a servant of the Lord would anoint the person for the task God wanted him to do. God's prophets, priests, and kings were anointed before they started serving Him.

At a special ceremony, oil would be poured on the person's head as a sign of God's Spirit being poured on the new leader. From that time on, the Spirit would give that person the ability to do what God wanted him to do.

VERSE FOR TODAY

Jesus said, "The Spirit of the Lord is on me, because he
has anointed me to preach good news to the poor."
LUKE 4:18

DAVID

A good shepherd

After Samuel had anointed David, he left and went back to Ramah, while David went back to his father's flock of sheep in the fields.

Day and night David stayed with his sheep to make sure they were well cared for. He let his sheep graze in fields of lush grass. He led them to quiet streams where the rushing water would not frighten them. He used his rod to scare off wild animals and his staff to gently lead the sheep away from places that were unsafe.

David wrote a psalm about God. He thought about the Lord as a Shepherd looking after him, just as he was looking after his father's sheep.

Why does Jesus call us sheep?

Have you been on a sheep farm or seen a flock of sheep grazing in a field? Perhaps you have seen a painting or photo of a shepherd leading his flock of sheep. Sheep don't seem very bright, do they? If someone at school were to call you a sheep, you would probably feel rather upset. Why would Jesus call us sheep?

Like sheep, we need to follow a shepherd, otherwise we would end up following each other and get lost (Luke 15:4-6). Like sheep, we cannot defend ourselves (1 Peter 5:8). Like sheep, we don't know where the dangers lie (Proverbs 3:26).

Don't worry too much about being called a sheep – you have the best Shepherd looking after you. He loves you so much that He gave His life to save you. Besides, those who are not part of His flock are called goats – and that is far worse (Matthew 25:32).

VERSE FOR TODAY
We all, like sheep, have gone astray, each of us has turned to his own way.
ISAIAH 53:6

DAVID

A fearless shepherd

One day, while David was taking care of his father's sheep, a lion carried away one of the lambs. When David struck the lion, it turned on him, so he grabbed it by the throat and beat it to death, saving the little lamb.

At another time a bear came to take one of the lambs. David went after the bear and attacked it, rescuing the helpless lamb.

Why would a shepherd risk his life for a silly sheep?

If you were a sheep, would you feel safe having a shepherd like David? David did not only care about his sheep; he was brave and strong enough to protect them!

A shepherd's job is to look after a flock of sheep. However, there are two kinds of shepherds: a good shepherd who will do anything to keep his sheep safe, and one who only looks after sheep because he needs money. Someone who is paid to look after sheep does not care when a wolf comes to snatch away one of the sheep. Even if the sheep scatter, he will not risk his life to bring them back.

Jesus said, "I am the good Shepherd. The good Shepherd lays down his life for the sheep" (John 10:11). Because His sheep belong to Him and are precious to Him, Jesus not only risked His life, He gave His life!

Jesus is the only Shepherd who knows every one of His sheep by name (John 10:3-4). When He calls us, we recognize His voice because we have learned to trust Him.

Jesus is also the Gate (John 10:9). Every sheep that goes through the gate is kept safe because thieves cannot come and steal them. We can only be kept from the devil when we come to God through Jesus the Gate.

VERSE FOR TODAY

Know that the LORD is God. It is he who made us,
and we are his; we are his people, the sheep of his pasture.
PSALM 100:3

DAVID

A musical shepherd

While David was out in the fields watching his father's sheep, he had lots of time to pray and write beautiful songs of praise to the Lord.

Meanwhile, King Saul who was living in a fancy palace, was not happy. He was moody and unhappy most of the time. After Saul had disobeyed God, the Spirit of the Lord left him. To make matters worse, Samuel had told him that God would take away his kingdom and give it to someone else, someone who loved God.

One of Saul's servants told him that he would feel better if someone played him gentle music. Another servant happened to know about David and told Saul about his talent for playing the harp. So Saul ordered them to fetch David.

David started playing beautiful music for Saul and Saul liked him. Whenever Saul became grumpy, David's music would calm Saul's spirit and he would feel much better.

What kind of music should I listen to?

The Lord has given people the gift of creating beautiful music. How happy the Lord must be when we make music to honor Him – either by singing or by playing a musical instrument (Psalm 150:3-6).

The Lord does not mind what your favorite song is or what kind of music you like. The more good music you listen to, the more you will enjoy the different kinds of music from other generations and countries of the world. However, as far as possible, avoid listening to songs that dishonor the Lord by their words (some of which may be difficult to hear and recognize).

VERSE FOR TODAY

Speak to one another with psalms, hymns and spiritual songs.
Sing and make music in your heart to the Lord.
EPHESIANS 5:19

DAVID

An army scared stiff

The Philistines were at war again. Their army had lined up on one side of a valley; the Israelites had set up camp on the other.

A huge man from the Philistine army came out and challenged the Israelite army. He wore bronze armor and carried a long spear. A soldier walking in front of him carried his shield. The Philistine shouted across the valley to the Israelites; "I dare the Israelite army to choose someone to fight me. If he wins, we will be your slaves; but if I win, you will be our slaves."

When Saul and his men heard Goliath's challenge they were terrified!

Is the enemy of God stronger than I am?

Goliath, a giant in the Philistine army, was enormous. Not even the bravest soldier in Saul's army wanted to take up Goliath's challenge to fight him, no matter how big the reward.

Unlike Goliath, our enemy cannot be seen. We don't know what the devil is planning or what his army is doing. The devil puts his evil plans into the hearts of people who allow him to control them. They then go out and do the devil's dirty work through the evil deeds we see in the world. Only when we see the evil around us do we know how and where the devil is working.

It is foolish to take on the devil's army in our own human strength. Acts 19:11-16 shows the difference between conquering the devil in the strength of the Lord and trying to fight the devil with human strength. It is only with the power of God's Spirit in us that we can fight against the attacks of the devil. When we resist the devil by using the powerful words from the Bible, he runs away from us – defeated! (James 4:7).

VERSE FOR TODAY

Be self-controlled and alert. Your enemy the devil prowls around like a roaring lion looking for someone to devour.
1 PETER 5:8

DAVID

How dare he say that!

Day after day, Goliath mocked the army of the living God; yet not one of the Israelite soldiers was brave enough to fight the Philistine giant. During that time, Jesse asked his youngest son David to take some grain and loaves of bread to his brothers in Saul's army.

Early the next morning, David left someone in charge of the sheep and set off for the valley of Elah. When he got there, the Israelites and Philistines were taking up positions for battle. David took the food he had brought to the officer in charge of the food supplies. Then he ran off to look for his brothers and found them – ready for battle. As he talked to them, Goliath the Philistine started challenging the Israelites as he had done before.

"Listen to his challenge," the Israelites said to David as Goliath kept mocking God's people, and God Himself (verse 45).

What should I do when someone mocks God?

Do you feel angry when someone mocks God or laughs at you for believing in Jesus? Do you wish that God would prove Himself in a powerful way right there in front of everyone?

What did Jesus do when He was mocked? (Matthew 27:30-31). He did not defend Himself or threaten those who laughed at Him. What did Jesus do when they insulted Him? (Mark 15:29). He forgave them! (Luke 23:34). Jesus could have called down thousands of angels, but instead He chose to show us how much He loves us.

God is patient and merciful – He even loves those who mock and insult Him. When you hear someone mock God, you can ask the person not to talk that way, and you can pray that he or she may find the way to God.

VERSE FOR TODAY

"But I tell you that men will have to give account on the day of judgment for every careless word they have spoken."
MATTHEW 12:36

DAVID

Go back to your sheep!

When David heard Goliath's challenge for someone from the Israelite army to come and fight him, he asked some of the men standing around, "What reward will a man get for killing that Philistine?"

Eliab, David's eldest brother, heard David asking about the reward and said angrily, "What are you doing here? What about the sheep you are supposed to be taking care of? You just think you're big stuff! All you want to do is watch the battle."

"What have I done now?" David replied. "I only asked a question."

Some men who heard what David said went to tell King Saul who immediately called David. When David was brought before Saul, David said, "No one should be afraid of this Philistine! I will go and fight him."

Am I too young to be useful to God?

David was a young shepherd. He had never used weapons of war – and he definitely wasn't a trained soldier! What chance did David stand against the mightiest warrior in the Philistine army?

However, when someone is willing to trust God for strength, age and size don't matter.

Some may try to discourage you from doing what God wants you to do because you are too young. They might say, "Wait until you are older and understand things better." If you have thought about starting a prayer group, or a Bible reading group, do it and God will use you to conquer giants!

VERSE FOR TODAY

Don't let anyone look down on you because you are young, but set an example for the believers in speech, in life, in love, in faith and in purity.
1 Timothy 4:12

DAVID

The armor of God

King Saul had some doubts about David's ability to fight the huge Philistine. David was just a boy! Yet no one else had been willing to take on Goliath, so Saul said, "May the Lord be with you." Then he gave David his armor.

David put on Saul's bronze helmet and coat of armor. Then he strapped Saul's sword over the armor. As David walked around, he realized that the armor was too heavy for him, so he took the armor off and headed down the valley without it.

How can I protect myself from the devil's attacks?

David was about to face the fiercest warrior in the Philistine army with a stick and a sling. David didn't need Saul's armor because he was already wearing God's armor. King Saul may have shaken his head in unbelief, but the battle had already been won in David's mind.

You can also be on the winning side by putting on God's armor (Ephesians 6:14-17):

- Tie the Belt of Truth tightly around your waist so that you do not get tripped up with wrong ideas about God.
- Protect your heart with the Breastplate of Righteousness; let purity and goodness guard your heart from sin.
- Wear the Gospel of Peace shoes so that you can spread the Good News of God's love everywhere.
- Carry the Shield of Faith so you can stop the burning arrows of doubt.
- Put on the Helmet of Salvation, which you get when you ask Jesus to become Lord of your life.
- Use the Sword of the Spirit, which is God's Word.

VERSE FOR TODAY

Therefore put on the full armor of God, so that when the
day of evil comes, you may be able to stand your ground,
and after you have done everything, to stand.
EPHESIANS 6:13

DAVID

What a shot!

The Philistine giant could not believe his eyes when he saw David coming toward him. All David had to fight with was his shepherd's stick, a sling and five smooth stones he had found in a stream.

Goliath started walking toward David to get a better look. "What's that stick for?" he asked. "Am I a dog?" He swore at David and said, "I will give your body to the birds and animals to eat!"

David replied, "You have a sword, a spear and a javelin. I come with the Lord God Almighty on my side. Today, everyone will see that the Lord does not need swords or spears to save His people."

David took a stone from his pocket, put it in his sling and hurled it at Goliath. The stone hit Goliath on the head and he fell to the ground. Then David ran up to Goliath and used his sword to cut off his head.

How do I get rid of a giant in my life?

Goliath would just not stop! Day after day he came out to mock the Israelites. Each day he stood there laughing, the Israelites felt more helpless and defeated. If it weren't for Goliath, they may have had the courage to attack the enemy.

You have probably faced many problems and tackled each one with courage. Yet there may be a Goliath-sized obstacle inside you that seems to be there all the time – laughing at you day after day. It may be a bad memory that keeps you from trusting others; it may be a fear that keeps you from doing your best; it may be difficulty with schoolwork; or it may be the way you see yourself. Go get that giant! Pray for courage, then face your problem head-on in God's strength and with God's armor.

VERSE FOR TODAY
For everyone born of God overcomes the world.
This is the victory that has overcome the world, even our faith.
1 JOHN 5:4

DAVID

Best friends

When Saul saw how David had gone out to fight Goliath, he asked the commander of the army to bring David to him.

From that day on Jonathan, Saul's son, became best friends with David and promised to be his friend forever.

Saul sent David on many raids, and each time David and his group of men went out to fight the enemy, he won the battle. Saul was pleased with David so he made him an officer in his army.

How do good friends become best friends?

To have a best friend you must be a best friend. Jonathan and David became best friends because their friendship was built on a solid foundation.

Personality: Friends become friends because they like each other – they just seem to fit together. Compare Jonathan's act of courage with David's (1 Samuel 14:1; 17:36).

Selflessness (sharing): Jonathan gave David what was most special to him (1 Samuel 18:4). When Jonathan gave David his robe, he was taking off the clothes of a prince and putting them on David – he did not mind if David became king. Jonathan also gave David his armor and sword to defend himself.

Trust (loyalty): Jonathan and David trusted each other completely and through their steady trust came a deep loyalty. Jonathan was willing to stick up for David even though it almost cost him his life (1 Samuel 20:33).

Faith (belief): They had the same strong faith and purpose – to please God in everything. Compare Jonathan's daring trust in the Lord (1 Samuel 14:6) with David's bold trust (1 Samuel 17:37).

VERSE FOR TODAY

He who loves a pure heart and whose speech
is gracious will have the king for his friend.
PROVERBS 22:11

DAVID

Music and cheers

As King Saul's soldiers returned home from their victorious battles with the Philistines, women from the nearby towns would come out to meet King Saul. They made music, danced, and sang a joyful song: "Saul has killed thousands; but David, tens of thousands."

Saul did not like this song at all because it made David look a lot better than him. Saul became angry. "Why do they only sing about thousands for me? Soon they will want David to be their king." From that day on, Saul became very jealous of David and tried to get rid of him; but everyone else liked David because he was such a good leader.

How should I respond to compliments and praises?

How would you feel if you were to receive a medal or a prize for an achievement? It may be hard to describe your mixed emotions as you go up to receive your award in front of a cheering crowd. You may have feelings of joy, pride, nervousness, or even embarrassment.

People respond differently to the compliments and praises they receive for doing something well. There is nothing wrong with accepting a person's kind words, and it is polite to thank someone who pays you a compliment. Perhaps you could use the opportunity to give God the glory by thanking Him openly.

When David was praised he did not stop leading his men to victory, neither did he play down his abilities. He did, however, acknowledge that God had helped him (Psalm 54:4). In contrast, the New Testament tells of a king who loved the praises of men. When they called him a god, he just loved it and took all the glory! Well, read what happened to him (Acts 12:21-23).

VERSE FOR TODAY

Because of the service by which you have proved yourselves,
men will praise God for the obedience that
accompanies your confession of the gospel of Christ.
2 CORINTHIANS 9:13

1 Samuel 18:17-22, 28-30

DAVID

Jealousy, courage and love

David had become popular all over Israel and Saul was jealous. He thought, "I will get David to fight in the fiercest battles so that he gets killed by the Philistines – then I will not need to kill him myself."

Michal, one of Saul's daughters, fell in love with David. Saul was pleased when he found out about this and ordered his officers to tell David, "All Saul wants from you as payment to marry Michal is a hundred dead Philistines."

David wasted no time in showing his love for Michal and came back with proof that he had killed two hundred Philistines. So Saul allowed Michal to marry David, but planned to use her to trap him.

What can I hold on to when life becomes hectic?

So much had happened in David's life since he had left his peaceful life as a shepherd to join Saul's army. Do you think David sometimes longed to be back with his sheep in the field?

Within a short time, David had become famous throughout the land. He had also become a commander in Saul's army. As a shepherd he had only heard of the Philistines; now he faced them in battle day after day. Then there was Saul, the jealous king who kept on trying to get rid of him. And now David had married Saul's daughter. It had all happened so fast. Imagine all the different feelings that tumbled around in David's heart.

Life has peaceful moments when we have time to look at flowers and watch the clouds changing shape. Suddenly things change and we feel unsafe, like a small boat being tossed about on a stormy sea.

For David, there was only one thing that would never change: the fact that God was in control of his life. Knowing that made all the difference!

VERSE FOR TODAY
You will keep in perfect peace him whose mind is steadfast,
because he trusts in you.
Isaiah 26:3

DAVID

An idol in bed

One day, Saul was in one of his bad moods again. He was sitting with his spear in his hand, listening to David playing his harp. As a deep hatred and anger filled Saul's heart, he lifted his spear and threw it at David. David jumped out the way and ran for his life.

Then Saul sent his men to watch David's house and kill him the next day. Michal, his wife, warned him: "If you don't escape tonight, they will kill you in the morning." Then she helped David escape through a high window and put a life-sized idol in his bed.

When Saul's men came to get David, Michal told them that he was sick. But when the men went back to tell Saul he said, "Carry him here in his bed so that I can kill him." So the men went back to fetch David and discovered that it was only an idol in the bed. Saul was furious that his own daughter had tricked him and that she had let David escape.

Was David afraid of Saul?

David had not been afraid to face Goliath, who was far bigger and fiercer than King Saul. If David had the courage to face Goliath, why was he so afraid of someone like Saul? Why would he run away from him?

David's courage came from knowing that he was doing what God wanted him to do. When he faced Goliath, there was no doubt in his mind about what God wanted him to do.

David also knew that, although God had chosen him to be the next king, his time to rule had not yet come (1 Samuel 24:6). He was not going to take over from God and do things on his own, as Saul had done. He was waiting for God's perfect time.

VERSE FOR TODAY

My times are in your hands; deliver me from
my enemies and from those who pursue me.
PSALM 31:15

DAVID

An arrow for David

Saul had arranged a feast for one of the regular celebrations. David was expected to attend the feast, but instead he decided to hide in the fields for a few days. He said to Jonathan, "If your father asks where I am, tell him that I have gone home to Bethlehem." Then they arranged that Jonathan would go to the field and give David a signal that would show whether it was safe for David to return to Saul, or whether he should run away.

When Saul – who had planned to kill David – found out that David was not at the feast, he was furious. He shouted at Jonathan for being David's friend, and threw a spear at him. So Jonathan went out to where David was hiding and shot some arrows. Then he called to his servant, "Isn't the arrow still farther away? Hurry up!" These words were a sign to David that his life was in danger and that he should run for his life.

Why did David have to wait so long to become king?

Samuel had anointed David as the new leader of God's people. David had proved his courage by defeating Goliath and winning many battles. He was also a respected leader and commander in the army. On the other hand, Samuel told Saul that God had rejected him as king of Israel.

Time was passing and nothing seemed to be happening. What was the hold up?

As humans, we can't know and understand God's complete plan. Often we only see the obvious, not what God is doing to prepare the hearts of people. To prepare a heart that is faithful takes time. It may take years for God to bring about the changes that will make us ready to do the task He has planned for us.

VERSE FOR TODAY

Humble yourselves, therefore, under God's mighty hand,
that he may lift you up in due time.
1 Peter 5:6

DAVID

1 Samuel 25:1-13

A mean sheep-owner

MAY 16

One day, Nabal, a rich man who owned land and many sheep, prepared a feast for his family and his shepherds. David, who had protected Nabal's shepherds from thieves and enemy raiders, sent some of his men to ask Nabal for some of the food or whatever he had.

Nabal refused to give David's men a single thing and sent them away saying, "Who is David? I don't even know him."

When David's servants told him what Nabal had said, David was furious and commanded four hundred men, "Put on your swords and come with me."

How do most quarrels start?

A quarrel starts when two or more people disagree about something. Each one believes he or she is right and angry words may end in a fight.

Do you remember how the first quarrel between two people started? They were brothers. Cain was jealous of Abel because Abel's sacrifice was pleasing to the Lord, and his was not. Instead of doing what was right, the jealousy that burned in Cain's heart led him to kill his brother.

The sinful desires of selfishness, pride, revenge, and jealousy stir up angry emotions that keep us from thinking clearly. Because we are selfish, we don't try to understand how the other person feels.

Do you think Nabal should have given David some food? Did he even know who David was, or had he asked David to keep his shepherds safe? Do you think David had a right to ask for food? When he didn't get it, did he have the right to threaten or kill Nabal?

To avoid quarrels, rather try to see things the way the other person does.

VERSE FOR TODAY
What causes fights and quarrels among you?
Don't they come from your desires that battle within you?
JAMES 4:1

DAVID

The peacemaker

Abigail wasted no time in thinking of a plan to stop David and his men from killing her husband Nabal. She took two hundred loaves of bread, some wine, five sheep, grain, cakes of raisins and figs. She loaded everything on donkeys and told her servants to go on ahead. She didn't tell Nabal that she was going out to meet David.

When Abigail saw David coming, she bowed down with her face to the ground. "My master," she said, "let me take the blame for what has happened and do not pay any attention to what Nabal said. The Lord will make you king because you are fighting His battles. Please take this present and do not take Nabal's life. And when the Lord has made you king of Israel, you won't have to feel guilty for having taken someone's life unnecessarily."

Then David said, "Praise the Lord who sent you to me today. Thank God for your good sense and for keeping me from taking revenge."

How can I end a quarrel between my friends?

How does one stop a fight or a quarrel in a fair way? Abigail knew that unless she did something, someone was going to get hurt. Let's see what she did to bring peace to an ugly situation:

- She didn't take sides. Although Abigail was married to Nabal, she tried to understand how David felt.
- She made an effort. Abigail gave of her own food, worked out a clever plan, and used her servants (see verse 18-19).
- She took a risk. She put herself between Nabal and David (see verse 23-24).
- She helped David see the bigger picture. Abigail convinced him not to do something he would regret later (see verse 30-31).

VERSE FOR TODAY

Peacemakers who sow in peace raise a harvest of righteousness.
JAMES 3:18

DAVID

1 Samuel 26:1-12, 17-21

While the king slept

Some men came to Saul and told him that David was hiding in the desert. So Saul went out with three thousand of his best soldiers to find David.

David and the men with him were hiding in a cave. That night David asked one of his men to go with him to Saul's camp. So David and Abishai crept into the camp where Saul and his soldiers were sleeping. Abishai said to David, "God has put the enemy in your power. Let me kill him."

But David said, "No! God has made him king. It is not right for us to take his life. But let's take his water jug and his spear and get out of here."

They left the camp without waking a single soldier. Then David crossed to the other side of the valley and shouted to Saul's commander, "Abner! Aren't you the greatest man in Israel? Why did you not protect your master, the king? Look around you. Where is the king's shield and his water jug?"

When Saul heard that it was David, he was ashamed of what he was doing. "I have done wrong," he said. "I will never harm you again because you have spared my life." So David went on his way and Saul returned home.

Should I respect ungodly leaders?

Imagine if there were no traffic officers to stop people who ignore the rules of the road, or imagine if there weren't any rules at all. People would drive on the wrong side of the road and race through intersections, not caring for the safety of others.

If a traffic officer does not believe in God it does not give us the right to disobey or ignore him. Similarly, our parents, teachers, and everyone else who keeps order in a country should be obeyed and respected – whether they believe in God or not.

VERSE FOR TODAY

Obey your leaders and submit to their authority.
HEBREWS 13:17

1 Samuel 30:1-3, 16-25

DAVID

The raid

One day, when David and his men got back to the town where they were staying, they found that the Amalekites had attacked the town, burnt everything and taken the women and children. David prayed and asked the Lord, "Shall we go after the raiders and will we catch them?" The Lord answered and told David to go after them.

So David and his men set out to find the Amalekites, but along the way, some of David's men were too exhausted to carry on and stayed behind. The others went on and attacked the raiders, taking all their possessions. They also rescued their wives and children.

When those who had gone out to fight got back, they didn't want to share what they had brought back with those who had stayed behind. But David said, "Everyone must get the same; those who guarded the supplies must get the same as those who went into battle."

Is everyone's work for the Lord equally important?

Do you think that David's defeat of the Amalekites was more important to God than looking after sheep? We may think that a shepherd's task of defending sheep against wild animals is not as important as defending a country against their enemies. Yet to God the most important thing is not what we do for Him, but whether we are obedient and faithful. God was pleased with David whatever he did.

Each of us has been given a task in God's kingdom. When we do it well, God trusts us with another, maybe bigger and more difficult task. When David had proved his faithfulness and courage by looking after his father's sheep, God knew that he was ready to look after His people.

VERSE FOR TODAY
The man who plants and the man who waters have one purpose,
and each will be rewarded according to his own labor.
1 CORINTHIANS 3:8

DAVID

Tragedy strikes

When David came back from his battle with the Amalekites, a young man arrived with bad news.

The Philistines had attacked Saul's army on the mountain of Gilboa. The fighting was fierce and in the chaos of battle an arrow hit and wounded Saul. Saul killed himself by falling on his own sword. Jonathan and his brothers also died in the battle with those who had not already fled.

When David heard about the death of Saul and Jonathan, he tore his clothes and cried bitterly until evening.

How can I comfort someone whose friend has died?

You would probably feel a little uneasy talking to a friend who has lost someone through death. It would seem out of place to talk about everyday things, and yet it may feel awkward to talk about death. When you meet your friend, you need not try to look or feel as sad as your friend does, but rather show your genuine care.

Sometimes it is best not to say too much, but just to sit quietly with your friend. She will feel your love even though you don't say much. If your friend would like to talk, ask her what she admires most about the person who died, or ask her to tell you about the fun times that she remembers having together.

Tell your friend how it makes you feel to see her so sad. You can tell her that God loves her very much and feels sad with her. Encourage her to tell God how she feels. If your friend doesn't feel like praying, you could ask if it would be okay to say a prayer for her. Pray that God will help her to feel His great love and care.

VERSE FOR TODAY

Even though I walk through the valley of the shadow of death, I will fear no evil, for you are with me; your rod and your staff, they comfort me.

PSALM 23:4

DAVID

David becomes king

David was thirty years old when the leaders of the tribes of Israel came to him and said, "You are one of us. Even when Saul was our king, you led the people of Israel into battle, and the Lord promised that you would rule His people."

Then they anointed David as their king and he ruled Israel for forty years. David captured the walled city of Jerusalem and ruled from there. The city became known as The City of David.

How can I let Jesus be King of my life?

Would you like to have a real king in your life and become part of his kingdom? You can! You can let the King of the whole universe rule in your life from this moment on. He is the best King you could ever have – a King who loves you, who is powerful, and a king who lives forever.

The King wants you to:
- obey Him (John 14:23)
- serve Him (John 15:16)
- be loyal to Him (Luke 16:13)
The King will:
- keep you safe (John 10:28)
- let you live in peace (John 14:27)
- give you what belongs to Him (Romans 8:17)
- give you a new life that never ends (John 3:16).

All you need to do is tell Jesus that you want Him to be your King. You then become part of God's Kingdom and receive ETERNAL LIFE. By asking Jesus to become your King, you allow Him to live and rule in your heart.

VERSE FOR TODAY
I will exalt you, my God the King; I will praise your name for ever and ever.
PSALM 145:1

DAVID

The Covenant Box comes back

Now that David was finally king, his first thought was to bring the Covenant Box back to where it could be kept safe. It was still at Abinadab's home. David's men took it and placed it on a cart drawn by oxen. Everyone was dancing and making a joyful noise.

As they came to the threshing floor of Nacon, the oxen stumbled, and Uzzah reached out to take hold of the Covenant Box. The Lord God was angry with Uzzah for touching the box, and Uzzah died there next to it. David was angry because the Lord had punished Uzzah; but he was also afraid, so he took the box to the house of Obed-Edom.

Could the Word of God ever disappear?

Do you remember what Moses put inside the Covenant Box? Look up 1 Kings 8:9 to see what it was – and if it was still there? Yes, after all this time the commandments were still in the box because the Lord was very strict about anyone touching it. Only the priests whose special job it was to carry it were allowed to touch it.

The commandments were more than just a set of rules. God had made a promise (covenant) that those who keep His rules will be His people, and that He will love them and care for them (Psalm 103:17-18).

God has given us the Bible with commands and promises: commands we must obey, and promises that God will keep. He has also given a strict warning to anyone who tries to change a single word in the Bible (Revelation 22:18-19). That is why we can trust the Bible because God's Word will never change or disappear.

VERSE FOR TODAY

"Heaven and earth will pass away, but my words will never pass away."
MATTHEW 24:35

DAVID

Dancing for joy

The Lord blessed Obed-Edom and his family while the Covenant Box was at his house. After a few months, when David heard how the Lord had blessed him, he went out with some of his men to fetch it.

Then David and the Israelites took the Covenant Box to Jerusalem with shouts of joy and the sound of trumpets. As the box was brought into Jerusalem, David danced and jumped around with joy. Afterwards, he gave everyone bread, meat and raisins to celebrate the happy occasion.

How can I show my joy in worship?

What do sports fans do when their team wins a nail-biting match? What do you do when you get really excited? Do you feel like jumping up and down or shouting out aloud?

If you get excited about praising God, you might find it difficult to sit still (without tapping your feet or twitching a finger). That is how David felt when the Covenant Box came home. He was overjoyed and so was everyone else. The people were shouting with joy and blowing trumpets.

God loves it when we get excited about Him, just as He gets excited about us (Zephaniah 3:17). When you worship God, you can clap (Psalm 47:1); you can sing and shout (Psalm 108:1); and you can make music and dance (Psalm 149:3). You should remember though, that your worship should be honoring to the Lord. You should never become disrespectful by the way you show your enthusiasm.

David's wife, who was watching him as he entered the city, was not happy with the way he danced in front of everyone. But David did not mind about what she thought because he was dancing to honor the Lord.

VERSE FOR TODAY

Speak to one another with psalms, hymns and spiritual songs.
Sing and make music in your heart to the Lord.
EPHESIANS 5:19

DAVID

2 Samuel 7:1-7, 12-13

A palace and a tent

Things started to settle down in the palace. The Lord had kept David safe from his enemies, and now he was king of Israel. However, David started feeling a little uneasy in his heart. He called the prophet Nathan and said, "Here I am, living in a beautiful palace while God's Covenant Box is being kept in a tent."

Nathan replied, "Do whatever you are thinking because the Lord is with you."

But that night the Lord said to Nathan, "Tell David that he is not the one to build the Temple for Me to live in. I will make one of his sons king and he will build the Temple for Me."

Is a church building important?

If God is everywhere, why was it so important for David to build a Temple for the Lord to live in?

If we can pray to the Lord and read our Bibles wherever we like, why is it important to go to a church building?

The Bible tells us that all those who believe in Jesus are a part of His body, the Church. That means every believer fits into a special place like a living stone in His Temple (1 Peter 2:4-5).

But if we, as living stones, are scattered all over the place and never get together, no one would even know that we are part of one big Church. If we only watched a preacher on TV or listened to a sermon on the radio, it just wouldn't be the same as going to worship the Lord together with other believers.

When we get together, God is there!

VERSE FOR TODAY

I rejoiced with those who said to me, "Let us go to the house of the Lord."
PSALM 122:1

DAVID

David's prayer

After Nathan told David that the Lord wanted one of his sons to build the Temple, David was very happy. He went to the Tent of the Lord and prayed.

David said to the Lord, "I am not worthy of what You have done for me. Now You are doing even more by making this promise about my son. You have done these things to teach me. How great You are Sovereign Lord. There is none like You! And now Sovereign Lord, do what You have promised."

Can a king have a king?

Is there anyone greater than a king? Would you dare to tell a king that he is actually not the greatest? Probably he wouldn't be happy to find out that he is not the greatest after all.

David realized that there is someone much greater than he was. Even though he was the king of a great nation, he knew that God had put him there and that God could replace him.

David learned that joy and peace come from knowing that there is someone higher and more powerful than him. The joy he had felt as a shepherd was still in his heart and, even as a king, he still relied on God. David said, "Listen to my cry for help, my King and my God, for to You I pray" Psalm 5:2.

When David was a shepherd he thought like a shepherd and prayed to God as his Shepherd (Psalm 23).

Now that David was a king, he thought like a king and spoke to God as the Sovereign Lord (verse 27). By calling God Sovereign, he was saying that God is his King – the King of kings.

VERSE FOR TODAY

On his robe and on his thigh he has this name written:
KING OF KINGS AND LORD OF LORDS.
REVELATION 19:16

DAVID

Adopted as his son

One day David asked, "Is there anyone left of Saul's family because I would like to show him kindness for the sake of Jonathan." Jonathan, David's best friend had been killed in a battle.

Ziba, one of Saul's servants told David that Jonathan had a son Mephibosheth. When he was five years old, news of Saul and Jonathan's death reached the city. The nurse who was looking after Mephibosheth picked him up and fled. She was afraid that he would be killed too. But as she ran she tripped and dropped him. Mephibosheth became crippled in both legs.

When Mephibosheth was brought before David, David said, "Don't be afraid, I will be kind to you for the sake of your father Jonathan. I will give you all the land that belonged to your grandfather Saul." And from that day on Mephibosheth ate at David's table as one of his very own sons.

Can I belong to two families?

Do you know what it means to be adopted? A son or daughter can be taken in by a new family and become a true child of that family, even though he or she was not born into that family.

When Mephibosheth was adopted into David's family, he was treated as if he had been born into David's family. From one day to the next he became a king's kid.

There is no need for a family to adopt you if you already have parents looking after you. But you can be adopted into God's family. When you let Jesus rule in your heart, you become a King's kid as well!

VERSE FOR TODAY

In love he predestined us to be adopted as his sons through Jesus Christ, in accordance with his pleasure and will.

EPHESIANS 1:4-5

2 Samuel 11:2-5, 12:1-10, 13

DAVID

The stain

MAY 27

One evening, while David was walking on the flat roof of his palace, he saw a beautiful woman having a bath. He told his servants to find out who she was and bring her to the palace. When David found out that she was married and that her husband was in his army fighting the Ammonites, he sent a message to the commander telling him to move Uriah to the front ranks where the fighting was fiercest. David wanted Uriah to get killed so he could marry his wife Bathsheba.

Uriah did get killed and David married Bathsheba. What he had done was wrong in the Lord's eyes. So the Lord sent the prophet Nathan to show David that he had taken something very precious from someone else. Then David confessed his sin and said, "I have sinned against the Lord."

Will the Lord ever forgive me for something bad?

Do you have old clothes that are stained? Maybe there is a blob of ink or paint that just won't go away completely, no matter how many times it's been through the wash.

What David did was really bad! He wanted something (someone) that didn't belong to him. He had Uriah killed and brought dishonor to the Lord. Do you think that David deserved to be forgiven after all that the Lord had done for him? No, David did not deserve forgiveness, and neither do we! No one has an excuse for the wrong things we do.

But God is gracious. That means, He will forgive us for every sin – no matter how big it is! Jesus loves us so much that He chose to be nailed to a cross so that His blood could wash away our sin and make our hearts white as snow.

VERSE FOR TODAY
Wash away all my iniquity and cleanse me from my sin.
PSALM 51:2

DAVID

A rebellion is planned

Absalom, one of David's sons did not follow God. He wanted to be king of Israel, so he gathered loyal followers around him by pretending to care for them and sorting out their problems.

Absalom wanted the followers to help him take over the throne of his father David. Eventually the number of Absalom's rebellious followers grew until they had become strong enough to fight David's men.

How does a rebellion start?

A person who rebels is one who goes against the structures and authorities that keep law and order. Structures are the rules and guidelines, while authorities are people who make up the rules and see to it that people keep them.

A country has laws to protect its people and make it possible for them to live in peace (1 Timothy 2:2). Your school has rules that keep children and teachers focused. Even a home has certain rules to keep the harmony between everyone.

A rebel disobeys the law and disrespects those in authority, whether it is a parent, a teacher, the leaders of a country, or even God Himself.

Before God created man, an angel in heaven decided to rebel against God. God threw him out of heaven (Isaiah 14:12). His name is Satan.

A rebellion starts when Satan puts rebellious thoughts in the mind of a person. If the person's heart is not filled with God, then anger, jealousy or pride which already fill his heart, feed those thoughts. Bad thoughts lead to bad actions and those actions influence others, and so the rebellion spreads.

VERSE FOR TODAY

Consequently, he who rebels against the authority is rebelling against what God has instituted, and those who do so will bring judgment on themselves.
ROMANS 13:2

The king's son dies

Absalom, who wanted to be king, was in a battle against the soldiers of his father's army. While Absalom was riding on a horse through some trees, his head got stuck in the branches, and he hung there helplessly while his horse kept on going. Joab, one of David's men found Absalom and killed him with a spear.

Someone went to King David and said, "Praise the Lord, your son who was fighting against you has been killed."

David went to his room and wept. "Absalom, my son Absalom," he cried. "If only I could have died in your place."

What is the greatest love of all?

Is it unusual for a father to love his son? No, it is natural for a father to love his children. But what if the son hates his father? What if the son gets an army to fight against his father? Surely if a father loves a son even then, his love must be very great. David loved his rebellious son so much that when he heard about Absalom's death, he cried, "If only I could have died in your place." We know that David had the love of God in his heart because Jesus said, "Greater love has no one than this, that he lay down his life for his friends" (John 15:13).

The greatest love anyone can show is to give his life for someone else. Jesus did that when He gave His life for you. If you want to know what the greatest love is, then see what the Bible says about God's love. "Very rarely will anyone die for a righteous man, though for a good man someone might possibly dare to die. But God demonstrates his own love for us in this: While we were still sinners, Christ died for us" (Romans 5:7-8).

VERSE FOR TODAY
This is love: not that we loved God, but that he loved us
and sent his Son as an atoning sacrifice for our sins.
1 John 4:10

SOLOMON

1 Kings 2:1-4, 10-12

An old king and a new king

MAY 30

King David was getting old, so he called his son Solomon in order to give him some important instructions. "Be confident and be determined," he said. "Do whatever the Lord your God orders you to do. If you obey the Lord's commands, He will keep the promises He has made."

Soon after this, David died and was buried in Jerusalem, the City of David. Solomon took over from David and became the new king of Israel.

One day, will I be able to do the difficult things my parents do?

As you watch your mom cooking, or see your dad sorting through piles of bills, do you wonder if you will be able to do all the things they do?

The responsibilities that your parents have are too great for you to worry about now!

However, when your parents give you chores to do around the house, they are teaching you to do some of the things that they do. By doing them well, you are showing your parents how responsible you are. They will know when you are ready to do tasks with greater responsibility.

David taught Solomon to become responsible and gave him all the instructions and plans he would need for building the Temple (see 1 Chronicles 28:10-21).

Your parents are not perfect – just as David wasn't perfect. So, even when they make a mistake, you still need to be obedient to them. When they tell you not to do something that they might have done at some stage, it is because they don't want you to get hurt by making the same mistakes.

VERSE FOR TODAY

Come, my children, listen to me; I will teach you the fear of the Lord.
PSALM 34:11

SOLOMON

A wise choice

Solomon was king. He loved the Lord and tried to please Him in every way. One day he went to Gibeon to offer sacrifices there. That night the Lord appeared to Solomon in a dream and said, "What would you like me to give you?"

Solomon answered, "I am very young and I don't know how to rule. Please give me the wisdom I need to rule Your people, and the ability to know the difference between right and wrong."

The Lord was pleased with what Solomon asked for, and said, "Because you have asked for wisdom to rule with fairness instead of asking for long life and riches, I will give you what you have asked for. I will give you more wisdom than anyone has ever had or ever will have, and I will also give you great riches and honor which you did not ask for."

Will God give me anything I ask for?

Don't you just love those stories where someone is given three wishes that come true? It is fun to imagine what it would be like to be given a wish like that. If you could ask for anything you liked, what would it be?

What would you tell the Lord if He asked you what you would like, knowing that it was for real, not just a fairy tale?

Jesus said, "If you remain in Me and My words remain in you, ask whatever you wish, and it will be given you" (John 15:7). Does it really mean that Jesus will give us whatever we wish for?

If what we ask for is good and it is what God wants to give us, He will. Look at the first part of what Jesus said. If we stay close to Him, we will pray for the things He wants us to have.

VERSE FOR TODAY

For the Lord gives wisdom, and from his mouth
come knowledge and understanding.
Proverbs 2:6

June

1 Kings 3:16-28

SOLOMON

Whose baby is it?

After King David died, his son Solomon became the new king of Israel and he was very wise.

One day, two women came to Solomon with a big problem. They were staying together in a house, and each one had a baby. When they awoke that morning, one baby had died. Now both women argued and said, "The living baby is my baby!"

Then Solomon said, "Bring the baby here so that I can cut it in half, then each of you can have half a baby."

When the real mother heard that Solomon was going to kill her baby, she said, "No, please don't kill my baby – rather give the baby to the other woman." Then Solomon knew that she was the real mother – because she wanted the baby to live – and he gave the baby back to her.

JUNE 1

How can a sword help me find out the truth?

Imagine if you were a king trying to get someone to tell the truth. Would you use your sword to threaten the person? What if the person insisted that he was telling the truth, would you be convinced? Without God's wisdom, a sword is only a weapon – not a lie detector!

God has given us a different kind of Sword. It is so sharp that it can pierce right into the heart of a person (without making him bleed). The truth of God's Word can show up a person's lies and deceit. "For the word of God is living and active. Sharper than any double-edged sword; it judges the thoughts and attitudes of the heart" (Hebrews 4:12).

By reading the Bible we, like Solomon, receive wisdom from God; and because God's Word is Truth, it helps us recognize the lies of the devil.

VERSE FOR TODAY

Take the ... sword of the Spirit, which is the word of God.
EPHESIANS 6:17

SOLOMON

Solomon prospers

During the reign of King Solomon, there was peace throughout Judah and Israel. Solomon had thousands and thousands of horses and many servants, and his twelve governors supplied him with the best food.

The Lord gave Solomon unusual wisdom and understanding. He knew so much that it was almost impossible to test his knowledge. He wrote three thousand proverbs and over a thousand songs. He knew all there was to know about plants and trees, and about animals, birds, reptiles and fish.

Solomon ruled over a very large country, and the kings ruling in nearby countries had to pay taxes to him.

Will God also bless me with wealth if I follow Him?

In the Old Testament, people who were blessed by God received His protection or became wealthy, or both. He also blessed people by giving them many children and allowing them to live a long life. Can you think of some examples of the characters you have read about so far? Here is a clue: Their names start with A and J.

Jesus said that we should not only think about getting treasure (wealth) here on earth where thieves can steal it, and where moths and rust will destroy it. We should rather store up treasure in heaven – where it is kept safe for us to enjoy when we get there.

God's blessings are much greater than money and things (that don't last anyway). Instead, He gives us a share of His eternal riches (Romans 8:16-17); and more than long life on earth – eternal life in heaven. By blessing us with His Spirit, we can be truly happy now, and for all eternity!

VERSE FOR TODAY
How much better to get wisdom than gold,
to choose understanding rather than silver!
PROVERBS 16:16

SOLOMON

The Temple is built

King Hiram had always been a friend of King David. When he heard that David had died and that Solomon was king, he sent some of his men to see him. Solomon sent a message back with them saying, "God did not allow my father to build the Temple, but He did promise that his son would build it. So I have decided to build the Temple. I need the help of your men to bring me cedar wood from Lebanon."

King Hiram was pleased to help. He got his men to chop down trees, which they floated down the coast. Solomon built the Temple with strong stone walls lined from top to bottom with cedar wood on the inside.

And the Lord said, "If you obey all My laws and commands, I will do what I promised. I will live here among My people in this Temple and I will never abandon them."

JUNE 3

What has happened to God's Temple?

The Temple that Solomon built was not only beautiful, its walls were made of huge blocks of stone. It was built to last! Yet, we read in 2 Chronicles 36:19 that the Temple was completely destroyed by the Babylonians.

Although the Temple was rebuilt many years later, it was never as beautiful as the Temple Solomon built. Many who had seen the first Temple wept when they saw how much smaller the new Temple was going to be (Ezra 3:12). And even this Temple was destroyed (Luke 21:6).

Are you also sad that God doesn't have a beautiful, big Temple to live in anymore? God doesn't need a Temple built with stones. He lives in the most beautiful Temple of all – in the hearts of those who love Him (1 Corinthians 6:19).

VERSE FOR TODAY
"We heard him say, 'I will destroy this man-made temple and in three days will build another, not made by man.'"
MARK 14:58

SOLOMON

1 Kings 10:1-10

A queen comes to visit

JUNE 4

As Solomon's fame spread, the Queen of Sheba heard about his wisdom and traveled to Jerusalem to meet him. The queen was amazed when she saw Solomon's palace, all his servants and the loads of tasty food. "Praise the Lord your God, for He has shown just how pleased He is with you," she said.

The queen asked Solomon the most difficult questions she could think of – yet there was nothing too difficult for him to explain. Then she gave Solomon the gifts she had brought along, including heaps of gold and jewels. Solomon also gave the queen everything she wanted, as well as many other gifts.

Where can I go for words of wisdom?

It is good to seek wisdom! (Proverbs 3:13). Many wise words have been spoken since time began, and some wise sayings may be helpful in certain situations. However, wisdom from the Bible is more than good advice. God's treasure of wisdom in the Bible leads to everlasting life. When you bury the pearls of wisdom from God's Word in your heart by learning verses from the Bible, you can use those truths over and over, whenever you need God's wisdom to make a decision.

Reading the Bible increases your knowledge; doing what it says leads to godliness; applying the truths in the right way at the right time shows wisdom. We can only be truly wise when our relationship with the Lord is right. "The fear of the Lord is the beginning of wisdom; all who follow his precepts have good understanding" (Psalm 111:10). If you want to be wise, start by using the handbook that was written by the One who created us.

VERSE FOR TODAY

Who is wise and understanding among you? Let him show it by his good life, by deeds done in the humility that comes from wisdom.
JAMES 3:13

1 Kings 11:3-12, 41-43

SOLOMON

Solomon turns away from God

Solomon became unfaithful to God and sinned against the Lord by worshiping the heathen gods of his wives. He even built special places to worship the gods.

The Lord appeared to Solomon twice and warned him not to worship the foreign gods, but he did not listen to the Lord. So the Lord said to Solomon, "Because you have deliberately disobeyed Me, I will take the kingdom away from you. However, for the sake of your father David, I will only take a part of it away and it will only happen after you have died." Solomon ruled Israel for forty years, and after he died, his son Rehoboam became king.

Why would a wise man do something foolish?

At what age did you start walking? By now, you should be quite good at walking. Yet even as you grow up, you slip and fall or trip over things. It doesn't matter how long you have been walking or how good you are at walking, when you take your eyes off the path, you are likely to stumble.

Solomon must have been pretty confident that he was wise enough to solve any problem. He knew almost all there was to know about the world around him, and he owned more than he could use in a lifetime. Yet, what would have made the wisest person on earth do something so foolish as to worship silly gods thought up by heathens?

There is a danger of knowing, but not doing; knowing what is right, but not doing it. Wisdom is only useful if it is put in to practice. Jesus said, "But everyone who hears these words of Mine and does not put them into practice is like a foolish man who built his house on sand" (Matthew 7:26).

JUNE 5

VERSE FOR TODAY

When pride comes, then comes disgrace, but with humility comes wisdom.
PROVERBS 11:2

JOB *

(*His name is pronounced Jobe)

A good man

Long ago, there was a man named Job who lived in the land of Uz. He was a good man and worshipped God. Job had seven sons and three daughters. He also had thousands of camels and sheep, donkeys and many servants.

One day, while the angels were presenting themselves to God, the devil went with them. The Lord said to Satan, "Have you noticed my servant Job? There is no one on earth as faithful as he is."

Satan answered, "Job only worships You for what he gets out of it. You have always protected him and everything he owns. If You took everything away from him he would curse You to Your face."

JUNE 6

How can I convince others of my motives?

"You're only helping Mom so you can get something out of her!" Does that kind of talk sound familiar? Job was a good man just minding his own business. He was careful not to do anything that was wrong. The Lord had been watching Job, just as He watches everything we do. This is what the Lord said about Job, "There is no one on earth as faithful and good as he."

On the other hand, the devil immediately found fault with Job, accusing him of being good only because he wanted the Lord to bless him. One way in which God could prove that Job's motive was pure was to allow the devil to take away everything he owned.

You need not convince others of your reason for doing what is right. Your love and faithfulness will prove your good intentions.

VERSE FOR TODAY

Live such good lives among the pagans that, though they accuse you of doing wrong, they may see your good deeds and glorify God on the day he visits us.
1 PETER 2:12

Disaster strikes

Job was a good man and the Lord blessed him. The devil had been talking to the Lord about Job and was given permission to test Job's faithfulness, but not to harm him in any way.

So the devil went off to start his attack against Job. One day, raiders came and stole all of Job's oxen and donkeys. Then lightning struck and killed all the sheep and shepherds. Other raiders came and stole all Job's camels and killed his servants. And while his children were having a feast at the home of the eldest, a storm swept across the house and made it collapse, killing all his children. When Job heard what had happened, he got up and tore his clothes with grief, but he did not sin by blaming God.

JUNE 7

Will I ever be tested in a way that I can't handle?

Do you hate tests at school? Are you sometimes nervous as you wait for the test papers to be handed out, afraid that it will be too difficult or that you won't remember everything? Tests are not much fun! However, once you have written the test and received your marks, you can see just how well you did.

Similarly, we can only know how strong our faith is if it is tested. Through trials, hardships and temptations, our faith is tested and strengthened. The devil doesn't know whether we will pass or fail the test – but God does!

Jesus knew that his friend Peter was going to face the toughest test of his life. He knew that although Peter would fail this test by denying Him, he would not lose his faith completely. Jesus said to him, "I have prayed for you, Simon, that your faith may not fail" (Luke 22:32). Jesus does not keep us from facing problems, but He will help us overcome them.

VERSE FOR TODAY
And God is faithful; he will not let you be tempted beyond what you can bear. But when you are tempted, he will also provide a way out so that you can stand up under it.
1 CORINTHIANS 10:13

Another test for Job

Once again, when the angels came before God, the devil appeared there with them. The Lord asked him, "Have you noticed My servant Job? The last time you came, you persuaded Me to let you attack him for no reason – and even then he has stayed faithful."

The devil replied, "The only reason Job hasn't cursed You is because he is completely healthy."

And so the Lord allowed the devil to make Job sick. The devil made sores break out all over Job's body. Yet, even though his body was terribly sore all over, Job did not sin or turn against God.

Does sickness come from God?

People have different ideas about the reasons and causes of sickness. While it is not always clear why someone gets sick, there are a few things about sickness we can learn from the Bible:

Before Adam sinned, creation was perfect in every way. Sin brought sorrow, pain and death into the world; and we are a part of that imperfect world (Romans 8:22).

At times, God has used sickness as a punishment for sin. Gehazi, a servant of Elisha got leprosy because he sinned (2 Kings 5:26-27).

God may use someone's sickness to bring glory to Him – often by healing the person (John 9:3).

Our body is like a flimsy tent (2 Corinthians 5:1-3).

We cannot understand God's ways and His purpose. However, when you are sick, you can be sure that Jesus cares for you – He feels a tender compassion for those who are sick (Matthew 14:14).

VERSE FOR TODAY

Jesus said, "This sickness will not end in death. No, it is for God's glory so that God's Son may be glorified through it."

JOHN 11:4

JOB

"Friendly" advice

When three of Job's friends heard how he was suffering, they decided to go and comfort him. Job's children had died, all his animals had been stolen, and now his body was covered with sores.

At first, Job's friends didn't even recognize him, but when they did, they tore their clothes to show how upset they were. They sat in silence with him for seven days. Then, one by one, each of them started telling Job why all this had happened to him. One said that Job had sinned against God, while another said that he was being punished for something his children had done. However, Job could not think of any wrong he or his children had done.

How can I encourage someone who is feeling down?

We all go through times when almost everything seems to go wrong. Perhaps you've noticed your mom or dad looking upset, or a friend who seems down in the dumps.

Have you been discouraged or worried lately? If you have, you can feel and understand what the other person is going through. That makes it easier to say the right thing to them because you can say what you would have liked to hear when you felt that way. "God comforts us in all our troubles so that we can comfort others. When they are troubled, we will be able to give them the same comfort God has given us" (2 Corinthians 1:4).

Rather than trying to point out possible reasons for what happened (like Job's friends did), let your friend to tell you how he/she feels. If your friend also seems upset with you, it is only because you are listening and allowing her to get rid of her frustration and anger.

VERSE FOR TODAY

Therefore encourage one another and build each other up,
just as in fact you are doing.
1 THESSALONIANS 5:11

JOB

God speaks

After Job and his friends had had long discussions about the likely cause of his problems, the Lord Himself spoke to Job out of a storm.

God said to him, "Who are you to question what I do? Where were you when I made the world? Who waters the dry land and put the planets in space? The Lord asked Job many such questions and then gave him a chance to speak."

But Job said, "I have said foolish things. What can I answer? I will not say anything else because I have already said more than I should."

Can we ever really know God?

If it were possible for you to have a conversation with an ant, think of some questions you would ask the ant. "Do you know how to tie a shoelace? Are you able to take the dog for a walk? Do you know how to add and subtract?"

Maybe God smiled as He looked around at His creation and asked Job about things that are so obvious and easy for Him to do.

As humans, we sometimes think we are very clever and very powerful. We can work out how far the moon is from the earth, and we can make powerful bombs to destroy big cities. But who keeps the planets spinning at the right speed and in their right path? And who keeps the sun shining with the heat of a million atom bombs?

We will never be able to know and understand God fully. Paul puts it like this: "Oh, the depth of the riches of the wisdom and knowledge of God! How unsearchable His judgments, and His paths beyond tracing out!" (Romans 11:33).

JUNE 10

VERSE FOR TODAY
For who has known the mind of the Lord that he may instruct him?
But we have the mind of Christ.
1 Corinthians 2:16

More than before

After the Lord had finished speaking to Job, He said to Job's friends; "I am angry with you because you did not speak the truth about Me. Now go make a sacrifice to Me! Job will pray for you and I will answer his prayer."

The three friends did what the Lord told them to do, and after Job had prayed for them the Lord gave Job twice as much as he had before.

Job had children again; seven sons and three beautiful daughters. Once again he owned thousands of camels, sheep, donkeys and cattle. He lived to a very old age – long enough to see his grandchildren and his great-grandchildren.

Will my problems ever come to an end?

As surely as spring follows winter and morning follows a dark and lonely night, so God will bring you through your times of trouble. David said this in one of his psalms: "Weeping may remain for a night, but rejoicing comes in the morning" (Psalm 30:5).

God had not left Job, even though it seemed – for a while – as though he had been abandoned. Little by little, God started putting Job's life together again. Job could not have done this by himself because he had absolutely nothing left.

God rewards faithfulness. God had kept a record of everything the devil had taken away. The devil had his chance to turn Job's heart against God, but Job had passed the test! God was so pleased with Job that it seemed as though He couldn't wait to give Job back everything that had been taken from him. In fact, the Lord gave Job a lot more than he had before!

VERSE FOR TODAY
For our light and momentary troubles are achieving for us an eternal glory that far outweighs them all.
2 CORINTHIANS 4:17

ELIJAH

Not a drop!

After the death of King Solomon, his kingdom divided and was ruled by two kings. Jeroboam ruled the ten tribes of Israel in the north, while Rehoboam the son of Solomon ruled Judah's two tribes in the south.

After a number of kings had come and gone, Ahab became king of Israel. He sinned even more than the kings before him and married a wicked woman named Jezebel. Ahab and Jezebel worshipped the heathen god Baal.

Elijah, a prophet of God, said to King Ahab, "In the name of the living God of Israel, I tell you that there will be no dew or rain for the next few years."

Then the Lord told Elijah to go east and hide near the brook Kerith. "You can drink from this brook," the Lord said, "and I have commanded ravens to bring you food."

Elijah obeyed the Lord and went to the brook. There, the ravens brought Elijah bread and meat every morning and every evening.

Can one leader cause everyone to suffer?

We have many examples of how one person – a powerful leader – can cause much suffering and hardship in a country. Many big wars have been started by the decision of a single person, and thousands of people have been killed because of the stubbornness and greed of one person. King Ahab's sin brought hardship for many.

In some cases, the people themselves chose their leader – not knowing how he would turn out. We should remember to pray for our leaders so that they will let God lead them (1 Timothy 2:1-3).

VERSE FOR TODAY

Do any of the worthless idols of the nations bring rain? Do the skies themselves send down showers? No, it is you, O Lord our God. Therefore our hope is in you, for you are the one who does all this.
JEREMIAH 14:22

ELIJAH

The widow's last meal

The stream where Elijah had been getting water had dried up because it hadn't rained for a long time. So the Lord told Elijah to go to a certain town. When Elijah got to the town, he saw a widow gathering firewood and said to her, "Please give me a drink of water, and could you give me some bread as well?"

The woman answered, "Believe me, I don't have any bread. All I have left is a handful of flour in a bowl and a drop of olive oil in a jar. I am gathering firewood to make one last meal for my son and I before we die."

"Don't worry," Elijah replied. "The bowl will not run out of flour, neither will the jar run out of oil until the Lord sends rain again." So the widow went to prepare the meal for Elijah; and while the drought lasted, the flour and the oil did not run out.

Who looks after missionaries and evangelists?

Most adults either work for somebody or they have their own business. They are paid by the firm they work for or live off the money they make from their business.

If missionaries and evangelists work for the Lord, then who pays them? Yes, the Lord does reward them, but they still have the everyday expenses of food, clothes and other things.

God uses those who earn money to give some of what they earn to those who spend their lives telling others about Jesus. You too could be part of God's plan to help missionaries! You could give some of your pocket money to missions or donate used books and other things to missionary kids.

VERSE FOR TODAY

In the same way, the Lord has commanded that those who preach the gospel should receive their living from the gospel.
1 CORINTHIANS 9:14

ELIJAH

A mother sees God's power

The widow and her son now had enough food for themselves and for Elijah. God was taking care of them in a special way. One day, the son of the widow became very ill. He got worse and worse, and finally died. The widow said to Elijah, "Did you come here to remind God of my sin and cause my son to die?"

"Give me the boy," Elijah said. He took the boy upstairs and laid him on the bed. He asked the Lord why He had done this to the widow who had been so kind to him. Then he prayed, "Lord, bring this child back to life."

So the Lord answered Elijah's prayer and the boy started breathing again! Then Elijah took the boy downstairs to his mother and said, "Look, your son is alive!"

Where do small children go when they die?

It is especially sad when a baby or young child dies. It seems as if he or she has missed out and didn't get the chance to live life fully. Death is very sad for those left behind. We miss the joy of showing our love and care, and we miss the closeness of that special relationship. Happy relationships bring joy to our lives, and when someone is taken from us, it feels as though a chunk has been ripped from inside us.

Although life feels like a very long journey, we are actually on earth for just a short while compared to the time we will be together in heaven. Jesus said, "Let the little children come to Me, and do not hinder them, for the kingdom of heaven belongs to such as these" (Matthew 19:14). All those who have a heart (an attitude) like a child will go to heaven to be with their heavenly Father, and Jesus will be there to welcome them.

VERSE FOR TODAY

By his power God raised the Lord from the dead, and he will raise us also.
1 CORINTHIANS 6:14

ELIJAH

Baal cannot hear

It had not rained for three years, just as Elijah had said. Then Elijah went to King Ahab and told him to get the prophets of Baal and everyone else together on Mount Carmel. Elijah told them, "Take a bull and put it on an altar with wood. But do not light a fire. I will do the same. The God who answers by sending fire is the true God."

The prophets of Baal spent all day praying to their god. By the end of the day, when Baal had not answered their prayers, Elijah said, "Come, gather around." He built an altar and dug a trench around it. Then he prepared the bull, laid it on the altar, and told the men to pour water all over it. So they drenched the altar until the water filled the trench.

Elijah prayed, "Answer me, Lord, so that these people will know that You alone are God." When he had finished praying, God sent a fire that burnt up the sacrifice, the wood and the stones and even dried up the water.

How should our lives be different from those of unbelievers?

Imagine if players from two opposing teams wore the same colors. That would be confusing!

God wanted to make it clear that His people could not serve two gods. They needed to make up their minds whose side they were on.

"Do not conform any longer to the pattern of this world, but be transformed by the renewing of your mind" (Romans 12:2). In other words, don't become like the ungodly people of the world by fitting in so perfectly that no one would even know you are a Christian. Remember that you can't be on both sides. You have been chosen to be on the winning side!

VERSE FOR TODAY

Choose for yourselves this day whom you will serve ...
But as for me and my household, we will serve the Lord."
Joshua 24:15

ELIJAH

A whisper in the desert

JUNE 16

King Ahab told his wife Jezebel about how Elijah's God had sent fire that burned up the altar; and how Elijah had ordered the prophets of Baal to be killed. Jezebel was furious! She sent a message to Elijah; "May the gods strike me dead if I don't do to you what you did to the prophets of Baal!"

Elijah was afraid and fled for his life. He found a cave where he could spend the night. Suddenly, the Lord spoke to him and said, "Go out and stand on the mountain, for the Lord is about to pass by."

First, the Lord sent a furious wind that shattered the rocks, but the Lord was not in the wind. After the wind there was an earthquake, but the Lord was not in the earthquake. After the earthquake there was a fire, but the Lord was not in the fire. After the fire came a gentle whisper. When Elijah heard it, he covered his face and went and stood at the entrance of the cave and God spoke to Him.

Does God speak with a voice of thunder?

God spoke – and all of creation came into being. By His words the earth was formed and every creature was given life. To do that, God's voice must be very powerful!

When we hear a loud clap of thunder roll across the dark sky, we get an idea of how it would sound if God were to speak (see Joel 3:16). Yet, God does not want to scare us by using His loud voice when He speaks to us.

When God speaks to us, He doesn't shout at us from heaven. He uses the quiet voice of the Holy Spirit in our hearts to speak to us, just like the gentle whisper Elijah heard. In fact, if we don't get away from the noise of life and quietly spend time with Him, we may not even hear His voice.

VERSE FOR TODAY
"... How faint the whisper we hear of him!
Who then can understand the thunder of his power?"
JOB 26:14

ELIJAH

A helper

The Lord had appeared to Elijah and told him to anoint Elisha as the prophet who would take over from him. So Elijah went from there and found Elisha plowing with oxen. Elijah took off his cloak and put it on Elisha as a sign of God's Spirit of power on him.

Elisha asked if he could first say goodbye to his father and mother. Elijah replied, "All right, go."

So Elisha went to say goodbye to everyone. He killed his oxen and used the wood from the plow to make a fire and cook the meat. After giving the meat to the people, he went off to become Elijah's helper.

Will I have to leave home to follow Jesus?

"Come and follow Me!" Jesus said, as He called the men who would make up His team of disciples (see Mark 1:17-20 and Mark 2:14). The call was so strong that none of those chosen for the team asked Jesus how long they would be away or where they were going. God had been preparing their hearts, and when Jesus called them, they just left everything and followed Him.

God had been watching Elisha and saw that he was the right person to take over from Elijah. Elisha did not seem surprised or confused, almost as though he had been expecting God to do something big in his life.

When you hear people talk about following Jesus, it doesn't mean that you must wait for Jesus outside with your suitcase packed. What it means is that you must follow the example of Jesus, living the way He did. And as God prepares your heart, you too will be ready to go anywhere when He calls you.

VERSE FOR TODAY

Jesus replied, "No one who has left home or brothers or sisters or mother or father or children or fields for me and the gospel will fail to receive a hundred times as much in this present age."
MARK 10:29-30

ELIJAH

A chariot of fire

Elijah knew that his time on earth was almost up. God had told him to coach Elisha to take over his task as a prophet. As they stood at the edge of the River Jordan, Elijah took off his cloak, rolled it up, and struck the river with it. The river parted and they crossed over on dry ground. As they walked together, Elijah asked Elisha, "What can I do for you before I am taken away from you?"

"Let me have even more of the Spirit's power than you had," Elisha replied.

Elijah said, "You have asked a hard thing, but if you see me when I am taken from you, God will give you what you have asked for."

As they walked together, a chariot of fire pulled by horses suddenly appeared. Elijah was taken up to heaven by a whirlwind and Elisha saw him go up.

Is it possible to get to heaven without dying?

Most people want to go to heaven, but few think about how they'd get there. To get to heaven, our bodies have to be changed. God must give us new heavenly bodies (1 Corinthians 15:53), and for this to happen, our old bodies must die. Elijah went to heaven without actually dying. What a way to go! If you had a choice, you would probably like to go that way too!

For believers, this will actually happen when Jesus comes back to take us up to heaven. He will come at a time no one expects, and all those who love Jesus will meet Him in the air. We will be changed in an instant and be with Him forever. So, be ready at all times because you may be one of those who will go straight to heaven without dying.

VERSE FOR TODAY

After that, we who are still alive and are left will be caught up together with them in the clouds to meet the Lord in the air. And so we will be with the Lord forever.

1 THESSALONIANS 4:17

ELISHA

The test

Elijah had been taken up to heaven and now Elisha was on his own. Because Elisha had seen Elijah as he was taken, he knew he had been given an extra portion of the Spirit's power. But now everyone wanted to find out whether he was really a prophet. The people from Jericho came to him and said, "This is a wonderful city, but the water makes people sick."

So Elisha said, "Get me some salt in a bowl." Then he took the salt and threw it in the spring, saying, "This is what the Lord says, 'I have made this water pure and it will no longer cause people to die.'" And the water was pure from that day on.

How can I know that the Spirit of God lives in me?

One way in which a prophet can show that his message is truly from God is by doing miracles. When God works in amazing ways through His servants, it gives them the authority to speak as though God is speaking.

The people of Jericho had had a problem with their water for some time. Now they had a chance to get their water problem sorted out, and also to find out whether Elisha was for real.

How do your friends know you are for real? The only way someone can tell that the Spirit of God lives in you is by seeing your fruit. Just as you can tell a fruit tree by its fruit, people can tell what is in your heart by the fruit in your life. The Spirit lets fruit appear as you live out the goodness that God has put in your heart. "The fruit of the Spirit is love, joy, peace, patience, kindness, goodness, faithfulness, gentleness and self-control" (Galatians 5:22-23).

VERSE FOR TODAY

(Jesus said) "And I will ask the Father, and he will give you another counselor to be with you forever – the Spirit of truth. ... You know him, for he lives with you and will be in you."
John 14:16-17

The morning glow

When King Ahab of Israel died, the king of Moab rebelled against Ahab's son Joram, the new king.

King Joram was being threatened, so he – together with the king of Judah and the king of Edom – went to see Elisha the prophet. Elisha told him, "Dig ditches all over the valley, and even though you will not see any rain, the valley will be filled with water for you and your animals to drink."

When the Moabites heard that the three kings had come to fight against them, they got up early the next morning to prepare for battle. As the sun was rising, the pools of water looked red in the morning light and the Moabites thought it was blood. "The kings must have fought against each other," they said. "Let's go and raid their camp!" So they did, but the armies of the three kings defeated the Moabites and then destroyed their fields and towns.

How should I deal with nasty comments?

Are nasty comments making you feel embarrassed, worthless and unwanted?

If God could use the glow of the morning sun to give the Israelites victory against attacks, He can shine His love into your situation too! If other kids are trying to make you miserable, the Lord can change your situation as He did for the Israelites. Pray until you feel the warmth of Jesus' love shine into your life and bring healing to your hurting heart.

Jesus is the best friend anybody could wish for. He will never leave you, no matter what! Remember that Jesus made you special, and that is what you are. Enjoy being the person you were made to be!

VERSE FOR TODAY

But for you who revere my name, the sun of righteousness
will rise with healing in its wings. And you will go
out and leap like calves released from the stall.
MALACHI 4:2

ELISHA

Jars of oil

One day, a prophet died before he could pay back the money he owed a man who had lent him the money. The man told the widow that if she didn't pay back the money, he would sell her two sons as slaves to get his money.

When she told Elisha what had happened, he said, "What do you have in your house?"

"I have nothing except a little oil," she replied.

"Go ask all your neighbors for empty jars, as many as you can get," Elisha said. "Then go inside, shut the door and start pouring the oil into the jars."

The woman did as Elisha had told her, and as she poured the oil into the jars, it just kept flowing. The woman went back to Elisha and told him what had happened. So Elisha said, "Now go sell the oil, and with the money you make you can pay your debt and live off what is left."

JUNE 21

Can I be joyful all the time?

"Rejoice in the Lord always. I will say it again: Rejoice!" (Philippians 4:4). Is that actually possible? Is it possible to be happy all the time?

Usually we think of happiness as the pleasant emotion we have when everything goes our way. Paul, who told the Philippians to rejoice, was not having an easy time at all! He spent a lot of time in prison. Of course he wasn't happy about being tied up and beaten, yet he sang songs of joy to God.

Joy comes from inside us! Joy does not depend on others or the things around us. It comes from knowing that Jesus loves us and He is with us. Let the joy of Jesus fill you to overflowing as He anoints you with oil of joy.

VERSE FOR TODAY

Therefore God, your God, has set you above your companions by anointing you with the oil of joy.
PSALM 45:7

ELISHA

Enough room(s)

Elisha once stayed with a man and woman in Shunem. One day the woman said to her husband, "I know that this is a holy man of God. Let's build a small room on the roof of the house, and put in a bed, a table and chair, and a lamp. Then he can stay with us whenever he comes this way." So they built the room.

Then one day, while Elisha was in his new room, he called the woman and said to her, "About this time next year, you will have a son." And the woman became pregnant and had a son the following year, just as Elisha had said.

What is hospitality?

Have your parents ever invited someone to stay in your home for a few days, or even months?

The Holy Spirit has given some people the gift of hospitality. People with this gift are really good at making others feel welcome – whether it is just for a meal or to stay for a while. Whether you have the gift of hospitality or not, you too can make others feel welcome. "Offer hospitality to one another without grumbling. Each one should use whatever gift he has received to serve others …" (1 Peter 4:9-10).

Although the woman and her husband did not have enough space at first, they made a plan. You might not be able to invite others to your home now, but you can share what you have.

You can also show new kids around at school or introduce someone new at church to your friends. Simply share what you have with others – even if it is your big smile!

VERSE FOR TODAY
Share with God's people who are in need. Practice hospitality.
ROMANS 12:13

ELISHA

The faithful slave girl

Naaman was a commander in the Syrian army and was respected by the king because he had won many battles. But Naaman had a problem: he had a terrible skin disease which causes a slow and horrible death.

In one of their raids against Israel, the Syrian army had captured and brought back Israelites slaves. Among them was a little girl who ended up as a servant of Naaman's wife. One day she said to her mistress, "If only my master could go to the prophet in Israel he would be cured of his disease."

When Naaman heard about the prophet in Israel, he went to the king and told him what the girl had said. The king of Aram immediately wrote a letter to the king of Israel and said to Naaman, "Go to Israel, and take this letter with you."

JUNE 23

Can my faith be strong even though I'm young?

Would you have dared to be as brave as the little servant girl was? Naaman was a commander of a big army, and he didn't become commander by being nice! The girl probably didn't even know the name of the prophet in Israel. She also didn't know whether the prophet would heal someone from Syria. She simply trusted God.

She knew that it is easy for God to do things that seem impossible – she had faith! God gave her the confident assurance to tell her mistress about the prophet. Although she knew that she'd be in big trouble if her master came back unhealed, she was obedient to God's voice in her heart. There was absolutely no doubt in her mind that God could heal her master!

VERSE FOR TODAY

Jesus replied, "If you have faith as small as a mustard seed,
you can say to this mulberry tree, `Be uprooted and planted
in the sea,' and it will obey you."
LUKE 17:6

ELISHA

The king can't help

Naaman set out on a journey from Syria to Israel to find the prophet who could cure him of his skin disease. He took along some silver and gold, beautiful clothes and a letter that his king had written.

After a long journey, he arrived in the city of the king of Israel and handed him the letter which said, "This is my officer Naaman. I want you to cure him of his skin disease."

When the king read the letter, he was very upset and tore his clothes. "How can your king expect me to cure you? Does he think I am God? He just wants to pick a fight with me!"

Elisha heard what had happened and sent a message to the king: "Why are you so upset? Send the man to me and I will show him that there is a prophet here who serves the living God."

Should I go to a doctor or pray for healing?

When you feel sick, your mom probably tucks you up in bed and gives you some horrible tasting stuff that makes you better. Some sicknesses are so bad that we need to see a doctor or even a specialist. God will not be upset when your mom takes you to the doctor even though you have prayed and asked Him to make you better.

Think of what you do when you have toothache. Do you ask God to fill your cavity or do you let a dentist fill it?

In most cases, God uses doctors and medicines to make us better. And when doctors don't have a cure for an illness, God still has the same power to heal us in miraculous ways! So even if you go to a doctor, you can still trust God to heal you and make you strong again.

VERSE FOR TODAY
People brought to Jesus all who had various kinds of sickness,
and laying his hands on each one, he healed them.
Luke 4:40

ELISHA

The unbelieving commander

Naaman went with his chariot and horses to the house where Elisha the prophet lived. When he arrived at the house, Elisha told his servant to give Naaman this message, "Go to the Jordan River and dip in the water seven times and you will be cured."

Naaman was upset because Elisha had not even come out to speak to him and cure him right there on the spot. Then Naaman added, "Besides, aren't the rivers back home good enough? I could have washed in them and be cured."

But Naaman's servants said, "Sir, surely if the prophet had told you to do something difficult you would have done it. Why don't you just go down into the river and do what the prophet told you."

So Naaman went down to the Jordan River, and when he had gone in and dipped in it seven times, he was completely cured and his skin became like that of a young boy.

How can I overcome my doubt?

Children learn to trust their parents first and then they start trusting others around them. Unfortunately sooner or later, someone will let you down.

Because we usually think of God in a human way, we wonder whether He, too, will let us down – especially if He has not answered our prayers in the way we had hoped. Naaman expected to be healed in a certain way; but when things worked out differently, he almost gave up.

One way in which you can grow in your faith and trust God more is to read the Bible. By reading about God's faithfulness through thousands of years we can know for sure that God will never change.

VERSE FOR TODAY

Consequently, faith comes from hearing the message,
and the message is heard through the word of Christ.
ROMANS 10:17

ELISHA

The dishonest servant

Naaman was so grateful that he had been healed, he said to Elisha, "Now I know that your God is the only God. Please take this gift as a sign of my gratitude."

But Elisha replied, "I will not accept the gift." Even though Naaman tried to persuade him to take it, Elisha refused. So Naaman went on his way. But Gehazi, Elisha's servant, heard them speaking and decided to get something out of Naaman for himself. Naaman had not gone far when Gehazi caught up with him. "My master sent me to tell you that two prophets have just arrived and that he could use the gifts you wanted to give him," he said.

Naaman gladly gave Gehazi what he had asked for. When Gehazi got back, Elisha asked him where he had been. "I didn't go anywhere!" Gehazi lied.

Then Elisha said to him, "Is this the time to take money and clothes for yourself? Because you have done this, you will get the skin disease that Naaman had."

Does a little dishonesty really matter?

Gehazi may have thought to himself, "Seeing that Naaman really wants to show his gratitude and Elisha doesn't want the gift, I'll take the gift and everyone will be happy." It seemed a sensible thing to do – and no one would know!

Dishonesty in "little" things leads to dishonesty in "bigger" things. When someone is dishonest, others lose their respect for that person and find it harder to trust them with other things. Let your heart and mind be pure so that your heavenly Father can trust you with bigger things.

VERSE FOR TODAY

"Whoever can be trusted with very little can also be trusted with much, and whoever is dishonest with very little will also be dishonest with much."
LUKE 16:10

ELISHA

The axhead

One day, the group of prophets said to Elisha, "The place where we meet is too small for us. Let's go to the Jordan River and cut logs for a new building." Elisha was happy with the idea and went along with them.

As they were chopping down trees, one of the axheads came off the handle and fell into the water. "Oh sir," the man cried, "it was borrowed!"

"Where did it fall?" Elisha asked. So the man showed him the place. Then Elisha cut a stick and threw it into the water. The axhead floated to the surface and the man was able to lift it out of the water.

Why do things go wrong even when we work for God?

Imagine being part of a team of workers building something for God's kingdom. Surely God wouldn't allow anything to go wrong when you are doing your best for Him. Yet, even when some of the prophets were building a bigger place in which to meet, something happened to frustrate them and slow them down.

There are different reasons why things go wrong when we are serving God. The devil isn't going to sit with his arms folded watching people get excited about serving God. Although his power is limited, he will try his best to disrupt the work.

God also has reasons for allowing things to go wrong, even when we are doing something for Him. When we do things for the Lord, we sometimes become proud of what we are doing. He lets things go wrong to remind us to rely on Him – to do things His way and with His strength.

VERSE FOR TODAY
And we know that in all things God works for the good of those who love him, who have been called according to his purpose.
ROMANS 8:28

ELISHA

The unseen force

The king of Syria was at war with Israel. Elisha was able to warn the Israelites about where the Syrians were making their camp. When the king of Syria found out that it was Elisha who was telling the Israelites about their movements, he sent his army with horses and chariots to surround the city where Elisha was staying.

Early the next morning, when Elisha's servant got up and saw that the enemy had surrounded the city, he cried out, "My master, what shall we do now?"

"Don't be afraid," the prophet replied. "Those who are with us are more than those who are with them." Then Elisha prayed, "Lord, open his eyes and let him see!" Immediately, Elisha's servant was able to see horses and chariots of fire covering the hillside and surrounding them.

Do angels really protect us?

Have you heard people talk about a guardian angel? How would you like to have your own invisible bodyguard? The Bible says, "For He will command his angels concerning you to guard you in all your ways" (Psalm 91:11). Doesn't it make you feel special that angels have been given the responsibility of looking after you and keeping you from harm!

When you face danger or feel alone, you may not be aware of your helpers in the unseen world. Elisha's servant was not aware of the army of angels protecting them. He only realized how safe they actually were when the Lord allowed him to see the spiritual forces around them. Can you think of someone else in the Bible who was looked after by an angel? (Clue: D __ n __ el 6:22).

VERSE FOR TODAY

"See that you do not look down on one of these little ones. For I tell you that their angels in heaven always see the face of my Father in heaven."
MATTHEW 18:10

ELISHA

A dying city

The king of Syria led his whole army against Israel and surrounded the city of Samaria. No one could go in or out! People inside the city became very hungry because there was no food. But Elisha told the king, "This is what the Lord says, 'By tomorrow there will be plenty of food again.'"

There were four men outside the city wall who had a sickness called leprosy. They said to each other, "We have nothing to lose. We are going to die anyway so let's go to the Syrian camp." They didn't know that the Lord had made the Syrians hear the sound of a large army of horses and chariots, which made them run for their lives.

When the four men reached the camp, nobody was there. As they went into one tent after another they found gold, silver, clothing, and food. Then they said to each other, "Come, let's go tell everyone!" So they rushed back to the city to give the other Israelites the good news.

JUNE 29

Is there really a treasure inside me?

Don't you love those stories where the most unlikely character becomes the hero? Well, the four beggars lived outside the city for a reason! They had an ugly skin disease and were thrown out of the city.

However, when they found the enemy camp deserted with lots of treasure and food left behind, they were far better off than those starving inside the city. The beggars could have been spiteful and kept it a secret, but they went back to share the good news. The way they looked on the outside was no longer important – the message they had, was!

It doesn't matter what we look like on the outside, we have a precious treasure inside us – the good news of Jesus. Share it with others!

VERSE FOR TODAY

But we have this treasure in jars of clay to show that this all-surpassing power is from God and not from us.

2 CORINTHIANS 4:7

JONAH

Go tell those people

One day, the Lord spoke to the prophet Jonah and said, "Go to the city of Nineveh and tell the people that I know all about their wicked deeds."

But Jonah didn't want to listen. Instead of going to Nineveh, he went to a coastal town called Joppa and boarded a ship going to Spain. When the ship was far out at sea, the Lord sent a great storm. The ship was in danger of sinking and the sailors were terrified. They started throwing the cargo over the side and prayed to their gods for help.

Earlier on, Jonah had gone to his cabin and fallen fast asleep. When the captain of the ship found him there, he said, "How can you be sleeping? Get up and pray to your God to save us!"

Meanwhile the sailors were drawing lots to find out who was responsible for the storm. When it became obvious that Jonah was the guilty one, the sailors asked, "Is all this your fault? What are you doing here? Where do you come from?" Jonah told them that he was running away from God.

Does God care about wicked people too?

God loves us because it is in His nature to love – not because we are good. God is love (1 John 4:16) so we don't have to do anything for Him to love us!

God loves every person on earth so much that He sent His Son Jesus to die for our sins so that anyone who believes on Him will not die in sin, but live forever with Him (John 3:16). Romans 5:8 tells us that God loved people even before they believed.

Yes, God loves sinful people, but He does not love the bad things they do. That is why He sent people like Jonah to tell them about forgiveness and following God's way.

VERSE FOR TODAY

Jesus answered them, "It is not the healthy who need a doctor, but the sick. I have not come to call the righteous, but sinners to repentance."
Luke 5:31-32

July

JONAH

Jonah 1:11-2:1, 10

The bottom of the ocean

Now that the sailors knew that the storm at sea was Jonah's fault, they asked him what they should do so that the storm would stop.

"Throw me into the sea," he said, "and it will be calm."

At first, the sailors did not want to throw Jonah overboard, but when the storm grew worse, they picked him up and threw him into the sea. At once, the sea became calm.

The Lord had planned for a huge fish to swallow Jonah – and from deep inside the fish, he prayed to God.

For three days and nights, Jonah was trapped inside the dark stomach of the fish. Then the Lord heard Jonah's prayer and made the fish spit him out onto a beach.

Once again, the Lord told Jonah to go to the city of Nineveh to preach to the people; so Jonah obeyed and went to Nineveh.

JULY 1

Can we actually run away or hide from God?

What made Jonah decide to run away? As a prophet, he should have known better. So why didn't he want go to Nineveh?

In Jonah's mind, the people of Nineveh were enemies – they were heathens that did not deserve God's forgiveness. Jonah thought that if he took a ship going in the opposite direction that nothing, and no one, could get him to Nineveh. Soon it would be "impossible" for him to get to Nineveh, and he'd be so far away that his conscience wouldn't even bother him.

Adam also disobeyed God and thought he could hide from Him. It is foolish to hide or run from God: He knows exactly where we are anyway. When we run from God's loving arms, we are sure to run into BIG trouble!

VERSE FOR TODAY
Where can I go from your Spirit? Where can I flee from your presence?
PSALM 139:7

JONAH

From riches to rags

The city of Nineveh was so big that it would have taken three days to walk around it. Jonah started telling everyone the message God had given him: in forty days Nineveh would be destroyed. The people believed the message of God. They decided to put on rags and go without food to show how sorry they were.

When the king heard the message, he stepped down from his throne, took off his royal robe, and put on scratchy cloth. He even went to sit in a pile of ashes. He sent out an order that no one was to eat or drink anything, and that everyone was to pray to God and ask for forgiveness. The king thought, "Maybe if we stop our evil ways, God will change His mind and not be angry with us anymore."

How can the heart of a wicked sinner be changed?

God had warned His own people the Israelites many times about their pride and their worship of heathen gods. But their hearts did not change toward Him. (Not even the prophet Jonah had a humble, obedient spirit.) Yet God gave this heathen nation just one chance to change – and that was all they needed. They immediately humbled themselves and asked for forgiveness. After hearing Jonah's warning, they stopped their evil deeds straight away.

If you push something hard enough, it will move. If you make something hot enough, it will melt. But how can you change the heart of a person? What can make a wicked person want to be good? Only the Spirit of God can change a person. "It is not by might nor by power, but by My Spirit," says the Lord (Zechariah 4:6). Only the Holy Spirit can change the heart (spiritual attitude) of a person.

JULY 2

VERSE FOR TODAY

"I will give them an undivided heart and put a new spirit in them;
I will remove from them their heart of stone and give them a heart of flesh."
EZEKIEL 11:19

JONAH

"It's not fair!"

God was merciful toward the people of Nineveh. He changed His mind about destroying the city when the people showed that they were truly sorry for their sin.

Instead of being happy that the people actually listened to his warning, Jonah was upset that God was not going to destroy the city after all. "I knew You are a loving and merciful God; always patient and kind and willing to forgive," Jonah complained.

Then Jonah went to sit outside the city and sulk. So the Lord showed Jonah how selfish he was for only thinking about himself and not about the thousands of people who would have died without knowing the right way.

Why was Jonah so upset when God was merciful?

Suppose there is a special club at your school that only specially chosen kids may join. After a very long time, you are finally allowed to become part of the club. A few weeks go by and someone suggests that two younger kids – whom you don't like – be allowed to join. How would you feel about letting them be part of the special club?

Jonah didn't mind being part of a nation that God had chosen to bless. He may have thought that God's special favor was not only a privilege – it was his right. He felt that Israel was better than the heathen nations around them and that they deserved God's blessing. When Jonah saw how merciful God was to others, he became jealous and angry.

Be happy when you see God being kind to others, remembering that next time you could be the one needing His mercy and forgiveness.

VERSE FOR TODAY
God said, "I will have mercy on whom I have mercy,
and I will have compassion on whom I have compassion."
ROMANS 9:15

AMOS

Stealing from the poor

The kingdom of Israel had split: there was a Northern kingdom (still called Israel), and a Southern kingdom (now called Judah). God spoke through different prophets who preached to the people in Israel and in Judah. Amos was a prophet who preached to the people in the Northern Kingdom, where some had become very rich while others lived in poverty.

God told Amos to say this to the rich: "You sell honest men as slaves and poor men for a pair of sandals. You trample down the weak and helpless and push the poor aside. Of all the nations on earth, you are the ones I have cared for. This is why your sin is so terrible, and for that I will punish you."

What should I do when someone can't pay me back?

Jesus told a story about a servant who owed his master a lot of money. When he couldn't pay it back, the king ordered him to be sold as a slave to pay his debt. The servant begged the king to be patient with him. The king felt sorry for the servant and forgave him his debt. But later, when this same servant met someone else who owed him money, he was not willing to forgive the other person his small debt (Matthew 18:23-35).

God was angry because the rich Israelites demanded their money back from the poor – even though they themselves had more than enough to live on. What made God even more angry was that they sold others into slavery, forgetting that they themselves had been rescued from slavery in Egypt.

If someone owes you something that they can't give back, remember that things should never become more important than people. If you are kind to others, God will be kind to you!

JULY 4

VERSE FOR TODAY

"But love your enemies, do good to them, and lend to them without expecting to get anything back. Then your reward will be great, and you will be sons of the Most High."
LUKE 6:35

AMOS

Holidays and parties

Amos the prophet said to the people of Israel, "God will be your helper if you hate evil and love what is good."

Then Amos told them, "This is what the Lord says; 'I hate your religious feasts. When you bring Me your sacrifices and offerings, I will not accept them. I cannot stand the noise of your songs and the sound of your harps. What I want from you is a flood of justice and streams of goodness.'"

What does God think about our religious celebrations?

Why would God tell the Israelites that He hated their religious celebrations when He had told them to have these feasts?

God does not tell us to do things without a reason. The reason for the celebrations was to get everyone to take a break from their busy lives and think about their faith. One of the feasts was to give thanks by bringing the first part of their harvest. Another was to sacrifice an animal for the forgiveness of their sins. Then there was a feast to remind them of how God had brought them out of Egypt.

But instead of remembering how good God had been to them, they used the celebration as an excuse to have a big party. And so, a festival that was meant to make people think about God and rejoice in His goodness turned into a noisy party where everyone forgot about God.

Paul says that each person should decide which days have a special meaning, and which are just ordinary days. It is up to you to decide which occasions are important to you. If they are meant to remind you about the Lord, let them be meaningful by making Him welcome at the celebrations – and in your heart!

JULY 5

VERSE FOR TODAY

One man considers one day more sacred than another; another man considers every day alike. Each one should be fully convinced in his own mind.
ROMANS 14:5

HOSEA

God proves His faithfulness

After the ministry of Amos, God called Hosea to carry on preaching to the people of Israel. His message to the people was to stop their idol-worship and turn to God.

The Lord spoke to Hosea and told him to marry a woman who would be unfaithful to him. God was showing Hosea (and Israel) how He felt about their unfaithfulness to Him. Hosea's wife chose to love other men, just as Israel had chosen to worship heathen idols instead of their Lord.

Even though Hosea's wife ran away from him to go live with other men, he loved her so much that he went out and looked for her. He paid silver to buy her back so that she could stay with him once again.

Is there going to be a real wedding in heaven?

When a man and a woman get married, they promise to love each other and be faithful to one another. God had kept His promise of love and faithfulness – His people had not! He compares His relationship with Israel to the relationship between a husband and wife. We, the Church, have now become the bride of Jesus Christ!

As Hosea showed his love for his wife by paying the price to get her back, so Jesus came to the world to look for us and save us, and bring us back to God. But Jesus did not buy us back with silver – He bought us with His precious blood by dying for us (1 Peter 1:18-19).

Now that we – as the Church – are the bride of Jesus, we must stay pure and be ready for Him. We do not know when He is coming to take us to be with Him. When He does, there is going to be a wedding in heaven, and we will live with Jesus forever!

JULY 6

VERSE FOR TODAY

Let us rejoice and be glad and give him glory! For the wedding of the Lamb has come, and his bride has made herself ready.
REVELATION 19:7

HOSEA

Hosea 6:1-6

But I did say sorry!

Hosea the prophet pleaded with the people who had turned from God, saying, "Come let us return to the Lord who has hurt us, for He will be sure to heal us again. He has wounded us, but He will bandage our wounds. Let us try to know Him better, and He will come as surely as the sun rises, and the rain falls in early spring."

The Lord said, "Your love disappears like the morning mist or like the dew when the sun comes up. I don't want your sacrifices; rather show mercy to others. Give me your honor and worship instead of your animal sacrifices."

What does 'repent' mean?

How would you feel if someone hurt you on purpose, then said, "Oops! Sorry!" and hurt you again. Do you think such a person is really sorry for what he did to you? No! Well this is exactly the way God felt about His people. They were pretending to be sorry by offering sacrifices, but in their hearts they had chosen to love their money and idols instead of loving God.

To repent means that you are truly sorry for what you have done. A prayer of repentance could be like this: "Dear Father, once again I have messed up and disappointed You by what I did. I am really sorry that I did something I knew was wrong. Please forgive me and make my heart clean. Lord, I don't want to make the same mistake again, so please help me to stay close to You and rely on Your strength when I am tempted."

God's grace is big enough to forgive you every time – no matter how often you sin or how "big" the sin. All God wants is to see that you are truly sorry and that you are willing to change.

JULY 7

VERSE FOR TODAY
Godly sorrow brings repentance that leads to salvation and leaves no regret.
2 CORINTHIANS 7:10

HOSEA

The promise of new life

Once again, the Lord spoke to His people through Hosea, telling them what He was going to do for them one day. "I will bring My people back to Me. I will love them with all My heart, and I will no longer be angry with them. I will come to them like rain on the dry land and they will blossom like flowers. They will be alive again with new growth and have the sweet smell of cedar trees.

Once again I will protect them and they will flourish like a garden and be fruitful like a vineyard. They will have nothing more to do with idols and I will answer their prayers and take care of them. It is from Me that all their blessings will come."

What is grace?

Have you done something really bad that made you feel ashamed and guilty? You were probably afraid that someone would find out what you had done and be punished. Perhaps you tried to be extra helpful or did something good to cover up the sin.

How would you feel if someone came to you and said, "I will take the blame for what you did; in fact, I will take your punishment as well. I will even take away that awful feeling of guilt."

What a relief to know that Jesus has taken the blame for us. He has taken the sin of the whole world on Him. But Jesus does not only forgive; He takes us in as His children He blesses us with every good thing. That is grace!

- Forgiveness – Isaiah 53:6
- Acceptance – Luke 15:11-24
- Blessing – Ephesians 1:3

JULY 8

VERSE FOR TODAY
For it is by grace you have been saved, through faith – and this not from yourselves, it is the gift of God.
EPHESIANS 2:8

ISAIAH

The vineyard

The Lord spoke through Isaiah – the first prophet to the people of Judah – saying, "Listen as I sing you a song about my friend and his vineyard:

My friend had a vineyard on a fertile hill;
He built a winepress and tower.
He planted and pruned the vines with skill.
But every last grape was sour!"

Israel was the vineyard of the Lord and the people were the vines He had planted. The Lord of the vineyard expected the very best because He had done everything He could, but the sin of the people made the grapes sour.

How can I keep from turning sour?

JULY 9

Do you like eating lemons? If you do, then you would probably like sour grapes too! Most people plant a vine to get tasty, sweet grapes; and if they want something sour, they may plant a lemon tree as well. But imagine if you had decided to enjoy a glass of sweet grape juice and it tasted awfully sour. (Pull a face to show how disgusted you would be.)

We can become sour by having a wrong attitude (like not forgiving someone). But sour people are not friendly, happy people. If you are struggling to be sweet, ask Jesus to prune away those things in your life that keep you from bearing good fruit. As you live in the sunshine of God's love and let the Holy Spirit's goodness flow into you, you will please Jesus – the Gardener of your life – and be a blessing to many.

VERSE FOR TODAY

Jesus said, "I am the true vine, and my Father is the gardener. ... Every branch that does bear fruit he prunes so that it will be even more fruitful."
JOHN 15:1-2

ISAIAH

"I will go!"

Uzziah, the king of Judah, had died. In that same year, Isaiah saw the Lord sitting on His throne. Around Him were flaming creatures, each with six wings. They called out to each other, "Holy, holy, holy! The Lord Almighty is holy, and His glory fills the whole earth."

Isaiah said to himself, "There is no hope for me! I am doomed because the words I speak are sinful – and now I have seen the Lord Almighty!"

Then one of the creatures flew down and touched his lips with a glowing coal from the altar, saying, "This has touched your lips, and now your sin and guilt has been taken away."

Then Isaiah heard the Lord say, "Whom shall I send? Who will be our messenger?" Isaiah immediately answered, "Here am I. Send me."

Does God still have prophets?

God mainly used prophets to bring His message to the people living in Old Testament times. Today, we have preachers, pastors and evangelists who bring God's message to us from the Bible.

During the time of the prophets, God spoke directly to them, telling them exactly what to say. The prophets did not have the complete Bible from which to preach. In fact, much of what they said now forms part of the Old Testament. At that time the New Testament had not yet been written.

Today, we have the complete Bible as God wanted it to be. It is God's message written by people who were guided by the Holy Spirit. As in the time of the prophets, God is still looking for messengers to spread the good news of His love and forgiveness. Would you be willing to say, "Here I am, Lord. Send me"?

JULY 10

VERSE FOR TODAY

We proclaim him, admonishing and teaching everyone with all wisdom, so that we may present everyone perfect in Christ.

COLOSSIANS 1:28

ISAIAH

Words of encouragement

Isaiah told King Hezekiah that the Babylonians would attack and raid Jerusalem, carrying off everything the people owned and taking them to Babylon as slaves. But there was hope! Isaiah encouraged the people that a time would come when the Lord would bring them back and God's glory would be seen by the whole world.

This is what the Lord said: "All people are like the grass of the field. They don't live much longer than wild flowers, which bloom for only a short while. Yet, even though the grass withers and the flowers fade, the Word of God stands forever. The Lord is coming to rule with power, bringing with Him a reward for His people. He will care for His flock like a shepherd and carry the young ones in His arms. He will gently lead the mothers and carry the little lambs close to His heart."

JULY 11

Is there hope for people living in this messed-up world?

Isaiah told the people living in Judah that things would go from bad to worse. In spite of many, many warnings, the people no longer followed the Lord's commands. God would let the enemy take them as captives to a far-away place so that their hearts would return to Him. But God did not want them to lose hope. He knew that the years of slavery in Babylon would set their hearts free from wanting to worship idols.

As in Isaiah's day, godless people today are making our world an unsafe and unfriendly place; but we should not become discouraged by the evil around us. All this will change when Jesus comes again. He will lead us like a gentle shepherd and keep us safe forever. Be encouraged: Jesus said that He is coming back soon, bringing with Him a reward for His faithful ones!

VERSE FOR TODAY

(Jesus said) "Behold, I am coming soon! My reward is with me, and I will give to everyone according to what he has done."
REVELATION 22:12

ISAIAH

A new thing

The Lord told His people through the prophet Isaiah that He would rescue them from the Babylonians.

He said to them, "I am the Lord, your King. I am the One who made a way for you through the sea and who led the Egyptian army to destruction. But don't hold onto the past and keep thinking about what happened. Look! I want to do something new, and it has already started to happen: I will make a road through the wilderness and give you streams of water in the desert."

If I go the wrong way, does God have another plan?

The Lord had rescued His people from the Egyptians and made a way for them through the sea and the desert. Maybe they were wondering whether God would ever do miracles like that again. Were those days over? Would God rescue them from slavery a second time? Bringing them out of Egypt was only the first part of God's plan. That is why He said; "Do not hold onto the things that happened long ago – watch for the new thing I am going to do!"

Perhaps you are worried that one day you might mess up God's plan for your life. We sometimes go the wrong way and it feels like we're in the desert, far from God. However, like the streams in the desert that Isaiah wrote about, the Living Water of God's Spirit will flow into your life (John 7:38-39).

God will also make a highway for Jesus to come right into your situation (Mark 1:1-3). This highway goes through the wilderness, which means that there is a way out! So, even when you do mess up, God will make a new plan. He will do a new thing in your life. Isn't that exciting!

JULY 12

VERSE FOR TODAY
But one thing I do: Forgetting what is behind
and straining toward what is ahead.
PHILIPPIANS 3:13

ISAIAH

Isaiah 52:13, 53:1-9

The Messiah

God loved His people! Although they had been taken as slaves to a distant land, God went with them wherever they went. The Lord promised that He would bring them back to their land, and back to Himself.

There was only one way for God to rescue His people from their sin: He would send Jesus to earth where He would suffer and die to conquer sin. He would be beaten and bruised so that people wouldn't recognize Him.

Jesus took the suffering that should have been ours. He was wounded to take away our sins. Yet, even though He was treated harshly and beaten for the wrong things we have done, He did not complain once.

Why did Jesus have to suffer?

It is hard to understand why Jesus had to die to make it possible for God to forgive sins. But it is even harder to understand why Jesus had to suffer so much pain by being beaten and then nailed to a cross.

When Jesus was praying in the garden the night before He was crucified, He knew that He would have to suffer. He said to His Father, "If at all possible, may I not have to go through with this, but I do not want My way; I want to do what You want."

Although we cannot fully understand why God the Father allowed Jesus to suffer, the Bible does tell us some of the reasons:
- to show His complete obedience (Philippians 2:8);
- to show His great love for us (1 Peter 1:18-19);
- to become a sacrifice for our sin (Hebrews 9:22);
- to feel and understand our suffering (Isaiah 53:3);
- to heal us (Isaiah 53:5, Matthew 8:16-17).

JULY 13

VERSE FOR TODAY

And being found in appearance as a man, he humbled himself and became obedient to death – even death on a cross!

PHILIPPIANS 2:8

MICAH

The Savior is promised

During the time of Isaiah, Micah the prophet also preached to the people of Judah. Even though he had warned them of judgment, his message was filled with hope for the future. This is what the Lord said through the prophet Micah: "Oh Bethlehem, you are one of the smallest towns in Judah, but out of you will come a great King who was alive before time began."

God would allow His people to be ruled by their enemies until the time when the mother gives birth to her child.

When the Lord comes, He will be the Shepherd of His flock. And they will live in safety, for His greatness will reach every part of the earth – and there will be peace!"

Did the Old Testament prophets know about Jesus?

During the time of the prophets, people were not able to see the whole picture of God's plan to save us from sin. They did not know that God would send His Son, Jesus, to earth hundreds of years later. Although the prophets spoke of a Savior who was to come (and Micah even prophesied where He would be born) they did not know that it would be Jesus. God's plan was a mystery to them (Romans 16:25-26).

After many years, when Jesus was born on earth as Micah had prophesied, Herod – who was king at that time – asked the religious leaders to find out if the prophets had said anything about a great king that was to be born. They searched the Scriptures and found this exact prophecy where Micah said that a ruler would be born in Bethlehem (Matthew 2:5-6).

JULY 14

VERSE FOR TODAY

The shepherds said to one another, "Let's go to Bethlehem and see this thing that has happened, which the Lord has told us about."
LUKE 2:15

MICAH

Pleasing God

Through Micah's preaching, the Lord reminded the Israelites living in Judah how He had brought them out of Egypt. Then Micah asked the people some questions they should have been asking themselves: "What should I bring to the Lord when I come to worship Him? Will the Lord be pleased with thousands of sheep or rivers of olive oil?"

"No, of course not," Micah said. "What the Lord wants from you is this: to do what is right, to show mercy, and to walk humbly with your God."

What does God expect of me?

Do you want to please God by the way you live? What do you think pleases God most? Some people do good (religious) deeds to show how good they are. But that doesn't impress God at all!

Jesus lived as a perfect example of a life that pleases God. Jesus showed fairness by defending a woman who had sinned and was about to be punished by men who were just as guilty of sin (John 8:3-11). He showed mercy by healing the ear of a man who had come to arrest Him (Luke 22:50-51). And Jesus showed humility by getting down on His knees and washing His disciples' dirty feet (John 13:3-5).

What God expects of you is not hard to do. This is what He wants from you:
- to be just and fair;
- to be merciful and loving;
- to submit to God in a humble way.

If you forget these three things, don't worry; just remember to do to others as you would want them to do to you (Luke 6:31).

JULY 15

VERSE FOR TODAY
And do not forget to do good and to share with others,
for with such sacrifices God is pleased.
HEBREWS 13:16

Zephaniah 1:1,
2 Chronicles 34:1-7

ZEPHANIAH

A young king pleases God

During the reign of King Josiah, God chose Zephaniah as a prophet to speak to the people of Judah. King Josiah was only eight years old when he became king after his father, Amon, was murdered. King Josiah pleased the Lord, as King David had done, and obeyed all the laws of God.

When he was a few years older, he started destroying the places where people worshiped the heathen gods until he had cleared the whole country of idols.

How can I be a good leader?

Maybe you have never thought of yourself as a leader. Yet others may be following your example without you even knowing it. That makes you a leader! A leader is not someone who just bosses others around. Here are a few things that will make you a good (or a better) leader:

- **Be courageous:** Being a good leader takes courage. People respect leaders who know what is truly important and stand up for what they believe in.
- **Be an example:** Do what is right and change what is wrong. Josiah found out all he could about living a life that is pleasing to God. Then as he grew older and saw all the wrong, sinful things around him, he did what he could to stop the evil.
- **Be loyal to God:** Serving God and doing what is right may make you unpopular with certain people. Josiah was not concerned about what people thought of him. Unlike his father, he chose to please God rather than people.

JULY 16

VERSE FOR TODAY
In everything set them an example by doing what is good.
TITUS 2:7

ZEPHANIAH

God's Word is found

While the Temple of the Lord was being cleaned up and repaired, Hilkiah the High Priest found the written instructions that God had given to Moses. "I have found the book of the Law!" he exclaimed; and he gave it to Shaphan who took it to King Josiah.

When the book was read aloud, Josiah ripped his clothes and said, "Go find out from the Lord about what is written in the book. God is angry with us because our fathers have not been doing what the book says."

Then the Lord gave Josiah this message: "Because you humbled yourself, tore your clothes, and wept before Me, My judgment against Jerusalem will not come until after you have died."

Has the Bible become outdated?

Have you ever skipped a meal or gone without food for a whole day? If you have, you obviously survived. But if you don't eat for days and days, you will run out of energy and become weak. In the same way, if we don't get our spiritual food by reading the Bible every day, we won't have the strength to face our daily struggles and resist temptation.

Without the written Word of God to guide them, God's people had lost their way. They had thrown away the map of life, thinking that they no longer needed the law that Moses had given them hundreds of years before. It just seemed so out-of-date! Idols were in fashion now – and God's rules told them that idol-worship is wrong. The people didn't realize that the Word of God is actually so up to date that it even tells us what will happen in the future. If only they had read it, they would have known what was going to happen to them (2 Chronicles 34:24-26).

VERSE FOR TODAY
Therefore my people will go into exile for lack of understanding.
ISAIAH 5:13

ZEPHANIAH

God's song of joy

The Lord allowed Zephaniah to see His plan for Jerusalem and Judah. Although the people would be taken to a distant country as slaves, eventually when the time came for them to return, they would be humble and obey the Lord once again. Their hearts would rejoice because God's punishment had ended and they were free again.

"The Lord will be joyful too!" Zephaniah told them. "He will be delighted with His people and sing about them like someone at a festival."

"The time is coming!" says the Lord, "I will bring the scattered people home and make them famous."

Does the Lord get excited about me?

Sometimes I feel like such a bore. I don't do anything exciting and I don't have exciting things to talk about. I'm not even excited about myself, how could anyone else get excited about me? If that is how you feel about yourself, there is great news for you!

It doesn't matter how you feel about yourself on a Monday morning, or when you look in the mirror. It doesn't matter if you are not a top performer in class or a star on the sports field. God gets so excited about you that He actually sings about you!

You may think that God has so many people to look after that He doesn't have the time to spend with you. Well, think about this: does it really matter to you how many hairs are on your head? God thinks it does! He knows the exact number (Luke 12:7). And if that is important to Him, think how much more important it is for Him to watch you, to love you, and to talk to you.

JULY 18

VERSE FOR TODAY

For the LORD takes delight in his people;
he crowns the humble with salvation.
PSALM 149:4

JEREMIAH

Jeremiah 1:4-10, 2:1-3

Remember!

Jeremiah lived during the reign of King Josiah. One day the Lord spoke to Jeremiah and said, "I chose you before you were born. I have a special purpose for your life: to be a prophet to the nations."

Then Jeremiah answered the Lord, "Almighty Lord, I am too young. I don't know how to speak."

But the Lord said, "Do not say that you are too young, but go to the people I am sending you to. Do not be afraid of them for I will be with you and will protect you." Then the Lord told Jeremiah to give the people of Judah this message; "I remember how faithful you were when you were young, how you loved Me as a bride loves her husband; how you followed Me through the desert. You belonged to Me alone; you were My special possession."

How can I keep my love for God from growing cold?

JULY 19

What does someone have to do to become lazy and unfit? Nothing! How does a friendship fizzle out? By doing nothing!

Over time, the Israelites stopped praying to God because they trusted in other gods. They stopped reading God's Law because they had lost it. They had stopped going to the Temple to worship God because they worshiped other gods. It was obvious that their love for God was no longer important.

Jesus said that in the last days (before He comes again), most people won't care about loving Him: "Because of the increase of wickedness, the love of most will grow cold, but he who stands firm to the end will be saved" (Matthew 24:12-13).

Let the warmth of His love keep you standing firm in your faith.

VERSE FOR TODAY

Jesus said to the Church at Ephesus, "You have forsaken your first love … Repent and do the things you did at first."
REVELATION 2:4-5

JEREMIAH

Don't boast

This is what the Lord said through his prophet Jeremiah. "The wise should not be proud of their wisdom, nor the strong show off their strength, neither should the rich boast about their wealth. If someone wants to boast, it should be about knowing and understanding Me, because My love does not change from day to day, and I do what is fair and right. These are the things that please Me."

Why is pride such a problem?

The Bible says that we should not think more highly of ourselves than we ought (Romans 12:3).

On the one hand we should never think of ourselves as worthless, ugly, or good-for-nothing. We are made in the likeness of God, which means that we are His beautiful, precious children. God wants us to feel good about ourselves – to love and accept ourselves (Galatians 5:14), because when we do, others can see the beauty of Jesus in us.

On the other hand, if there is one thing God hates, it is pride – the sin of believing that what we are and what we have comes from our own strength, ability and cleverness. Proud thoughts will grow in your head if you allow a proud attitude to take root in your heart.

Do not boast by what you say (words): Boastful words are a sure way to chase away friends and make a fool of yourself!

Do not boast by what you do (actions): Boastful actions lead to foolish bravery that can cause harm and injury.

Do not boast by what you think (attitude): A boastful attitude is the worst kind of pride because it is telling God that you don't need Him.

VERSE FOR TODAY

May I never boast except in the cross of our Lord Jesus Christ, through which the world has been crucified to me, and I to the world.
GALATIANS 6:14

JEREMIAH

Jeremiah 18:1-6

The potter

One day, the Lord told Jeremiah to go down to the potter's house. Jeremiah went there and found the potter making clay pots on his spinning wheel. Jeremiah noticed that whenever the pot that the potter was making did not turn out exactly right, he would take the clay and form something else.

Then the Lord said to Jeremiah, "Do I not have the right to do with the Israelites what this potter has done with his clay? You are in My hands like the clay in the potter's hands."

How does God mold me?

Have you ever shaped things with modeling clay? What do you do when something doesn't look right? You squeeze the clay into a ball and start over; perhaps trying something new. The clay that potters use is like sticky mud. If the clay is soft, it can be molded easily; if it is hard or lumpy, the pot is ruined.

We were formed out of the dust (or clay) of the earth (Genesis 2:7). Just as a potter keeps his eyes on the spinning lump of clay he is shaping, God keeps His eyes on us as He forms and molds us into His likeness. By using both hands to gently shape the vessel, the potter feels the clay all the time and knows just how hard to press it. Our lives are in God's loving hands as He gently works with us, for He knows how we are formed; He remembers that we are dust (Psalm 103:13-14).

God may use circumstances and relationships (people) in your life to smooth out rough places and make you ready for a special purpose. He knows that we are fragile and weak, so He carefully works on us to shape us into the vessel He wants us to be (Romans 9:21).

JULY 21

VERSE FOR TODAY
Yet, O Lord, you are our Father. We are the clay,
you are the potter; we are all the work of your hand.
Isaiah 64:8

JEREMIAH

God's discipline gives hope

King Josiah died, and after a time, Zedekiah became king of Judah. He did not follow the Lord as King Josiah had done. The Lord had promised Josiah that He would not bring disaster on Jerusalem as long as he was alive. But now, the destruction of Jerusalem was about to happen. Yet, even at this time, Jeremiah still pleaded with the people to leave their idols and turn back to the Lord.

Then, King Nebuchadnezzar of Babylon attacked the Israelites in Judah, raided the Temple of the Lord and took many men, women and children back to Babylon as slaves – just as the Lord had said would happen.

Jeremiah, who was still in Judah, wrote a letter to those who had been taken to Babylon, telling them of the Lord's promise: "When your seventy years in Babylon are over, I will show you mercy and bring you back home. For I know the plans I have for you; plans to prosper you and not harm you, plans to give you hope and a future."

What is the difference between discipline and punishment?

Discipline could be illustrated by a motorist who is fined for speeding and gets another chance to drive within the speed limit.

Punishment could be illustrated by a motorist who has been caught speeding. Because he refuses to slow down, his driver's license is taken away.

The Lord uses discipline to stop us from doing something that is wrong sinful. It is His way of correcting and training us. The Lord wants us to accept His discipline; not stubbornly rebel against it. Discipline is the loving action of our Father to keep us within His plan for our lives.

JULY 22

VERSE FOR TODAY

The fear of the LORD is the beginning of knowledge,
but fools despise wisdom and discipline.

PROVERBS 1:7

JEREMIAH

Jeremiah 38:4-13

Things get messy

JULY 23

Jeremiah told those who were still in Jerusalem that they would not be killed in battle or die of starvation if they surrendered to the Babylonians. But when the leaders heard Jeremiah's message, they went to tell King Zedekiah and asked that Jeremiah be killed.

The king answered, "Do whatever you want to do with him." So the men took Jeremiah and threw him into a deep, muddy pit, thinking that he would soon die.

However, when two of the men working in the palace heard what the others had done, they went and told the king, who ordered them to go pull Jeremiah out again.

Can people change God's plan for my life?

Nothing and no one can take you out of God's will or change His plan for your life! God already knew about every part of your life before you were born. He has a wonderful and perfect plan worked out for you.

There were three kinds of people who changed things for Jeremiah: those who were against Jeremiah because of his message; the king who didn't really care what happened to Jeremiah; and Jeremiah's friends who risked their lives to help him by speaking to the king.

When Jesus was on earth, there were people who wanted to crucify Him; there was Pilot the governor who didn't want to get involved; and then there were the disciples who were Jesus' friends.

God allowed people to bring trouble and change in the lives of Jeremiah and Jesus; and through people, His will was done – just as Jesus prayed that it would be.

VERSE FOR TODAY
Jesus said, "My sheep listen to my voice; I know them,
and they follow me ... no one can snatch them out of my hand."
JOHN 10:27-28

DANIEL

Not on the Menu!

As Jeremiah had prophesied, King Nebuchadnezzar of Babylon attacked the city of Jerusalem, taking many Israelites to Babylon as slaves.

Daniel was one of those who were captured. Soon after he arrived in Babylon, King Nebuchadnezzar ordered his chief official to choose the cleverest and best looking men from Israel to serve in his royal court. Ashpenaz, the chief official, selected Daniel and his three friends for a training program to teach them the Babylonian language and way of life. They were offered the best food and wine – straight from the king's kitchen.

Daniel made up his mind not to eat the rich, royal food or drink the wine offered to him. He said to the guard, "Test us for ten days. Give us only vegetables and water. Then compare us to the others who eat the royal food."

The guard agreed, and after ten days, Daniel and his friends looked healthier and stronger than the others who had been eating the king's special food. So the guard allowed it, and God blessed them.

Do I have to eat my vegetables?

Daniel and his friends were used to eating plain, healthy food. It is not surprising that they were so bright and healthy. Daniel knew that God, who created us, also provides us with all the natural food our bodies need. Daniel was determined to honor God by looking after his body. He also did not want to live a life of luxury while his fellow Israelites were suffering as slaves. Although Daniel's diet of vegetables was a personal decision, we can see that God was pleased with Daniel and blessed him.

Yes, you do need to eat vegetables to be healthy. Look after your body because it is the Temple of the Lord (1 Corinthians 6:19).

JULY 24

VERSE FOR TODAY
Everything is permissible – but not everything is beneficial.
1 Corinthians 10:23

DANIEL

The super-idol

King Nebuchadnezzar of Babylon ordered his workers to make a huge golden statue. When it was ready, he ordered the officials from all over the country to come and see it.

When everyone had gathered – including Daniel's three friends – there was a loud announcement: "People of all nations, races and languages; when you hear the sound of the trumpets and the music from the other instruments, you are to bow down and worship the golden statue. Anyone who does not bow to the golden statue that King Nebuchadnezzar has set up will be thrown into the blazing furnace."

And so, as soon as the people heard the sound of the instruments, they bowed down and worshipped the golden statue.

JULY 25

Is it wrong to admire a hero or superstar?

If you could get a huge autographed poster of the person you admire most, who would you choose? People may admire someone for their courage, their ability to lead, their physical strength, or for some other reason.

King Nebuchadnezzar had a dream about a statue (see Daniel 2:37). It gave him an idea to get the people to worship him like an idol. So he forced them to bow down to the statue as if they were worshiping him.

It is not wrong to look up to someone who is great or famous; but it is wrong to admire someone who is ungodly and then do the wrong things he or she does.

However, to follow the role model of a godly person is a good thing. Paul even told others to follow his example (Philippians 3:17). But remember, even good people are human. Jesus alone is perfect!

VERSE FOR TODAY

That at the name of Jesus every knee should bow,
in heaven and on earth and under the earth.
PHILIPPIANS 2:10

DANIEL

Bow or die!

King Nebuchadnezzar had instructed everyone to bow down to the golden statue he had set up. So when the music started playing, everyone bowed down to the statue – everyone, except Daniel's three friends, Shadrach, Meshach, and Abednego!

The king was furious and thought that they had not understood his instruction, so he decided to give them another chance. He told them that they would be thrown into a fire if they did not bow down. But the three men said to the king, "Our God is able to rescue us from the blazing furnace; but even if He does not, we will not bow down to your golden statue!"

Will God keep me from being bullied for my faith?

When King Nebuchadnezzar threatened Daniel's three friends with death, they knew that God would never leave them – in life or in death. They remembered the commandment: "You shall not have any other gods; and you shall not bow down to worship them" (Exodus 20:3-5).

In Psalm 91:14-15 it says, "God will save those who love Him and protect those who acknowledge Him as Lord. When they are in trouble and call on Him, He will answer them and rescue them." This Psalm promises us that God will rescue us from trouble when we pray to Him.

Does that mean we will never be harmed in any way? Paul suffered many beatings for preaching about Jesus. He was stoned and put in prison, yet even he was able to say, "The Lord will rescue me from every evil attack and will bring me safely to His heavenly kingdom" (2 Timothy 4:18). What Paul said helps us to realize that God will rescue us from every evil attack of the enemy even though we may be insulted or teased for loving Jesus.

JULY 26

VERSE FOR TODAY

Jesus said, "Blessed are those who are persecuted
because of righteousness, for theirs is the kingdom of heaven."
MATTHEW 5:10

DANIEL

Daniel 3:19-28

I am with you

Daniel's friends had refused to bow to King Nebuchadnezzar's statue and so they were thrown into a very hot furnace. It was so hot that even the guards, who threw the three men in, were burned to death.

Yet, as the king looked into the fiery furnace, he saw four men standing there. He got such a fright that he went up to the furnace and called them out. When they came out, not a single hair on their bodies had been burnt and their clothes did not even smell of smoke. Then the king praised their God – the true God – and made the three men officials in his kingdom.

Why does God feel so far away when I am in trouble?

If you have gone on a long car trip, you may have closed your eyes and dozed off on the back seat with a soft pillow and blanket. You wouldn't be able to see your father driving, yet you would have peace knowing that he was in control and that he would get you safely to your destination.

We don't have to see or feel God for Him to be close to us and in complete control. Some situations can be quite stressful, and it is natural for our emotions to get caught up in a crisis situation. However, it is also obvious that we can't rely on our emotions to feed our faith with peaceful feelings.

Through the prophet Jeremiah, God told the Israelites that He would be with them. He said, "Do not be afraid of the king of Babylon, whom you now fear. Do not be afraid of him, declares the Lord, for I am with you and will save you and deliver you from his hands" (Jeremiah 42:11).

One of the last things Jesus said to His disciples before He went back to heaven was, "Surely I am with you always, to the very end of the age" (Matthew 28:20). Jesus won't break His promise. He is always with you!

JULY 27

VERSE FOR TODAY

When you walk through the fire, you will not be burned;
the flames will not set you ablaze.
ISAIAH 43:2

Daniel 4:18, 24-34

DANIEL

The king eats grass

King Nebuchadnezzar had a strange dream that even his wisest advisors could not figure out. Eventually, the king called Daniel and told him the dream. When Daniel heard what the king had dreamt, he was afraid to tell him what it meant, but the king insisted that Daniel tell him the meaning.

"You will be driven away from people to go and live with wild animals," Daniel said. "For seven years you will eat grass out in the field and have no shelter. Then you will realize that God controls all the kingdoms of the world."

Daniel's words immediately came true. King Nebuchadnezzar was driven out from among his people. After seven long years, the king's mind became normal again and he started praising God and giving Him glory.

How can a bad experience lead us to God?

Imagine eating dry grass! You would have to be very hungry before grass starts looking tasty. People aren't meant to eat grass! Grass is for cattle and sheep – unless of course, like Nebuchadnezzar, you need to become as humble as a cow or as dependent as a sheep.

Jesus told the story of the son who rebelled against his father and left home to have a good life. He spent all his money on wild parties and sinful living. But when his money ran out, he needed to work and ended up feeding pigs. Eventually, he was so hungry that even the pigs' food started looking good (see Luke 15:11-20).

King Nebuchadnezzar, and the son who left home, rebelled against their father. They wanted to do their own thing and not rely on God.

When we run from God, He wants us back as part of His family.

JULY 28

VERSE FOR TODAY
Humble yourselves before the Lord, and he will lift you up.
JAMES 4:10

DANIEL

The banquet

King Nebuchadnezzar's son Belshazzar was the next king of Babylon. One night he invited a thousand special guests to a big party. While they were drinking wine, Belshazzar gave the order to bring out the gold cups and bowls, which his father had taken from the Temple in Jerusalem. Then he and his friends drank from the special cups that were made especially for the Holy Temple of the Lord.

Suddenly, a hand appeared and started writing on the wall where the light from the lamps shone brightly. The king turned as pale as a sheet and asked if anyone could read the writing, but no one could understand it.

In the end, Daniel was called in. He told the king exactly what his dream meant: "God has numbered the days of your kingdom and brought it to an end. You have been weighed and have failed the test. Your kingdom will be divided up and given to the Medes and Persians."

JULY 29

Why did God write a message the king couldn't read?

Can you read Greek, French or Chinese? Next time you find a paper with instructions in a foreign language, try reading it. It is pretty frustrating when you can't make any sense of what is written. King Belshazzar felt frustrated because he knew that the message on the wall was important.

Why would God write a message that the king couldn't understand? God didn't want the king just to read the words; He wanted a spiritual person to explain the deeper meaning to him.

Some parts of the Bible are hard to understand and only the Holy Spirit can help us grasp the meaning of God's words. God has also given us teachers, pastors and parents to explain the deeper meanings to us.

VERSE FOR TODAY

The man without the Spirit does not accept the things that come from the Spirit of God ... and he cannot understand them, because they are spiritually discerned.
1 CORINTHIANS 2:14

DANIEL

Nothing will stop me

On the same night that Belshazzar saw the writing on the palace wall, his kingdom was conquered by Darius – as Daniel had told him when he explained the message from God.

Darius chose Daniel, together with others, to look after the daily affairs of his kingdom. Daniel did everything so well that Darius wanted to put him in charge of the whole kingdom. The other governors were jealous and tried to find something wrong with the way Daniel did things. But they couldn't find a single thing because Daniel was so honest and reliable. So they persuaded the king to give a strict order that no one was to be allowed to pray to any god for thirty days, except to the king. Anyone disobeying the new law would be thrown into the den of lions.

The king signed the law – not realizing that this was a trap to get Daniel killed. When Daniel heard about the new law he went home. Then he went upstairs and knelt down in front of a window that faced Jerusalem. There he prayed to God – just as he had done every day.

Why did Daniel let everyone see he was praying?

After hearing about the king's law about praying, Daniel could have still prayed three times a day – but in a small room where no one would see him. He didn't even have to kneel for God to hear his prayers. He could have just thought the words of his prayer.

Even before Darius brought out a law to stop people praying, Daniel had decided in his heart that he was going to pray at his window every day. Daniel was not going to pray in secret and let others think he had stopped praying. Even the threat of death could not put out his light.

JULY 30

VERSE FOR TODAY
"You are the light of the world. A city on a hill cannot be hidden."
MATTHEW 5:14

DANIEL

The den of lions

King Darius had been talked into signing a law which said that anyone caught praying would be thrown to the lions.

However, Daniel still prayed three times a day – as he had done before. When Daniel's enemies saw him praying, they immediately went to tell King Darius. The king was very upset because he liked Daniel and couldn't change the law he had signed. So Daniel was arrested and thrown into a den of hungry lions. The king said to Daniel, "May the God you serve so faithfully keep you safe from the lions." Then the den was sealed with a huge stone.

King Darius went back to his palace, but he could not eat or sleep. Very early the next morning, he hurried to the den and called, "Daniel, servant of the living God! Has your God been able to keep you safe?"

To the king's great relief, Daniel answered; "O king! My God sent an angel to shut the mouths of the lions so they wouldn't hurt me."

JULY 31

Was Daniel afraid of the lions?

God has made us with emotions, which include the feeling of joy, love, anger … and fear! If God let us have these emotions, they cannot be bad. We must be careful that our feelings don't keep us from doing what God wants.

Fear becomes a problem when it keeps us from doing what is right. However, the Bible tells us that love drives out fear (see 1 John 4:18). When we love God, we trust Him; and when we trust Him, we are sure of His protection. Yes, Daniel may have been afraid of the lions, and if he was, his fear made his faith in God stronger than ever! Even David, who seemed fearless, wrote in a psalm, "When I am afraid, I will trust in You" (Psalm 56:3).

VERSE FOR TODAY

Rescue me from the mouth of the lions;
save me from the horns of the wild oxen.
PSALM 22:21

August

EZEKIEL

Ezekiel 2:4-7

They won't listen

Ezekiel was chosen by God to be a prophet to the Jews who had been taken captive by the Babylonians. God had allowed them to be taken as slaves to a distant country so they would turn back to Him.

However, the hearts of the people were hard, and it would take years for the people to turn back to God.

And so God encouraged Ezekiel and told him not to be afraid of the people. "Just keep telling the people whatever I tell you," God said, "whether they listen, or not."

What if my friends won't listen when I tell them about Jesus?

The Lord does not expect you to convince your unbelieving friends about the Bible, but simply to tell them that Jesus loves them and wants to be their Savior and friend.

Don't get into an argument with friends who don't believe the Bible. Instead, tell them what you know about God, sin and forgiveness. Be careful not to judge and criticize them, but rather tell them that everyone has sinned and needs Jesus to save them from sin. Let your love and kindness be seen in action.

Pray for your friends before you speak to them, and keep praying for them afterwards. By doing that, you are planting the seed of God's Word in their hearts. The Holy Spirit will keep working in their hearts.

Don't feel guilty if someone doesn't listen to you. Remember, sometimes a person needs time to think about what you said. So be patient – you may not see a change straight away.

AUGUST 1

VERSE FOR TODAY

Preach the Word; be prepared in season and out of season; correct, rebuke and encourage – with great patience and careful instruction.
2 TIMOTHY 4:2

Let's pretend

The Lord told Ezekiel that the people to whom he was preaching were only pretending to be interested.

"They are talking behind your back saying, 'Come let's go hear what the Lord has to say to us today.' Then they come and listen to you as though they really want to hear what you have to say, but they don't do what you tell them. They talk about Me as though they really love Me, but their hearts are greedy and they only think about money. You entertain them like one who sings love songs, or one who plays a musical instrument.

They hear your words but they don't put them into practice."

How can I make a Bible lesson or sermon more meaningful?

Some people go to church every Sunday, yet they show little spiritual growth. There are no exciting changes in their lives because they don't put into practice what they hear.

Here are some things you can do to keep growing in your faith:

- Pray that God will help you learn something new.
- Respect your teacher and listen carefully.
- Take part by looking up Bible verses and by asking questions.
- Write down words that will help you remember the main points of the lesson.
- Think about how your life is similar to that of the Bible characters.
- Ask God to help you practice what you have learned.

AUGUST 2

VERSE FOR TODAY

"But the one who hears my words and does not put them into practice is like a man who built a house on the ground without a foundation."

LUKE 6:49

EZEKIEL

Ezekiel 15:1-5

Dead wood

One day, the Lord asked Ezekiel, "What use is there for the wood of a dead vine? It can't be used for carving something useful and it doesn't even make good firewood! Trees of the forest are much better for that.

When you do use it for firewood and the wood becomes charred, it is even more useless than before.

Just as a vine that does not bear fruit is cut up and burnt, so I will remove Jerusalem and punish the people because they have chosen to be unfaithful to me. I will turn their country into a desert."

Am I bearing fruit?

We face many choices each day. Some choices are important, some are not. Some choices can be made for us; others can only be made by us. Some decisions can be changed, some cannot.

God's people had made their choice – and it was an important choice. Unfortunately, it was the wrong choice. They chose to be unfaithful to God. They had not slipped up in a moment of weakness or temptation; it was a choice they made on purpose. They had decided to worship idols, and their hearts were filled with greed instead of love for God.

A vine is not grown for its wood like a pine tree in the forest. A vine is grown to keep bearing fruit, year after year. Even after a tree is chopped down for firewood, a vine keeps blessing people with its fruit.

Jesus said that God is the Gardener. He cuts back every branch that bears fruit so that it becomes even more fruitful (John 15:2). We have been chosen to bear fruit – not end up as firewood!

AUGUST 3

VERSE FOR TODAY
"Every tree that does not bear good fruit is cut down and thrown into the fire. Thus, by their fruit you will recognize them."
Matthew 7:19-20

HAGGAI

The return to Jerusalem

After seventy years in Babylon, some of the Jews who had been slaves started returning to Jerusalem. God was bringing His people back to their own land as He had promised.

As the people started to settle down, their main concern was to build beautiful houses for themselves while the Temple of the Lord lay in ruins.

God spoke through Haggai the prophet, saying, "Don't you see what is happening to you? You have sown much, but harvested little. You have food, but not enough to fill you; you have clothes, but not enough to keep you warm. Can't you see why this has happened? Now go up to the hills and get wood to rebuild the Temple and I will be pleased."

Can one become too busy?

The Bible has a lot to say about those who are lazy (see Hebrews 6:12). God does not want us to be like a lazybones who never tries anything, does anything or achieves anything.

Yet, rushing from one activity to another and working like crazy is not what God had in mind for us either. One of the sins that the Israelites struggled with before they were taken to Babylon, was their constant longing for more money and things. Now that they had returned to Jerusalem, they became so busy with their own lives that they started shutting God out again. They must have looked like ants rushing around. God said, "Slow down! Stop being so busy with your own things. Rather put some time and energy into rebuilding the temple so that I can meet with you again."

God does not want our lives to be filled with so many things that there is no time left for Him! Give the best part of your day to the Lord.

AUGUST 4

VERSE FOR TODAY
Come near to God and he will come near to you.

HAGGAI

A promise of blessing

When Haggai told the Jews who had returned from Babylon that God wanted them to rebuild the Temple, they obeyed straight away. And as they began working on the Temple of the Lord, He encouraged them.

The Lord said, "Before you started working on the Temple, you would expect a big harvest, but there would be very little. I sent winds and hail to ruin everything you tried to grow. Today you have finished laying the foundation of the Temple. See what will happen now!

Although there is no grain left, and the grapevines and fig trees and olive trees have no fruit, I will bless you from now on."

Do I have to do things to be blessed?

It is only as the people started rebuilding the Lord's Temple that He promised to bless them. At this stage they had only laid the foundations, and already God was just waiting to pour out His blessing on them. He had wanted to bless them for so many years, but their disobedience had kept His blessing away. Now the trees would start bearing fruit again and the crops would grow tall. God's blessings would be like showers of rain.

Does that mean we have to do things to be blessed? God was not rewarding the people for what they did, but for being obedient! God had kept back His blessing so that the people would turn away from sin. Now that they were obedient and walking in His ways, the blessing He had been holding back could flow again.

Your obedience is important – whether it is to stop doing something wrong, or to do something that God has been telling you to do.

AUGUST 5

VERSE FOR TODAY

I will bless them and the places surrounding my hill. I will send down showers in season; there will be showers of blessing.
EZEKIEL 34:26

EZRA

Rebuilding the Temple

In the first year that King Cyrus became Emperor of Persia, he encouraged the Jews still in Babylon to go back to Jerusalem and help rebuild the Temple.

The Jews who went back were very excited about rebuilding the Temple. They gave money to pay the stonemasons who cut blocks of stone and laid them in place, and for the carpenters who did the woodwork.

They had dug deep trenches and laid a strong foundation. However, when some of the older priests saw the foundation of the new Temple, they were really disappointed because they remembered how much bigger the first Temple had been. But there were others who shouted and sang for joy because the foundation was the start of their return to worship.

Why are foundations so important?

Have you ever watched concrete being poured into a deep trench and thought, what a waste to dig a deep hole only to fill it again. Even though a foundation cannot be seen once the building is built, it has the most important work of all because the whole building rests on it. Without a foundation the building would crumble into a heap of rubble!

When our lives go through troubled times, we also need a solid foundation to hold us up and keep us strong. If our faith rests on Jesus the Rock, we have a sure foundation. Those who do not know what they believe are on shaky ground. When trouble comes, they don't know what to believe, or what to do. They suddenly feel weak and helpless, and their lives fall apart (Matthew 7:26-27). It is scary not to have someone mighty to depend on in times of trouble. Rely completely on Jesus. He is the Rock that will keep you standing firm in times of trouble.

AUGUST 6

VERSE FOR TODAY
For no one can lay any foundation other than
the one already laid, which is Jesus Christ.
1 CORINTHIANS 3:11

EZRA

Ezra 4:4-5, 6:3-8, 13-14

The Temple is finally finished

The Jews who had returned from Babylon were excited about rebuilding the Temple. But soon, the others who had stayed behind became jealous and tried to stop them. They sent messages to the king of Persia saying that these Jews were planning to rebel and not pay taxes to him. And so the work on the Temple stopped.

Years later, when King Darius came to power in Persia, he searched through the records of King Cyrus and found the scroll where Cyrus had ordered the Jews to rebuild the Temple.

Then Darius ordered that no one was to interfere with the building of the Temple, and he commanded the troublemakers to help. He also said that taxes were to be used to pay for the work. And so the Temple was completed at last and the people dedicated it to God.

How should I pray for our country's leaders?

God had worked in the heart of King Cyrus who sent many Jews back to Jerusalem and helped them with the Temple. When they became discouraged and stopped building, God used King Darius to get them going again. God used these kings to help rebuild their place of worship. When we pray for our leaders, God is able to do great things through them too. Pray that God will help …

- leaders make wise decisions.
- judges and rulers to know what is the right and proper thing to do.
- those in authority who have the power to make laws.
- those who enforce the law; that they will know how to deal with wrong-doing so that we can live peaceful lives.

AUGUST 7

VERSE FOR TODAY
I urge, then, first of all, that requests, prayers, intercession and thanksgiving be made for everyone – for kings and all those in authority, that we may live peaceful and quiet lives in all godliness and holiness.
1 TIMOTHY 2:1-2

Ezra returns home

Some years after the Temple was built, Ezra left Babylon with a second group of Jews and returned to Jerusalem. Ezra was not a prophet, but a scribe – someone whose job it was to write documents. He studied the Law, which the Lord had given to Moses, and taught it to others.

At that time, Artaxerxes was the king of Persia. He allowed Ezra and others to go back to Jerusalem and gave him gifts for the Temple.

Then Ezra gathered all those who wanted to return and told them to fast and pray that God would help them to have a safe journey. (Ezra did not want to ask the king for soldiers to protect them from enemies along the way because he had told the king that God blesses those who trust in Him.) So they prayed for the Lord to watch over them and their children.

The Lord kept them safe, and when they arrived in Jerusalem, Ezra gave the gifts of gold and silver to the priests of the Temple.

Why should we pray before going on a journey?

Hasn't God promised to look after us and protect us all the time? (2 Thessalonians 3:3). Why then should we pray for something the Lord has already promised to do? Surely that would show that we don't really trust Him.

Paul asked others to pray for his protection. He knew that while we are in the world there will always be an unseen war between good and evil (Romans 15:30-32). Through prayer and by faith in God, we strengthen our side and allow God's will to be done. And by asking for protection, we show that we are trusting in God – not in our own ability. Because we live in a world where things go wrong and where people do make mistakes, we should pray for God's care and protection.

AUGUST 8

VERSE FOR TODAY
But when our time was up, we left and continued on our way.
All the disciples and their wives and children accompanied
us out of the city, and there on the beach we knelt to pray.
Acts 21:5

NEHEMIAH

Bad news

King Artaxerxes had reigned in Persia for twenty years and Nehemiah served as his personal butler.

One day, Nehemiah found out that things weren't going well in Jerusalem. One of his brothers had brought news that the Jews who had gone back to Jerusalem were being mocked by the other tribes. He also found out that the wall around Jerusalem was still lying in ruins from when Nebuchadnezzar had invaded the city. Nehemiah was so sad that he didn't even eat.

One day, the king noticed that Nehemiah was not his usual self. "What's wrong, Nehemiah?" he asked. "Why are you so sad?"

Nehemiah replied, "Why shouldn't be sad when the walls of the city where my people live are broken down?"

Why was Nehemiah so sad about a broken-down wall?

How would you feel if you heard that a friend you had not seen for months didn't have enough clothes and often went to bed hungry because her mother was ill? You would probably feel the same as Nehemiah.

Although Nehemiah served in the king's palace, his heart was with his people back in Jerusalem. The problem was not only the wall; it was that the people acted as though they had been defeated. They didn't have the will or courage to defend themselves against the bad lifestyle of the ungodly tribes. Besides, some of these tribes were already living among them, and they were even marrying them.

Living among the ruins was not what God had promised. Nehemiah's heart wept because they were weak – like sheep without a shepherd.

AUGUST 9

VERSE FOR TODAY

When he saw the crowds, he had compassion on them, because they were harassed and helpless, like sheep without a shepherd.
MATTHEW 9:36

NEHEMIAH

During the night ...

After Nehemiah had told the king why he was so sad, King Artaxerxes said, "You may go to the land of Judah and rebuild the walls of the city where your people live."

The king also gave Nehemiah a letter for the keeper of the king's forest to supply him with wood for the city gates. He even sent along army officers to protect the group of Jews traveling back with Nehemiah.

When Nehemiah arrived in Jerusalem, he did not tell anyone why he had come. After three days, he and a few close friends sneaked out at midnight to inspect the broken wall. They stumbled around in the dark, going from one broken gate to another. Then they went back home.

How should I go about tackling a big task?

You are not likely to be asked to build a city wall, but you may have a school project or task that seems like a wall. For Nehemiah, building a wall around the city with heavy stones was a big task – too big to rush into.

Here are ideas that will help you get started with your task:

- Pray for God's help before you start.
- Ask God to give you good ideas and to guide you as you work.
- Set goals. If the project has to be completed by a certain day, divide the work into tasks. Remember, it always takes a bit longer than you think.
- Plan the task. What materials will you need? How much will it cost? Will you need help? What could go wrong?

Do your best. God is honored by a job well done.

Whether you need to complete a huge task or make an important decision, don't rush into it without talking to God first!

AUGUST 10

VERSE FOR TODAY

Suppose one of you wants to build a tower. Will he not first sit down and estimate the cost to see if he has enough money to complete it?

LUKE 14:28

NEHEMIAH

Nehemiah 2:17-20, 3:1-3

Get stuck in!

Nehemiah had gone out to inspect the broken-down wall around Jerusalem the previous night. Now he was ready to tell the leaders about his plan.

When they heard of his plan to rebuild the wall, they were excited and said, "Let's start building right away!" But there were a few leaders who were not happy about Nehemiah's plan. First they laughed at him; then they accused him of rebelling against the king of Persia.

But Nehemiah answered, "The God of heaven will help us. We are His servants – and we are going to build the wall!"

Then Nehemiah divided up the work so that small groups of people and families would be responsible for building a specific section of the wall.

Can anyone be a builder?

What does one need to do to become a builder? Do you think he would need to have special skills and do a special building course?

Well, most of the people who were given the task of rebuilding a certain part of the wall were not trained builders: they were just ordinary people doing ordinary jobs. There were priest, perfume makers, goldsmiths and traders. Even the children helped! The daughters of Shallum and the sons of Hassenaah helped repair their section of the wall.

Just as the people in Jerusalem had different jobs, we have different talents and gifts. Yet when we serve God, we should be prepared to help with the ordinary tasks too. Helping with chairs or tidying up are things we can do – even though we are gifted in other ways. Everyone should do his or her bit to build up the church. Each one should fit in with the next person to build a strong wall with no gaps where the enemy can get through.

AUGUST 11

VERSE FOR TODAY

By the grace God has given me, I laid a foundation as an expert builder, and someone else is building on it. But each one should be careful how he builds.
1 CORINTHIANS 3:10

NEHEMIAH

Rubble and other problems

As the people started rebuilding the wall around Jerusalem, Nehemiah's enemies became angry and teased the workers, saying, "Even a fox could knock down that wall!"

However, the people carried on building, and soon the wall was half its full height. Then Nehemiah's enemies planned to attack Jerusalem and cause confusion. But Nehemiah prayed, and God helped him find out about their plan. So from that time on, Nehemiah had half the people building the wall, while the other half guarded them.

How can I keep from being defeated?

The enemy will try everything to stop us from doing what God has called us to do. He tried to stop Nehemiah's work in two ways.

Firstly, he got some people to plan an attack on the workers. Ungodly people can hinder and obstruct our work for God.

Secondly, he tried to discourage them. Discouragement takes away our energy and enthusiasm to do good.

This is how Nehemiah handled the attack.

Nehemiah prayed (verse 9). God answered Nehemiah's prayer and helped him find out about the enemies' plan (read Ephesians 6:11).

Nehemiah expected trouble (verse 13). He made sure he would not be caught off guard and was ready for action (read John 16:33).

Nehemiah was practical (verse 13, 16). He placed armed guards around the workers (read Ephesians 6:16-17).

Nehemiah knew the importance of unity (verse 19-20). He told everyone to stand together (read Romans 15:5).

AUGUST 12

VERSE FOR TODAY

"Be strong and courageous. Do not be afraid or terrified because of them, for the Lord your God goes with you; he will never leave you nor forsake you."

DEUTERONOMY 31:6

NEHEMIAH

Nehemiah 5:14-19,
6:15-16

Leading by example

King Artaxerxes had made Nehemiah governor of Judah; and as governor, Nehemiah and his relatives were allowed to ask the people of the land for food and money.

However, Nehemiah did not take money from the people or ask them for help because they were struggling to survive. Nehemiah worked on the wall like everyone else, and he even fed a hundred and fifty people and their leaders every day.

In just over fifty days, the wall was finished and Nehemiah's enemies realized that the work of rebuilding the wall had been done with the help of the Lord.

Why should a leader be like a servant?

Have you ever played "follow-the-leader"? What is everyone supposed to do? The followers must watch the leader and do everything exactly the way the leader does it – because that is what followers do.

In real life, being a leader is a responsible job that should not be taken lightly because people watch their leader and follow his or her example.

Nehemiah knew the importance of being a good leader, so he didn't demand food and money from the people. He knew that those who followed and respected him would soon be doing the same. Taking food and money from people who were struggling was not right. Nehemiah had come to Jerusalem to help them, not to have an easy life and boss everyone around.

Jesus had the same attitude. He – the King of kings – humbled Himself and became a servant so that He could come and live among us and help rebuild ruined lives (Philippians 2:5-8).

AUGUST 13

VERSE FOR TODAY
"But you are not to be like that. Instead, the greatest among you should be like the youngest, and the one who rules like the one who serves."
Luke 22:26

ESTHER

The beautiful orphan

By now, many Jews had returned to Judah, while some had stayed on in Babylon, a city in Persia. King Xerxes became the new ruler of Persia, and in the third year of his reign, there were great celebrations. On the last day of the celebrations, the king (who was drunk) ordered his wife, Queen Vashti, to be brought to him. But she refused to come. The king was furious and gave an order that the queen was not allowed to see him ever again.

But after a while, when the king's anger had cooled down and he realized that he would never see Vashti again, he became moody. So the king's advisors suggested that they find a suitable woman to take Vashti's place.

There was a beautiful young woman named Esther whose family had been brought to Babylon as slaves by Nebuchadnezzar. She was an orphan, and her older cousin Mordecai had adopted her and raised her as his own daughter.

Can God care for an orphan like a father?

There are children, who through tragedy, have lost both their parents. That is very sad. An orphan is a child whose father and mother have died. Yet, there are homes where the father may no longer be part of the family for some reason – and that is just as sad.

God the Father has promised to take special care of orphans and the fatherless by being a father to them.

If your father is no longer with you, God is there for you. Even though God doesn't read you a story at night or check that your teeth are brushed, He will use others close to you to care for your everyday needs. Talk to Him as you would talk to your dad, and feel His gentle love (Isaiah 40:11).

AUGUST 14

VERSE FOR TODAY

A father to the fatherless, a defender of widows, is God in his holy dwelling.
PSALM 68:5

ESTHER

Esther 2:8, 10-11, 15-18

Esther becomes queen

King Xerxes had ordered the officials in his empire to find the most beautiful women in the country and bring them to his palace in the city of Susa. Esther was one of the chosen women.

She was brought to the royal palace where she was given pretty clothes to look good for the king. Meanwhile, Mordecai, the cousin who had adopted her, advised her not to tell anyone that she was Jewish.

Everyone admired Esther, and when the time came for her to be presented to the king, he liked her more than any of the other women. He fell in love with her! He put a royal crown on her head and made her queen in Vashti's place. The king gave a great banquet to honor Esther.

Can God use me for great things if I am just "ordinary"?

Esther grew up as an ordinary child. In fact, her people had been brought to Babylon as slaves – and she was an orphan.

God often uses ordinary people rather than great people whose hearts are filled with pride. Jesus said, "For everyone who exalts himself will be humbled, and he who humbles himself will be exalted" (Luke 18:14). Do you remember how God used ordinary people like Joseph, Gideon, David, and Daniel to do great things for Him?

Esther may have thought about the message that Jeremiah had sent the people in Babylon: "For I know the plans I have for you," declares the Lord, "plans to prosper you and not to harm you, plans to give you hope and a future" (Jeremiah 29:11). Life had been hard for Esther; yet God had blessed her so He could use her to bring hope to His people.

AUGUST 15

VERSE FOR TODAY

Brothers, think of what you were when you were called. Not many of you were wise by human standards; not many were influential; not many were of noble birth. But God chose the foolish things of the world to shame the wise.
1 Corinthians 1:26-27

ESTHER

The murder plot

King Xerxes had married Esther, and Mordecai her cousin became one of the king's officials. Esther had not told anyone that she was Jewish.

One day, two officials who guarded the entrance to the king's rooms became upset about something the king had done, and wanted to kill him.

Mordecai found out about the plot and told Queen Esther, who went to tell the king. When the king found out that the two officials had planned to kill him, he had them hanged. Then the king ordered that the whole story be written in a book in which the history of the empire was recorded.

When should I tell on someone?

"I'm going to tell Mom what you said!"

"Well then I'm going to tell her about the vase you broke last week!"

What should we do when we know about something wrong that someone has done or said? We should be honest and ask ourselves why we want to tell on that person.

Before you tell on someone about something that has happened, think about what it will do to your relationship with that person. Rather encourage the person who did wrong to own up. In this way he or she will be in control of the situation and it will keep your relationship with the other person friendly. A tattletale is never popular because we all slip up and make mistakes at some stage, and no one wants to get into trouble.

However, if someone does something dangerous; keeps doing something wrong in secret; or is planning to do something wrong, you should let an adult know about it. In this way you can help the person and stop something bad from happening.

AUGUST 16

VERSE FOR TODAY

"But I tell you that men will have to give account on the day of judgment for every careless word they have spoken."
MATTHEW 12:36

ESTHER

The VIP*

(*Very Important Person)

Mordecai had saved King Xerxes from being murdered, and although the details of what had taken place were written in a book, the king soon forgot about it.

Some time later, the king promoted Haman to a position above all the other officials. The king ordered that everyone should bow down to Haman as a sign of respect. But Mordecai would not bow down to him.

The officials asked Mordecai why he refused to bow down to Haman and tried to persuade him to obey the king's command. But Mordecai refused to bow or kneel before Haman. So the officials went and told Haman to see if he would let Mordecai get away with it. But Haman was furious and started thinking of a way to kill Mordecai and get rid of all the Jews.

Is it wrong to bow to an important person?

In some cultures, when greeting someone or leaving, it is polite to bow. For some, bowing is as common as shaking a person's hand, while for others it is something you would only do if you entered the throne room of a king.

Bowing to a person is a sign of respect. When we bow before God in prayer, it is more than a sign of respect; it is an act of humble surrender. We accept God's authority.

The Bible does tell us not to bow down to idols and gods (Leviticus 26:1), but it does not forbid us to bow down to a person. Yet it is just as wrong to bow down in adoration of a person as it is to bow down to an idol. Only God deserves to be worshiped because He is the King of kings and Lord of lords!

AUGUST 17

VERSE FOR TODAY

Come, let us bow down in worship, let us kneel before the LORD our Maker.
PSALM 95:6

ESTHER

Revenge on a nation

Haman's dislike for Mordecai turned into a deep hatred; not only for Mordecai, but for all the Jews still living in Babylon. It all started when Haman was made the chief official and Mordecai refused to bow to him.

Haman went to the King and said, "There is a certain group of people scattered all over your kingdom. These people have customs that are not like ours and they don't obey our laws. It would be best for you to give an order to kill every Jew in the empire. If you do this, I will pay you loads of silver to use as you wish."

The king was convinced. He took off the ring used for signing official laws and gave it to Haman, saying, "The people are yours; do whatever you like to them."

Why do certain groups of people dislike each other?

How would you feel if a hockey player (from a team that was known for cheating) asked to borrow your hockey stick?

To be honest, we are all guilty of judging the whole group by the actions of individuals in that group. When someone goes to a certain school, we may find ourselves acting differently or even being nasty toward that person because of the school he goes to.

Jesus doesn't treat people differently because they are part of a certain group. Every person is special to Him! He healed a leper who was treated as an outcast; He spoke to a Samaritan woman who was born into a hated tribe; He made friends with Zacchaeus who was a dishonest tax collector.

People sometimes judge others unfairly by thinking things that are not true. That is called prejudice, which means *judging before*.

AUGUST 18

VERSE FOR TODAY
"Do not judge, and you will not be judged.
Do not condemn, and you will not be condemned."
LUKE 6:37

ESTHER

For a time like this

When Mordecai heard about the king's order to kill every Jew in Babylon, he tore his clothes in despair. As the message spread from town to town, the Jews fasted and wept.

At first, Esther didn't know about the king's order, so she sent her assistant to ask Mordecai what all the fuss was about. Mordecai sent a message back, asking her to beg the king to have mercy on her people.

Esther was afraid of going to the king because by law, anyone who went to speak to him without being invited could be killed. But Mordecai said to her, "If you keep quiet at this time, God will use someone else. And who knows, maybe you were made queen for a time like this."

Is there such a thing as coincidence or fate?

Do things just happen by chance, or is there a plan and purpose for everything in life? If you throw a tennis ball into a crowd of people, at least one person is likely to get hit; and that person may ask, "Why me?" Was the person just in the wrong place at the wrong time?

When it comes to the everyday events in our lives, God leaves nothing to chance! We are far too precious for God not to be in control.

Esther was in the right place at the right time. God had everything under control when King Nebuchadnezzar brought her people from Jerusalem to Babylon. God planned that King Xerxes would banish Queen Vashti when she refused to appear before him. God made sure that the king would look for a new queen, and that Esther was chosen. Then God used Mordecai, Esther's cousin, to tell her exactly what to do.

When you live close to God, nothing can go wrong!

AUGUST 19

VERSE FOR TODAY

The LORD Almighty has sworn, "Surely, as I have planned,
so it will be, and as I have purposed, so it will stand."
ISAIAH 14:24

ESTHER

Fast and pray

When Queen Esther got Mordecai's message asking her to speak to the king, she sent this message back; "Gather all the Jews in the city and get them to fast and pray for me. Don't eat or drink anything for three days. My servant girls and I will do the same. Then I will go to the king – even if I must die for doing this."

After the three days, Esther put on her royal robes and went to stand at the entrance of the throne room. When the king saw her, he invited her in and said, "You may ask for whatever you wish and I will give it to you."

What is a fast?

A fast is not the opposite of "a slow". To fast means to go without food for a while. You are probably wondering why anyone would want to go without food. Well, there is a good reason and it has nothing to do with dieting.

Fasting helps our hearts draw closer to God because our hunger keeps on reminding us about Him.

Because fasting makes us weak, it helps us to be humble before God (Ezra 8:21). Fasting is a way of showing repentance (sadness for sins) (Jonah 3:7).

It helps us find out God's will when we ask Him to show us what to do (Acts 13:2-3). Some people fast when they pray about something that is very important (2 Samuel 12:16). Although some people (including Jesus) have fasted for forty days, a fast could be as short as skipping a meal. You could also decide to go without something else you might enjoy. The main thing is that a fast is between you and the Lord – a decision of your heart.

AUGUST 20

VERSE FOR TODAY

So we fasted and petitioned our God about this, and he answered our prayer.
EZRA 8:23

ESTHER

The king can't sleep

That night, the king couldn't sleep, so he ordered his servants to read his official diary to him. When they got to the part where Mordecai had saved his life, the king asked whether anything had been done to reward him. His servants answered, "No, nothing has been done."

Just then, Haman walked in; so the king asked him what he would do to honor someone. Thinking that the king wanted to reward him, Haman said, "The person should be dressed in royal robes and led through the city on horseback by the most important official."

"Good idea," the king said. "I want you to lead Mordecai through the city, crying out; 'This is the way the king honors those who honor him.'"

So Haman had to do as he was told. Afterwards he went home very angry and embarrassed.

Will mean, unfair people get punished?

Do you sometimes wish the worst on your "enemies"? Everyone feels like that towards those who make life unbearable for others – especially the weak. One of God's characteristics is His justice (fairness). Because we are made in His image, we too have a sense of right and wrong.

God is a fair Judge and knows all the facts! He knows about the things that have been done to you and the times you have been treated unfairly and said nothing. You can be sure that anyone who has been mean and hurtful to you will not get away with it.

So rather do what the Bible says; "Do not take revenge, my friends, but leave room for God's wrath, for it is written: 'It is Mine to avenge; I will repay,' says the Lord" (Romans 12:19). He will see to it that justice is done!

AUGUST 21

VERSE FOR TODAY
"For whoever exalts himself will be humbled,
and whoever humbles himself will be exalted."
MATTHEW 23:12

ESTHER

Esther's request

Queen Esther had prepared a special banquet for Haman and the king. At the banquet the king asked her, "Tell me what you want and you shall have it."

"All I ask is that I may live and that my people may live: someone is planning to kill us!"

"Who would dare do such a thing?" the king asked.

"Our enemy and persecutor is this evil man," Esther replied pointing to Haman. The king was furious and had Haman hanged that same day.

Later, Esther went to speak to the king again and kneeled at his feet. The king held out his golden staff to show that she was welcome in his presence. So Esther asked if there was a way to stop her people from being killed. But, because of their law, the king could not change the order he had signed. Instead, the king gave Mordecai permission to do whatever he could to help the Jews defend themselves, which they did.

Esther and Mordecai put a stop to the killing of God's people, and the king put Mordecai in charge of his whole kingdom.

Will God allow me into His presence?

Do you think that a mighty king would allow dirty, noisy kids to run into his throne room?

God does! God loves having children around Him, and although we aren't in heaven yet, we can go boldly to God in prayer and talk to Him about anything. The Lord is loving and merciful, and even though we don't deserve to come into His Holy presence, He lets us come right up to His throne in heaven because Jesus has washed us clean.

AUGUST 22

VERSE FOR TODAY

Let us then approach the throne of grace with confidence, so that we may receive mercy and find grace to help us in our time of need.

HEBREWS 4:16

MALACHI

A Messenger from God

By now, many of the Jews had returned from Babylon to Judah. They had restored the Temple in Jerusalem and rebuilt the wall around the city.

Yet, as time passed, the people started slipping back into their old sinful ways. They were unfaithful to God and untrue to their husbands and wives.

But God wasn't giving up on them. This is what the Lord said through the prophet Malachi; "I will send My messenger to prepare the way for Me. Then the Lord you are looking for will come to His Temple – the Messenger you long for will come and proclaim My covenant. He will come to purify His people."

Who was this promised Messenger?

Weren't all the prophets messengers of God who took His word to the people? How would this Messenger, whom Malachi spoke of, be different? God had sent many prophets, but the people had not listened to their message. Now God was going to send one more – His very own Son (read Mark 12:1-8).

The first messenger Malachi spoke of (in verse 1) would only prepare the way for Him. In Matthew 3:1-3 we read that John the Baptist was the one who prepared the way for Jesus.

The second Messenger is the One everyone was waiting for – Jesus. He is the One who would declare God's promise in the Temple.

When Jesus started teaching and preaching, He went to the synagogue and told the people that God's promise had come true (Luke 4:18-20). Jesus, the Son of God, is the Messenger who came to bring the good news of healing and freedom for all who believe in Him.

AUGUST 23

VERSE FOR TODAY
And this was his (John's) message: "After me will come one more powerful than I, the thongs of whose sandals I am not worthy to stoop down and untie."
MARK 1:7

Malachi 3:13-18

MALACHI

The list

The Lord spoke to His people through Malachi, saying; "You have said that it is useless to serve God and do what is right because it is the proud who are happy. It is the wicked who become richer and are not punished for their evil deeds."

When those who loved and respected the Lord heard Malachi's message, they started talking about it. Then the names of those who honored the Lord were written in a book: the name of every person who loved the Lord was written down.

This is what the Lord said about those who loved Him: "They shall be Mine for they are My treasured possession. Once again My people will see the difference between the godly and the wicked; the one who serves Me and the one who does not."

Is my name in God's book?

Have you ever stood in front of a large, shiny panel that lists the names of people who have been honored for their outstanding achievement? Wow! What an honor to have one's name listed with those top achievers and heroes. As you stare up at the printed names, have you secretly wished that your name were on the list?

Would you like your name to be on the most important list of all? It may be there already! If you have asked Jesus to be Lord of your life, your name is already written in the Book of Life. This is God's book, kept safely in heaven for that important day when those whose names are written in the Book of Life will be allowed to enter heaven and spend eternity with Him.

AUGUST 24

VERSE FOR TODAY

He who overcomes will, like them, be dressed in white. I will never blot out his name from the book of life, but will acknowledge his name before my Father and his angels.

REVELATION 3:5

ZECHARIAH

"I am too old"

For four hundred years, the Lord had not spoken to the people of Israel. There were no prophets – just a promise that someone would come to save people from their sin.

There was a priest named Zechariah. He was married to Elizabeth. They were good people who loved the Lord; and although they were old, they did not have children because Elizabeth could not become pregnant.

While Zechariah was in the Temple burning incense on the altar, an angel of the Lord appeared to him. Zechariah was surprised and afraid.

The angel said, "Do not be afraid, Zechariah. The Lord has heard your prayers. Your wife Elizabeth will have a son."

Zechariah answered, "How do I know that this will happen, for I am old and my wife is also old?"

Will God answer a prayer I have forgotten about?

When we ask God for something specific, there is no way we can know for sure how He will answer, or when He will answer. When we pray, and there seems to be no answer for a long time, does it mean that God has said "no" to our prayer? Or can it be that He will give us what we have asked for, but that we will have to wait before our prayer is answered?

Who knows how long Zechariah had been praying for a child. Now that he was old, he may have wondered whether he should stop praying, for it seemed as though God had a different plan.

Is there a point at which we should simply accept that God has answered our prayer, but not in the way we expected?

As long as the Holy Spirit keeps reminding you to pray – keep praying!

AUGUST 25

VERSE FOR TODAY

Devote yourselves to prayer, being watchful and thankful.
COLOSSIANS 4:2

Luke 1:18-25

ZECHARIAH

Zechariah is speechless

While Zechariah was busy in the Temple, the angel Gabriel appeared to him and told him that his wife would have a son. But because Zechariah was old and his wife could not have children, he doubted the angel's words.

Then the angel said to him, "Because you have not believed what I have told you, you shall not be able to speak until this promise comes true."

The people outside the Temple were wondering why Zechariah was taking so long. When he eventually came out, he could not speak, so he made signs with his hands to explain what had happened to him.

What is faith?

How would you have felt if you were Zechariah – having exciting news to share, yet not being able to speak?

Zechariah had been praying for a son for a long time. Now that the angel brought him the good news that his prayers had been answered, Zechariah doubted. Zechariah may have been praying the same prayer year after year, but he had lost hope and no longer expected God to answer. Is praying for the impossible not the same as faith?

Faith in God is trusting and depending on the Lord completely: believing in His power and relying on His faithfulness. The Bible puts it this way; "Now faith is being sure of what we hope for and certain of what we do not see" (Hebrews 11:1).

Have you wanted to ask God for something, but because it seems impossible, you have never prayed about it. Or have you prayed, but not really expected an answer. Ask God, and if it pleases Him to give you what you have asked for, it will come at the right time.

AUGUST 26

VERSE FOR TODAY

But when he asks, he must believe and not doubt,
because he who doubts is like a wave of the sea,
blown and tossed by the wind.

JAMES 1:6

MARY

A heavenly visitor

During the time that Zechariah's wife Elizabeth was expecting her child, the angel Gabriel appeared to Mary, a young woman engaged to Joseph. Joseph was a descendant of King David.

Gabriel said to Mary, "Peace be on you. The Lord is with you and has chosen to bless you." Mary was troubled by the angel's words and wondered what he meant.

"Do not be afraid, Mary," the angel said. "You will become pregnant and give birth to a son, and you will name Him Jesus. He will be great and will be called the Son of the Most High God."

"But how can this be?" Mary asked. "I am not even married yet."

"The Holy Spirit will come on you and the power of God will be over you like a shadow," Gabriel replied.

"I am the Lord's servant. Let it be as you have said," Mary answered.

Could Jesus have come to earth at any other time in history?

God chose a specific time in history to send Jesus to earth. There are many reasons why that time was the best time for Jesus to be born on earth. The Bible says, "When the time was right, God sent His Son ..." (Galatians 4:4).

All who put their faith in Jesus have eternal life because Jesus took their guilt and punishment on Himself when He died on the cross.

Those who lived before Jesus came to earth had to offer an animal sacrifice for their sins. Although that sacrifice could not take away their sin, it was an act of faith in the perfect Sacrifice – Jesus, who was to come. In this way, even the Old Testament people were saved by their faith (in Jesus).

AUGUST 27

VERSE FOR TODAY
He was chosen before the creation of the world,
but was revealed in these last times for your sake.
1 PETER 1:20

Luke 1:39-56

Mary's song of praise

After the angel had visited Mary and told her that she was going to have a son, she went to visit her cousin Elizabeth, who had also been promised a son – one who would make the hearts of the people ready to follow Jesus.

When Mary came to the house of Elizabeth and greeted her, the baby inside Elizabeth moved. Elizabeth was filled with the Holy Spirit and said to Mary, "You are blessed more than any other woman, for when I heard your greeting, the baby inside me jumped with gladness."

Then Mary started singing a beautiful praise song to God:

"My heart praises the Lord; My spirit is glad because of God my Savior, for He has remembered His humble servant. And from now everyone will call me blessed because of the great things God has done for me. Holy is His name."

How could I praise God with a song from my heart?

Do you like singing praise and worship songs? Have you ever thought of putting your own words of praise to a tune you know? You could even make up your own tune by first humming it until it sounds right. That is how many wonderful praise songs were written. David wrote in one of the psalms: "He put a new song in my mouth, a hymn of praise to our God" (Psalm 40:3). New songs keep coming from hearts that are filled with praise. How about putting some themes from Mary's song into your own words. Think of:

- God's power and might (verse 52)
- something He has done for you (verse 49)
- the promises He has kept (verse 54).

AUGUST 28

VERSE FOR TODAY
I will praise God's name in song and glorify him with thanksgiving.
PSALM 69:30

MARY

"Sorry, no room"

Mary stayed with Elizabeth for three months. When Elizabeth had her baby, everyone thought he would be given the name of someone in the family, but Zechariah wrote his name for everyone to see. As he wrote the name "John", Zechariah suddenly began to speak again.

At that time, Emperor Augustus ordered everyone to be registered in the town of their family tribe.

So Mary and Joseph, who were engaged to be married, left Nazareth and went to register in Bethlehem – the birthplace of King David.

When Joseph and Mary got to Bethlehem, the small town was over-crowded because of the many people that had come to register there. The time had come for Mary to have her baby, but there was no room for them to stay in the inn. Eventually, Mary and Joseph found a place for the baby to be born; and Mary wrapped Him in strips of cloth and laid Him in a manger.

Why was Jesus not born in a palace?

Jesus came to earth as a humble servant to show us that God cares for everyone – even the poorest people on earth. Jesus made Himself nothing, and took on the humble position of a servant (Philippians 2:7). He, the King of kings, willingly came to serve – not to be served. Jesus was laid in a feeding-trough for animals to show that Jesus came to earth with nothing.

What would you have done if you were the innkeeper the night Mary and Joseph were looking for a place to stay? Would you have cleared out your room and let them move in? Some people's hearts are so jam-packed with their selfish lifestyle that they have no room for Jesus. Have you invited Jesus into your heart?

AUGUST 29

VERSE FOR TODAY

"Here I am! I stand at the door and knock. If anyone hears my voice and opens the door, I will come in and eat with him, and he with me."
REVELATION 3:20

Shepherds in the field

At last the promised Savior had come. Jesus was born in Bethlehem, just as the prophets had said (see Isaiah 7:14, Micah 5:2).

There were shepherds spending the night in the fields nearby, taking care of their flocks. Suddenly, an angel appeared to them and the glory of the Lord shone all around. The shepherds were terrified, but the angel said to them, "Do not be afraid. I bring you good news of great joy. Today in the town of David, a Savior has been born to you. You will find the baby wrapped in strips of cloth and lying in a manger."

Then other angels appeared all around, singing, "Glory to God in the highest, and peace on earth to those with whom He is pleased."

When the angels had gone back to heaven, the shepherds said to one another, "Let's go to Bethlehem and see this thing that has happened."

So they hurried off and found Mary and Joseph and the baby, who was lying in a manger. When the shepherds saw Him, they told everyone what had happened.

Why did the angels appear only to shepherds?

Do you think the angels appeared to the shepherds because they were the only ones still awake, or was it because the angels didn't want to cause a disturbance in the peaceful town?

We can't say for sure why the shepherds were chosen to hear the good news about Jesus.

Jesus came to earth to be a Shepherd; to save His sheep from the prowling lion (the devil), and to lead us in green pastures of peace and goodness. He came to be the Shepherd who would give His life for His sheep.

AUGUST 30

VERSE FOR TODAY
And when the Chief Shepherd appears, you will receive the crown of glory that will never fade away.
1 Peter 5:4

Jesus is dedicated

A week after Jesus was born, Joseph and Mary took Jesus to the Temple in Jerusalem. He was to be dedicated and given the name Jesus – the name the angel had given Him.

They did this to obey God's Law given by Moses, which said that every first born son was to be dedicated to the Lord. They also offered a sacrifice as the Law said they should.

While they were at the Temple, a godly man named Simeon was led by the Holy Spirit to go to the Temple. The Spirit of God had told him that he would not die before he had seen the Lord's promise of a Savior.

When he saw Mary's baby, he took Jesus in his arms and gave thanks to God, saying, "Lord, You have kept Your promise. Now I can die in peace, for I have seen Your Salvation with my own eyes."

What does the name 'Jesus' mean?

After the angel had told Mary that she was going to have a baby, an angel appeared to Joseph in a dream and told him what would happen to Mary. "She will give birth to a son, and you are to give Him the name Jesus, because He will save His people from their sins" (Matthew 1:21).

The name Jesus comes from the name "Joshua," which means "God is our Salvation." God saves us through Jesus. Jesus became our Salvation when He died for our sins and saved us from death – eternal death.

When we ask Jesus to save us, He takes away our sin and gives us eternal life. That means, when we die, we go to live with Jesus in heaven forever!

AUGUST 31

VERSE FOR TODAY
"The virgin will be with child and will give birth to a son, and they will call him Immanuel" – which means, "God with us."
MATTHEW 1:23

September

MARY

Wise men from afar

When Jesus was born in Bethlehem, wise men (Magi) from the east came to Jerusalem and asked, "Where is the newborn King of the Jews? We saw His star in the east and have come to worship Him."

When King Herod – who ruled Judea – heard this, he became worried. He quickly called together the chief priests and teachers of the Law and asked them where their King was to be born.

"In Bethlehem," they replied, "for this is what the prophet wrote; 'Out of you, Bethlehem, will come a ruler who will be a Shepherd for My people Israel.'"

Then Herod called the wise men to a secret meeting and asked them when exactly they had first seen the star.

What made the Magi follow the bright star?

What do you think made this group of wise men leave their homes and travel far in the hope of finding a baby? And even if they did find a baby boy, how could they be sure that he was the one who would become a great king?

God had put a seed of expectation in their hearts – a hope that a mighty ruler would be born in their lifetime. Then one night, while looking at the stars, they saw it – a light, brighter than any star they had ever seen! They realized that this was the sign they had been waiting for; the sign of the Mighty King. Then the star moved – and by faith they followed it, trusting that it would lead them to the newborn King.

Jesus, the Bright Morning Star, is our sign of hope as He leads us to God. We can only find true joy when we follow Jesus, the Light of the world.

VERSE FOR TODAY

And we have the word of the prophets ... and you will do well to pay attention to it, as to a light shining in a dark place, until the day dawns and the morning star rises in your hearts.

2 Peter 1:19

MARY

Gifts for the King

After the wise men had gone to King Herod to find out about the newborn king, the star they had first seen in the east carried on moving. It led them to Bethlehem to the place where Jesus was.

They came to the house and found the small child with His mother Mary, and they bowed down and worshiped Him. Then they opened their treasures and gave Him gifts of gold, incense and myrrh.

Later, God warned them in a dream not to go back to tell Herod that they had found Jesus. So they returned to their country by another way.

Why did the Magi give Jesus such strange gifts?

If you were looking for a suitable gift for a toddler, you would probably go to a toy store or perhaps the children's department of a clothing store. Because you can't really ask a baby what it would like, you would have to choose something you thought was suitable.

Let's see why the wise men's gifts were probably the best gifts they could have given to Jesus. .

Gold is a gift that is usually given to a king. Gold reminds us that Jesus is the King of kings.

Incense was used in the Temple. The sweet smell of incense reminds us that our prayers and worship are like a sweet smell to the Lord.

Myrrh is a spice that was used when someone died. This might seem like the strangest gift of all, but it reminds us that Jesus came to earth to die for our sins (John 19:39-40).

If you would like to give Jesus the very best gift possible, let Him have your whole heart – just as you are.

VERSE FOR TODAY

"You are worthy, our Lord and God, to receive glory and honor and power, for you created all things, and by your will they were created and have their being."

REVELATION 4:11

MARY

Escape to Egypt

After the wise men had left, an angel of the Lord warned Joseph in a dream to leave Bethlehem and flee to Egypt.

So Joseph and Mary left the town of Bethlehem during the night and headed for Egypt with Jesus.

When Herod realized that he had been tricked by the wise men – who didn't come back to tell him where the baby was – he was furious! He ordered his soldiers to kill all the boys in Bethlehem under two years of age.

Meanwhile, Joseph and Mary stayed in Egypt where they lived in safety until Herod died. Then they returned to Judea, to the town of Nazareth, where Jesus grew up.

Why was King Herod so afraid of a baby?

The wise men had first gone to Herod to find out about the newborn king, thinking that he would know about a Jewish king. Herod must have wondered if he had missed something. How had these wise men from the east found out about this baby while he knew nothing about Him? Why hadn't anyone told him?

Herod had not been chosen by the Jews to be their king. The Romans who had conquered their country put him in charge. When he heard that a Jewish king had been born, he became jealous and afraid. Herod's selfish attitude took away his peace. He became so afraid that someone would take his throne that he had many innocent babies killed.

How different Herod's attitude was to that of the wise men: they left with hearts full of peace and joy; Herod's heart was full of anger and fear. But Jesus had not come to take Herod's throne – Jesus wanted his heart.

VERSE FOR TODAY

Jesus said, "My kingdom is not of this world. If it were,
my servants would fight to prevent my arrest by the Jews.
But now my kingdom is from another place."
JOHN 18:36

Luke 2:41-50

MARY

Jesus was a child

When Jesus was twelve years old, Mary and Joseph took Him to Jerusalem to celebrate the Passover Feast, as they had done every year.

When the feast was over, His parents returned home with a group of relatives and friends. They had traveled for a whole day before they realized that Jesus was not with the other children, as they had thought He was.

So Mary and Joseph returned to Jerusalem and found Jesus sitting with the teachers in the Temple, listening to them and asking them questions.

Did Jesus need to learn about God and the Scriptures?

It is a mystery we cannot understand; that while Jesus was on earth, He was completely human and completely God. From the time He was born until He went back to His Father in heaven, He was the only person to live a completely sinless life.

Jesus grew from a tiny baby to a young boy, and from a teenager to a young man. He had to learn things just as you do. As a toddler, He learned to walk; as a boy, He learned to play with other kids; as a teenager He learned to help His dad. He learned to read and write and get along with those who were mean.

Although the Bible doesn't tell us much about Jesus' childhood, we know that at the age of twelve, He knew enough about the Scriptures to talk to the leaders in the Temple about the things of God. Even though, by this time, Jesus knew that He was the Son of God (verse 49), it would seem that He didn't know everything, because He listened carefully to the teachers and asked many questions.

Never think that you're too young to understand things about God.

VERSE FOR TODAY

And Jesus grew in wisdom and in stature, and in favor with God and men.
LUKE 2:52

JOHN THE BAPTIST

Mark 1:1-8

Clothes of camel hair

When the time came for Jesus to start His ministry, the Holy Spirit led His cousin John to the desert where he lived on locusts and wild honey, and wore clothing made of camels' hair.

Crowds went out to the desert to hear the word of the Lord. John told the people to turn from their sins; and those who asked God for forgiveness, he baptized in the Jordan River.

He said to them, "There is someone coming after me who is more powerful than I am – someone whose sandals I am not worthy to untie."

Why did John go live in the desert?

You may have heard people say they feel God by getting close to nature.

The peaceful mood of a beautiful countryside can help us feel close to God. However, this is not because God lives in the things He created, but rather, because the wonders of nature help us to see how awesome God is.

Although a desert (or wilderness) may not be your idea of a beautiful surrounding, at least it is quiet out there. You would be excused for thinking that the desert is a strange place to preach to people, but here are at least three reasons why John went there:

He preached in the desert because that's the way God said it would be (Isaiah 40:3-5).

John wanted to get away from the busyness of the city to hear God's voice.

It was a good place for the people to hear John's message. Because they had walked so far to get there, they weren't likely to leave the moment they heard something they didn't agree with.

VERSE FOR TODAY

"See, I will send my messenger, who will prepare the way before me."
MALACHI 3:1

Jesus is baptized

While John was preaching, and baptizing people in the Jordan River, Jesus came from His hometown of Nazareth to be baptized as well. But John said, "I should be baptized by You, yet You are wanting me to baptize You?"

Jesus replied, "Do what I have asked, for I must do everything that is right." Then John baptized Jesus. As Jesus came up out of the water, heaven was opened, and the Spirit of God came down on Jesus like a dove. And a voice said from heaven, "This is My Son whom I love and with whom I am very pleased."

Why did Jesus ask to be baptized?

By being baptized, people show that they have asked God to forgive their sins and decided to live a life that is pleasing to God. John baptized the people by dipping them under the water (in this case, in the Jordan River).

It is easy to see why John thought it wasn't right for him – an ordinary man and sinner – to baptize Jesus, who is sinless. Because Jesus had never sinned, He didn't need to repent for His sin and be baptized.

Yet, this was the start of Jesus' ministry and He wanted to obey the Law of God in every way – even if it meant doing what was expected of sinners.

Three years later, on the cross, Jesus took our sins on Himself and died in our place (as if *He* had done wrong).

When Jesus was baptized, God spoke from heaven and the Holy Spirit came down on Jesus. This shows that God – who is one God – is also three persons: God the Father, God the Son, and God the Holy Spirit.

VERSE FOR TODAY

"Do not think that I have come to abolish the Law or the Prophets;
I have not come to abolish them but to fulfill them."
MATTHEW 5:17

ANDREW

"Follow Me"

SEPTEMBER 7

After Jesus was baptized, the Holy Spirit led Him into the desert to be tempted by the devil. There, in the heat of the desert, Jesus fasted for forty days. Every time the devil tempted Him, Jesus used Scripture to make the right choice. He never sinned.

Then Jesus began preaching to the people, telling them that the kingdom of heaven is near. As Jesus walked beside the Sea of Galilee, He saw two brothers, Simon (Peter) and his brother Andrew. Jesus said to them, "Come follow Me, and I will make you fishers of men." And they followed Him.

Later, Jesus saw two other fishermen, James and John, and called them too. Immediately, they left their boat and also followed Him.

Did the disciples know what it would cost to follow Jesus?

When people join a team or a club, they usually want to know what's in it for them. If they put effort or money into it, they usually expect something back, whether it is having fun, being honored, or getting a reward.

When the time came for Jesus to begin His ministry, He started choosing a team of helpers. These first disciples had no idea what lay ahead – and they didn't ask. Jesus simply said, "Follow Me," and they followed. They didn't know for how long, where they would sleep, or what was expected of them. Even though they hadn't known Jesus for long, they saw something in Him that helped them trust Him. They trusted Jesus enough to leave everything behind and follow Him – empty handed.

When Jesus calls you to follow Him – trust Him!

VERSE FOR TODAY

Jesus replied, "Foxes have holes and birds of the air have nests, but the Son of Man has no place to lay his head."
LUKE 9:58

ANDREW

Jesus' first miracle

While Jesus was in a town called Cana, He was invited to a wedding, together with Andrew and His other disciples.

During the celebrations the wine ran out, so Mary the mother of Jesus said to Him, "They have no more wine!"

Jesus replied, "Why are you telling Me? My time has not yet come." Later, Jesus told the servants to fill six big water jars with water. So the servants filled the jars to the brim. Then Jesus said, "Now scoop some out and take it to the master of the feast."

The servants did as they were told, and when the master of the feast tasted the water, it had been turned to wine.

Why did Jesus choose to turn water into wine?

A pianist is always careful when choosing the opening piece of music for a concert, because it gets people to sit up and focus on what is to come.

We don't know if Jesus had planned this miracle before the wedding, or whether the Spirit led Him while He was there. We do know that He wasn't going to be rushed into something that wasn't God's will (verse 4).

We would think that His first miracle would be the most important because it would show that He, the Son of God, had come to save the world. Yet Jesus did a miracle that simply helped someone out of an embarrassing situation. Although Jesus had come to save the world, He had also come to be with people. Jesus wanted to show that everyone is important to Him.

Jesus took water, used for everyday things like washing dirty feet, and used it to bless people. Jesus still takes our ordinary, everyday situations and changes them into a blessing as we allow Him to take control.

VERSE FOR TODAY

So whether you eat or drink or whatever you do, do it all for the glory of God.
1 CORINTHIANS 10:31

NICODEMUS

Born of the Spirit

There was a man whose name was Nicodemus. He belonged to a group called the Pharisees – religious leaders who often cared more about their own rules than they did about people. They did not believe the things Jesus taught and were jealous because many people had started to follow Him.

Nicodemus came to Jesus at night because he was afraid of being seen by the other Pharisees. "Master," he said to Jesus, "we know that You are a teacher from God who does miracles."

Jesus said to him, "I tell you the truth: no one can become part of God's kingdom unless he is born again."

"How can an old man be born again?" Nicodemus asked. "Can his mother give birth to him a second time?"

Jesus replied, "No one can come to God unless he is born of water and the Spirit."

Can I be born twice?

It is obvious that you've been born once. The proof is that you are alive. However, you can be born a second time – and this time the choice is up to you!

The first birth – When you were born into a family as a tiny baby, you became part of your family and took on the family name (your surname).

The second birth – When you become a child of God, you are born into His family and take on Christ's name – you become a Christian.

To be born again you must believe in Jesus, ask Him to save you, and trust Him to give you new life. The proof that you have become His child is that the Holy Spirit comes to live in you.

VERSE FOR TODAY

We know that anyone born of God does not continue to sin; the one who was born of God keeps him safe, and the evil one cannot harm him.

1 JOHN 5:18

John 3:9-21

NICODEMUS

The Savior of the world

Nicodemus, a respected leader and teacher who should have known about spiritual things, could not understand the truths Jesus spoke about.

So Jesus explained it this way: "Just as Moses lifted up the snake in the desert to bring healing to those who looked up at it, so God's Son must be lifted up [on a cross] to bring healing to the world.

God loved the world so much that He gave His one and only Son, that everyone who believes in Him will not die but have a new life that never ends. For God did not send His Son to earth to judge and to punish, but that every person can be saved through Him."

Did Jesus come to save our planet?

God, who created the world and everything on it, carefully watches every tiny part of His creation and keeps things going. He wants us to do our bit too by looking after our little part of this huge planet. We should care for animals and birds and plants, and be careful not to litter or waste.

However, when it says that God loved the world and sent Jesus to save it (verse 16-17), it doesn't mean that He sent Jesus to save this round planet we live on. The word "world" means all the people living on earth – the Eskimos, the Indians, the Africans, the Chinese, the Europeans, and everyone else living on the different continents of the world.

The Bible tells us that the world (the earth) will come to an end one day when God finally destroys it (2 Peter 3:10-12). God would not destroy something He loves, so we know that when we read, "God loved the world," it means that God loves every single person in the world – including you!

VERSE FOR TODAY

But in keeping with his promise we are looking forward to a
new heaven and a new earth, the home of righteousness.
PETER 3:13

THE SAMARITAN WOMAN

John 4:1-14

Living water

When Jesus and His disciples left Judea and headed back to Galilee, they had to go through the countryside of Samaria. At midday, Jesus rested at a well while His disciples went off to buy food in the village.

Just then, a woman came to draw water. Jesus said to her, "Will you give Me a drink?"

The woman was surprised that Jesus spoke to her because He was a Jew, and she was a Samaritan (Samaritans were hated by Jews). "Why do You ask me for a drink?"

Jesus said, "If you knew about the gift of God and who can give you this gift, you would have asked Him and He would have given you Living Water."

"Where would You get this Living Water?" she asked.

"Everyone who drinks of this water [from the well] will be thirsty again," Jesus replied, "But everyone who drinks of the water I give him will never be thirsty again!"

Can one drink Living Water?

Have you ever been really thirsty – so thirsty that your tongue feels completely dry? God created each person with a spirit that is "thirsty" to know Him and have a relationship with Him (see Psalm 42:1). Only Jesus can take away that thirst by giving us Living Water: the Holy Spirit.

Some people, like the woman at the well, try to satisfy their thirst for God in ways that aren't right, and so their spirits stay thirsty. When Jesus told the woman about the life-giving water He gives, she wondered about it. But the Living Water Jesus spoke of is not like the clear water one pours into a glass; it is the unseen Spirit of God that He pours into our hearts (Acts 2:17).

VERSE FOR TODAY

"Blessed are those who hunger and thirst for righteousness,
for they will be filled."
MATTHEW 5:6

THE SAMARITAN WOMAN

True worshipers

As the woman at the well spoke to Jesus, she realized that He knew a lot about spiritual things. She thought He was a prophet, so she started talking about the difference between the place where the Samaritans worshiped and where the Jews worshiped.

But Jesus said, "A time is coming when the place for worship will no longer be important. For God is Spirit, and those who worship Him must worship in spirit and in truth."

The woman said, "I know that the Messiah will come, and when He comes, He will explain everything to us."

Jesus replied, "I am He" [the Messiah].

How do I worship in spirit and truth?

Can a person who doesn't believe in God go to church, sing praise songs, put money in the offering basket, and say a prayer? Yes! Even someone whose heart is cold toward God can do things that look like worship but are just meaningless actions.

Worship is not what we do; it is an attitude of the heart. That's why Jesus said that true worshipers worship in spirit and in truth. Those who want to worship God in a meaningful way must worship Him from their hearts (in spirit), and in an honest way (in truth).

The Bible says, "Love the Lord your God with all your heart, all your soul, and all your mind." In other words, every part of you!

We should also be respectful in our worship, realizing that God is holy and powerful. Our lives are not in our hands, but in the powerful hands of God because we belong to Him (1 Corinthians 6:19).

VERSE FOR TODAY

Ascribe to the Lord the glory due his name;
worship the Lord in the splendor of his holiness.
PSALM 29:2

JESUS

Jesus heals the sick

When Jesus got to the town of Capernaum, a Roman officer came up to Him and begged for help. "Sir, my servant is sick at home and cannot move."

"I will go and make him well," Jesus said.

But the officer stopped Jesus. "I do not deserve to have You come into my house. Just give the order and my servant will be well again."

When Jesus heard this, He said to the people around Him, "I have never found anyone in Israel with faith like this!" Then Jesus turned to the officer and said, "Go home, and you will find your servant well."

Later, when Jesus arrived at Peter's home, He found Peter's mother-in-law sick in bed with a fever. Jesus touched her hand and the fever left her. Then she got up and started to serve them, and made them feel at home.

Can my faith make someone else well?

The Bible says that when we ask God for something, we must believe in order to receive what we have asked for (Matthew 21:22). But what if a person is so sick that he cannot pray? Will God answer the prayer of a friend who prays for the sick person? Yes! Asking God to do something for a friend is as easy as asking your mom to give your friend a lift home from school.

And if the person doesn't believe in God at all? There is a gap that separates an unbeliever from God. When you pray for your friend who doesn't believe in God, it is like standing in the gap between your friend and God (see Ezekiel 22:30). As God hears your prayer of faith, His grace will flow to your friend, helping him to put his faith in God.

VERSE FOR TODAY

Therefore confess your sins to each other and pray for each other so that you may be healed. The prayer of a righteous man is powerful and effective.

JAMES 5:16

Luke 5:1-11

PETER

"Because You say so!"

One day, Jesus stood on the shore of Lake Gennesaret and spoke to a crowd that came to listen to Him. The people started to push in so close to Jesus that He got into Peter's boat and asked Peter to push the boat a little way out on the water.

When Jesus had finished speaking, He said to Simon Peter, "Push the boat out into the deep water and let down your fishing nets."

"Master, we've worked hard all night," Peter answered, "and we haven't caught a thing! Yet, because You say so, I will let down my nets."

So Simon Peter and his fellow fishermen went out again. They let down their nets – and as they did, they caught so many fish that their nets started to break. Others came to help, and their boats almost sank because of all the fish.

Does Jesus know and understand my world?

Peter realized that Jesus knew the Scriptures and had the power to heal; yet Jesus grew up in the home of a carpenter in Nazareth – and Nazareth was not a fishing village! When it came to fishing, Peter knew everything there was to know – and this was definitely not the time to fish!

After a whole night's fishing, Peter had some doubts about the good of letting the nets out again, yet he listened to Jesus.

Do you sometimes feel that Jesus doesn't understand your world, your frustrations and your longings? Just as Jesus proved that He knew more about fishing than Peter did, so Jesus knows more about your world than you may have thought. Why don't you start talking to Jesus about your particular world?

VERSE FOR TODAY
For by him all things were created: things in heaven and on earth, visible and invisible, whether thrones or powers or rulers or authorities; all things were created by him and for him.
COLOSSIANS 1:16

JESUS

Luke 5:12-16

Jesus touches a man's life

SEPTEMBER 15

While Jesus was in one of the towns, He met a man covered with a bad skin disease. When the man saw Jesus, he went down on his knees, and with his face to the ground begged Jesus to cure him. "If You are willing," he said, "You can make me clean."

Jesus reached out and touched the man. "I am willing," Jesus said. "Be clean!"

The leprosy immediately left him and his skin became healthy again.

Although Jesus told him not to tell anyone about the healing, the news of what had happened spread all over. So many came to hear Jesus and be healed.

Why did Jesus reach out and touch the diseased man?

Although being sick is never fun, what makes up for it is the special care and attention we get from those who look after us. But that's not the way it was for this leper. Everyone avoided him, as they did all those who had the deadly disease. No one looked after him. No one touched him or even came close to him for fear that they too would get sick.

It wasn't his fault that he had leprosy, yet he suffered the pain of his dreadful sickness, and the pain of being rejected.

The man desperately needed healing and wanted to be cured of his leprosy, but he also longed for a friend to reach out and touch him.

When Jesus heals, He doesn't only get rid of the sickness, He becomes your friend. Jesus changes the lives of people by touching their hearts with His love. He heals the sickness of sin and takes away the sadness and pain that sin brings.

VERSE FOR TODAY
Praise the Lord, O my soul, and forget not all his benefits — who forgives all your sins and heals all your diseases.
PSALM 103:2-3

JESUS

Sharing and caring friends

One day, while Jesus was teaching in someone's home, a group of men came along carrying a paralyzed man on a sleeping mat. Because of the crowd that had gathered, they couldn't get into the house, so they went up onto the roof and lifted off some roof tiles. Then they lowered their friend down on his mat with ropes.

When Jesus saw him, He said, "Your sins are forgiven."

Some of those watching got upset and whispered, "How can this man forgive sins? Only God can forgive sins." But Jesus knew what they were thinking, and to prove that He had the power to forgive sins, He told the man to pick up his bed and go home. And at once the man was healed!

How can sharing change someone's life?

Have you recently invited a friend to your home and had your room look like a disaster zone by the end of the day? And when your friend left, you had to tidy up the mess!

The person at whose house Jesus taught might have thought how nice it would be to have Jesus visit him in his home. He had probably not considered that a crowd of people was about to take over his house, or that someone would rip open his roof. Just imagine the mess after everyone had left. Yet, one crippled man walked out of his house that day – healed, forgiven, and changed forever! Wouldn't you say it was worth it?

You may never know how wonderfully God is able to use your kindness to change someone's life. Be encouraged! Jesus sees when you have to clean up after everyone has left. The time and effort you spend to bless others will not go unnoticed!

VERSE FOR TODAY

"But when you give ... do not let your left hand know what your right hand is doing, so that your giving may be in secret. Then your Father, who sees what is done in secret, will reward you."
MATTHEW 6:3-4

MATTHEW

Who needs a doctor?

After Jesus had healed the paralyzed man, He went out and found a tax collector sitting in his small office. Jesus said to him, "Follow me."

So Levi got up, left everything and followed Jesus.

Later, Levi (Matthew) held a big feast at his house for his friends and fellow tax collectors, and invited Jesus as his special guest.

Some teachers of the Law complained to the disciples that Jesus was enjoying the company of tax collectors (who often cheated people by charging more tax than they should).

But Jesus answered them, "People who are well don't need a doctor, but those who are sick do. I have not come for those who are good [or think they are good], but for sinners who want to turn from their sins."

Does Jesus only want good people in His kingdom?

Did you know that everyone is a sinner – even the person who never seems to do a thing wrong? (Romans 3:10-12). There are people who think they will get to heaven because they are not as bad as others. They don't realize that even the "smallest" sin stains their heart as much as if they broke every commandment (James 2:10). No matter what they do or how hard they try, they cannot heal themselves or get rid of that stain.

Jesus is the only One who can cure the deadly disease of sin; He is the doctor of our souls. Jesus came to earth to invite all people to come to Him. He chooses sinners (like us) to become part of His kingdom. Jesus forgives all those who come to Him for healing. Then He makes us good (righteous) by placing His goodness into our hearts.

VERSE FOR TODAY

For the Son of Man came to seek and to save what was lost.

LUKE 19:10

JESUS

"Blessed are ..."

While Jesus was in Galilee, He said to His disciples:

"Blessed are those who trust God completely, for they will become part of God's heavenly kingdom.

Blessed are those who are sad, for in their sadness they will experience the loving comfort of God the Father.

Blessed are those who are humble and gentle, for they will receive what God has promised.

Blessed are those who long to do what God wants, for God will fill them with His Spirit.

Blessed are those who show mercy and are quick to forgive, for God will be merciful to them.

Blessed are those whose hearts are pure, for they will see God and live with Him.

Blessed are peacemakers who spread the peace of God to others, for they will be called the children of God.

Blessed are those who are treated harshly because they love God, for happy days are waiting for them in heaven."

What is a peacemaker?

When the angels told the shepherds about the birth of Jesus, they said, "Glory to God in the highest, and peace on earth to those with whom He is pleased" (Luke 2:14).

Being a peacemaker means more than stopping a fight at school or yelling at your friends to quit arguing. To be a peacemaker, we need to spend time with God so that His peace can fill our hearts.

VERSE FOR TODAY

Make every effort to keep the unity of the Spirit through the bond of peace.
EPHESIANS 4:3

PETER

Salt and light

Peter and the other disciples sat listening to Jesus as He taught them things they had never heard before.

Jesus said to them, "You are like salt here on earth! But if you are the same as those who do not love God, you will be like salt that has lost its flavor and become worthless.

You are the light of the world! Just as a city on a hill cannot be hidden at night, so the light of your good deeds will shine far and wide. Don't hide your light, but let it shine all around so that everyone will praise your heavenly Father for the good deeds you do."

How can I become salt?

Becoming salt has nothing to do with Lot's wife who turned into a pillar of salt because she disobeyed God. In fact, it is only by obeying God that you become salt.

As you allow God to use you, you become the salt of the earth. That doesn't mean you will suddenly taste salty, but rather, that you can make as much difference to the lives of those around you as a tiny bit of salt can make to a plate of tasteless food.

As salt is sprinkled over food to flavor it, so God has spread believers all around the world to flavor it with love. To check whether you have become salt, answer the following questions. Do you:
- keep your friends from doing wrong things?
- pray for those around you?
- tell others about Jesus or invite them to church?

If you have said yes to one or more question, YOU ARE SALT!

VERSE FOR TODAY

Let your conversation be always full of grace, seasoned with salt,
so that you may know how to answer everyone.

COLOSSIANS 4:6

PETER

Peter learns about anger

Jesus continued to teach His disciples about how to live a life that is pleasing to God. This is what He said about anger: "You all know that if a person murders someone, he will be judged. But now I tell you that even if a person is angry with his brother, or calls someone a fool, he is in danger of being judged."

Then Jesus told them, "If you are about to offer a gift to God and you suddenly remember that a friend has something against you, first sort out the problem with your friend, then offer your gift to God."

Is it okay to be angry?

God has created us with all the emotions we feel. Yet, unlike the emotions of happiness and love, anger seems like a bad emotion. You can, however, use your anger in a positive way. For example, you may be angry because the boy next door keeps kicking their dog. If your anger gets you to stop that from happening, you have used your anger in a positive way.

The Bible doesn't tell us not to be angry; but it does say that we must not let our anger cause us to sin. Showing your anger by breaking things, swearing, or hurting someone is wrong.

When you're angry, don't bottle it up. Rather …

- speak to the person who made you angry and tell him or her how you feel and why you feel that way.
- forgive the person who hurt or disappointed you.

Make something, read a book, draw a picture, or play with your pet.

Whatever you do, don't go to bed with anger burning inside you: it will spoil the start of a beautiful new day in the morning.

VERSE FOR TODAY

"In your anger do not sin": Do not let the sun go down while you are still angry.
EPHESIANS 4:26

JESUS

Jesus teaches about prayer

Jesus was teaching His disciples the things they needed to know to be good followers. He showed them how to live a godly life in the real world. Then Jesus taught them how to pray, "This is how you should pray:

Our Father in heaven, we honor and glorify Your Name.

May Your Kingdom come, and may Your will be done on earth as it is in heaven.

Please give us the food we need for today.

Forgive us for all the wrongs we have done, just as we forgive those who have hurt us in some way.

Do not lead us into tough trials, but keep us from temptation and the power of the evil one; for the kingdom and power and glory are Yours forever and ever.

Amen."

Is the Lord's Prayer an example of the perfect prayer?

Jesus prayed this prayer to teach His disciples the sort of things they should pray about. His prayer is also an example of the order in which we should pray about things. Jesus began His prayer by worshiping God, then He prayed for other things.

However, just because Jesus prayed this prayer, doesn't mean that it is the only prayer we should pray. Although it is the best example of a prayer, God wants us to talk to Him personally and not just repeat words without thinking about what we're saying.

VERSE FOR TODAY

And pray in the Spirit on all occasions with all kinds of prayers and requests. With this in mind, be alert and always keep on praying for all the saints.
EPHESIANS 6:18

JESUS

"Do not judge!"

Jesus and His disciples were spending some time alone on a hillside. As the disciples sat there listening, Jesus taught them truths about God's kingdom. "Do not judge others, or you will be judged," Jesus said. "For God will judge you in the same way that you judge others.

"Why do you get upset about the tiny speck of sawdust in your brother's eye, when you have a plank in your own eye? First take the plank out of your own eye, then you will be able to see clearly to take the speck out of your brother's eye."

Should we correct someone who has a bad habit?

Jesus said that we should not judge others, because in God's eyes, we are all sinners and do not have the right to judge. So how can we keep our friends from doing things that are wrong if we never say anything to them about their faults? Sometimes, we need to make someone aware of a bad habit, but we should always be careful how we do it.

Pointing out good ways to do things:
- makes a person aware of a problem in a sensitive way,
- offers understanding and support,
- gives hope for the future.

Pray for friends who have a bad habit. Show them what the Bible says about the right and wrong way to live, and set a good example. Remember, you don't need to judge someone – the Lord will take care of that.

VERSE FOR TODAY
Therefore judge nothing before the appointed time;
wait till the Lord comes. He will bring to light what is hidden
in darkness and will expose the motives of men's hearts.
1 CORINTHIANS 4:5

JOHN THE BAPTIST
Luke 7:18-23

"Are You the One?"

King Herod had put John the Baptist in prison. While John was in prison, some of his friends went to tell him about the miracles Jesus was doing. Then John sent them to ask Jesus if He was really the One sent from God, or if they should expect someone else.

When John's messengers found Jesus, they asked Him, "Are you really the One whom the prophet spoke about, or should we keep on looking for someone else?"

Jesus answered them, "Go back and tell John what you have seen and heard. The blind can see, the lame can walk, the deaf can hear, those who have leprosy are cured, and even the dead are raised to life. And tell him how even the poor have heard the Good News of God's love.

How happy are those who have no doubts about Me."

Is it a sin to doubt?

Everyone has doubts. If you were absolutely certain about everything, you would never need to exercise your faith.

Doubts that help us look for answers can lead to faith when we look for the answers in the right place – the Bible.

Doubts that get us to disobey, or take our eyes off Jesus, lead to sin. The Bible says that the person who keeps doubting is like a wave that is tossed about by the wind (James 1:6).

John was in prison. He wasn't able to see the miracles Jesus was doing. He may have even wondered why Jesus didn't do a miracle to get him out. But John did something about the doubts that troubled him: he sent his followers to find out the truth from Jesus.

VERSE FOR TODAY
Jesus said, "... Blessed are those who have not seen and yet have believed."
JOHN 20:29

Luke 8:4-8, Matthew 13:18-23

JESUS

Scattered seed

Wherever Jesus went, people kept coming to hear what He had to say. A large crowd had gathered around Him, so Jesus told the people a story to help them understand how the Word of God works in the hearts of people.

"One day, a farmer went to sow seed. As he scattered the seed, some fell on the path where it was stepped on and eaten by birds. Some seed fell on rocky ground. When the seeds sprouted, the plants dried up because the soil was hard and dry. Other seed landed among the weeds, which grew with the small plants and choked them. But some seed fell on good, fertile soil and grew into a large crop which gave a hundred times more seed than was planted."

Can a seed really grow in someone's heart?

The seed that Jesus spoke of in the story is the Word of God. God's Word reaches the hearts of people in different ways, either by hearing it, or by reading the Bible. The soil is the heart of a person. When God's Word touches a person's heart (spirit), it starts growing as the person thinks about it, understands it, believes it and then does what it says.

Some people don't want to hear the Word of God and they harden their hearts so that the seed cannot even start to grow.

Some people hear the words of Jesus and believe for a while, but when times of difficulty and testing come, they give up.

Some people listen to the Word, but the worries, riches, and pleasures of life make them forget what they heard.

But some people hear the Word and do what it says. They have a good heart where the words of Life grow and grow!

VERSE FOR TODAY

No one who is born of God will continue to sin, because God's seed remains in him; he cannot go on sinning, because he has been born of God.

1 JOHN 3:9

JESUS

Luke 8:22-25

Jesus calms the storm

SEPTEMBER 25

One day, Jesus got into a boat with His disciples and said to them, "Let's cross to the other side of the lake."

So they set out, and as they sailed, Jesus fell asleep. While He was sleeping, a strong wind started to blow, and as the waves washed over the side of the boat, it filled up with water.

The disciples woke Jesus, saying, "Master, Master, we're going to drown!"

Jesus got up and said to the wind and waves, "Be calm!" At once, the wind died down and the big waves flattened out. Then Jesus said to His disciples, "Where is your faith?"

The disciples were amazed and afraid. They said to one another, "Who is this man, that even the wind and the waves listen to Him?"

Can Jesus calm stormy emotions too?

Emotions are feelings caused by things that happen *around* us, or things that happen *to* us. Some situations can make us feel peaceful and happy; others make us feel sad, embarrassed, angry or afraid.

On a windless day, a sailing boat goes nowhere. A boat needs some wind to take it from one point to another. But wild storms can cause a boat to be tossed around like a cork.

At times you may feel as though you are in a storm because of something that has shaken your confidence. It may be a problem at school, or maybe there are changes happening in your life. Jesus calms the helpless feeling of being thrown about by waves of trouble!

Although your situation may not change straight away, Jesus can bring peace to the stormy emotions in your heart.

VERSE FOR TODAY
And the peace of God, which transcends all understanding,
will guard your hearts and your minds in Christ Jesus.
PHILIPPIANS 4:7

Mark 6:7-13

THE DISCIPLES

Disciples go out in pairs

Jesus called His twelve disciples together and told them to go out in pairs to do God's work.

He said to them, "Don't take anything for the journey except a stick. Don't take money or food. Wear sandals, but don't take extra clothes.

"When you get to a home where people welcome you, stay with them until you leave that town. If you get to a town where people don't listen to you or welcome you, leave the town. Don't even let the dust of that town stick to your shoes."

So the disciples went out and preached the message they had heard from Jesus. They commanded evil spirits to come out of people, and they healed many who were sick.

Why is it good to do things as a team?

We don't know who went with Peter, but whoever went out with him must have had a great experience! The Lord probably knew that Peter needed someone responsible who would think things through – and perhaps stop him from doing something silly.

When we work together in pairs or small teams, it isn't long before we realize that each of us is different. Each one has certain strengths (things we are good at), and some weaknesses. By working in a team, we can learn new ways of doing things by watching others do things *they* are good at. There are many advantages when we work together. Here are just a few:

- We can encourage one another when things get tough.
- We learn to pray for each other's needs.
- We get things done that we couldn't do alone.

VERSE FOR TODAY

In all my prayers for all of you, I always pray with joy because of your partnership in the gospel from the first day until now.

PHILIPPIANS 1:4-5

JESUS

Mark 6:30-31, John 6:1-13

Jesus feeds a great crowd

The disciples, who had gone out to teach and preach, returned to Jesus very excited and told Him all that had happened. Jesus said to them, "Come with Me to a quiet place and get some rest." They got into a boat and crossed the Sea of Galilee to get away from the crowd. But when the people saw them, they ran around the lake to the other side.

Jesus went up a hill and sat down with his disciples. When He looked up and saw the great crowd coming toward Him, He asked, "Where will we get enough food to feed all these people?"

Peter's brother Andrew said, "There is a boy here with five small loaves of bread and two fish."

Jesus took the loaves and fish and gave thanks to God. Then He broke the loaves and gave the pieces to the disciples to hand to the people. He also divided the two fish in the same way. When everyone had eaten enough, Jesus said to His disciples, "Let nothing be wasted. Gather up the food that is left." When they had collected all the leftovers, they had twelve baskets full.

What did Jesus teach about wasting and littering?

If Jesus could feed more than five thousand people from one boy's lunch, He could have made as much food as He wanted, whenever He wanted. Yet Jesus did not use His power to make loads of delicious food for Himself and His friends. Jesus showed us that we should …

- not always want the best or most expensive things;
- not litter the countryside (or any other place);
- be grateful for what we have, and give thanks to God.

VERSE FOR TODAY
Jesus said, "I am the bread of life."
JOHN 6:48

Matthew 14:22-33

PETER

"Come, Peter!"

After Jesus had fed the crowd, He told the disciples to get into the boat and go to the other side of the lake. Meanwhile, Jesus went up the hill to pray. When evening came, Jesus was alone. By this time His disciples were far out on the lake and a strong wind was tossing their boat around.

Early the following morning, while it was still dark, Jesus walked out to them on top of the water. When the disciples saw someone walking toward them, they were very scared.

But Jesus called out, "Don't worry, it's Me!"

Peter called back, "If it is really You, Lord, tell me to walk to You on the water."

"Come!" Jesus replied. So Peter got out of the boat and walked to Jesus on the water. But when Peter looked around and saw the wind and waves, he was afraid and started to sink. At once, Jesus reached out His hand and caught Peter. "You of little faith," Jesus said, "why did you doubt?" Then they got into the boat and the storm died down.

Why did Jesus let Peter sink?

Peter wanted to step out of the boat and walk to Jesus: this showed his courage. Peter asked Jesus about getting out of the boat: this showed his wisdom. Peter hopped over the side of the boat and walked out to Jesus: this showed his obedience.

Jesus is the One who created the laws of nature, and He can change them whenever He wants. While Peter kept looking at Jesus, his faith was strong and he walked on the water. Even if your faith is weak, Jesus is always with you.

VERSE FOR TODAY
When I am afraid, I will put my trust in you.
PSALM 56:3

PETER

Peter gets it right

One day, Jesus asked His disciples and important question: "Who do people say that I am?"

His disciples answered, "Some say You are John the Baptist, others say You are Elijah. Then there are those who say that You are Jeremiah or some other prophet."

"What about you?" Jesus asked. "Who do you say I am?"

Peter answered, "You are the Christ, the Son of the living God."

"You are blessed, Peter," Jesus said. "This truth was not shown to you by a person, but by the Father in heaven. You are Peter [the rock], and on this rock I will build my church; and not even the evil of hell itself will be able to stand against it."

Was Jesus a prophet?

If someone said to you that Jesus was just a good man, or that He was a prophet, would you agree?

We know that Jesus was good. In fact, He was sinless! But was Jesus a prophet? A prophet is someone who hears a message directly from God and tells people what God said. Old Testament prophets often did miracles and told the people things that would happen in the future. When something did happen as they said it would, it showed that their message was truly from God.

In some ways, Jesus was a prophet. He spoke the Word of God; He did many miracles; and He told us of things that would happen in the future.

However, Jesus is the Son of God! All the other prophets died and were buried: Jesus lives forever and sits at the right hand side of God the Father.

VERSE FOR TODAY

In the past God spoke to our forefathers through the prophets at many times and in various ways, but in these last days he has spoken to us by his Son.
HEBREWS 1:1-2

PETER

Peter's amazing experience

Jesus went up a high mountain with Peter, James and John to be alone and to pray. While they were on the mountain, a change came over Jesus: His face shone like the sun and His clothes were dazzling white. Just then, Moses and Elijah appeared and started talking to Jesus.

Peter, who had dozed off, woke up and blurted out, "Lord, it is so wonderful to be here! I can make three shelters: one for You, one for Moses, and one for Elijah."

While Peter was still speaking, a shining cloud came over them, and a voice said, "This is My own dear Son with whom I am pleased – listen to Him!"

The terrified disciples fell with their faces to the ground, but Jesus touched them saying, "Don't be afraid."

How did Jesus make His face shine?

On a rainy day, when the sky is a misty gray, we say that the sun isn't shining (because we can't see it). Yet if we could rise above the clouds, we would see that the sun is shining, and in fact has never stopped shining.

Jesus has never stopped shining either! From before time began, the brightness of His holiness has been shining and will carry on shining forever. His light is so bright that we won't even need the light of the sun in heaven. The Lord God will give them light" (Revelation 22:5).

Just as we suddenly see the sun shine through a break in the cloudy sky, the three disciples were allowed to see the glory of Jesus for a short while. As the rays of light streamed from His body, they saw His sinless glory. Jesus didn't have to do anything to shine: He IS the Light (John 8:12).

VERSE FOR TODAY

The LORD make his face shine upon you and be gracious to you.
NUMBERS 6:25

October

THE DISCIPLES

The greatest and the least

While the disciples were on their way to Capernaum, they got into an argument about which of them was the greatest. When they arrived in Capernaum, Jesus asked them, "What were you arguing about while we were walking along the road?"

The disciples were embarrassed and didn't answer. Calling the twelve together, Jesus sat down and said, "If someone wants to be first he must put himself last, and if he wants to be great he must be the servant of all."

Jesus brought a child to stand in front of them and gave him a hug. Then He said, "Whoever welcomes a child welcomes Me, and whoever welcomes Me, welcomes the One who sent Me. The one who becomes the least – he is the greatest."

If I am the least, when do I become great?

Being last and least has nothing to do with how fast you are or how young you are. No one likes being at the bottom of the pile, being last in the queue, or coming last in a race. And being least definitely doesn't mean that you are unimportant!

Jesus didn't say to His disciples that they *are* the least, but that they should *become* the least. Becoming the least is something we choose to do – whether we happen to be the fastest or slowest, tallest or shortest.

The one who is least has a kind and humble attitude. He doesn't think of himself as being too important to kneel down and make a child feel welcome. In God's Kingdom, those who are greatest are the ones who see the good in others, who encourage them, and who make friends with the lonely. When you choose to put others first, you become the greatest.

VERSE FOR TODAY

All of you, clothe yourselves with humility toward one another, because, "God opposes the proud but gives grace to the humble."
1 PETER 5:5

OCTOBER 1

JESUS

The cost of following Jesus

One day, when Jesus and His disciples were walking along the road, a man said to Jesus, "I will follow You wherever you go."

Jesus replied, "Foxes have holes and the birds of the air have nests, but the Son of Man has no place to lie down."

Later, Jesus said to another man, "Follow Me!"

But the man replied, "Sir, let me first wait until my father has died, then I will follow You."

Jesus replied, "Let those who don't have eternal life take care of things like that. You go and tell people about the kingdom of God."

Someone else said, "I will follow You, Lord, but let me first go home to say goodbye to everyone."

Jesus said to him, "Anyone who is distracted from doing the work I have planned is like a farmer who tries to plow in a straight line, but keeps looking behind him."

What does it cost to follow Jesus?

If you were to ask a sports coach if you could join the A team, do you think he would invite you to play in a match without training? No, he'd tell you about the many hours of training and practice that lie ahead. Fitness and skill only come with training and lots of practice!

Jesus told the man who was interested in joining His team that being a follower would not be easy. When we join Jesus' winning team, we can expect things to be tough! We must learn the rules and study examples of others in the Bible. We must listen to the Holy Spirit who is our coach. We must stay spiritually fit by praying every day.

VERSE FOR TODAY

I press on toward the goal to win the prize for
which God has called me heavenward in Christ Jesus.
PHILIPPIANS 3:14

Luke 10:25-37

JESUS

The Good Samaritan

One day, an expert on the Law of Moses came to Jesus and tried to trap Him by asking Him what a person must do to live forever. Jesus first asked him a question and then explained what it means to love your neighbor.

"There was once a man who was walking along the road from Jerusalem to Jericho when robbers attacked him. They stripped off his clothes, beat him and left him half dead beside the road.

A priest happened to be going down the same road. When he saw the wounded man, he crossed to the other side and walked on.

Later, a Levite who worked in the Temple came along. But he, too, left the wounded man and carried on walking.

Then a Samaritan came along. When he saw the man, he felt sorry for him. He kneeled down, cleaned the man's wounds and bandaged them. Then he put the man on his donkey and took him to an inn where he was cared for until he got better."

OCTOBER 3

How can I be a "Good Samaritan"?

When you have hurt yourself and someone has helped you, that person has been like the Good Samaritan to you. Perhaps you would also like to show your kindness by helping someone in need.

Why not ask your mom to show you how to clean a graze, put on a plaster, and tie a bandage. Although you may not find someone beaten up at the side of the road, you won't have to go far to find someone who has been hurt in a different way.

Some may have been hurt because of what others have said or done. You can bring healing to a wounded heart by being a loyal friend.

VERSE FOR TODAY
The entire law is summed up in a single command:
"Love your neighbor as yourself."
GALATIANS 5:14

MARY

Sitting at the Master's feet

As Jesus and His disciples went on their way, they came to a village where a woman named Martha welcomed Jesus into her home. Martha had a sister named Mary who went to sit at the feet of Jesus and listened to Him.

But Martha became upset because of all the work she had to do. She went to Jesus and said, "Lord, don't You care that my sister is just sitting here and has left me to do all the work by myself? Tell her to come and help me!"

"Martha, Martha," Jesus said. "You are worried and upset about many things. There is only one thing that is really important. Mary has discovered it, and it won't be taken away from her."

What is the most important thing in life?

If you were to ask different people what the most important thing is to them, you would get many different answers. Some may say that being happy is really important; others might choose a good education, health, being rich, or having a loving family. People spend time and energy on that which is most important to them.

To Martha, it was important to have things work out just right; and when Jesus came, she wanted everything to be perfect. When things weren't going exactly as she wanted, she got all worked up. Yet Jesus would have been just as happy to have a simple meal. Actually, He would have preferred Martha to relax and join the conversation rather than fuss over things that didn't really matter. What is the most important thing in your life? To Mary, it was spending time with Jesus.

One day, the earth and everything we own will be gone (2 Peter 3:7). Will that which is important to you now still be around then?

VERSE FOR TODAY

"My sheep listen to my voice; I know them, and they follow me."
JOHN 10:27

The kingdom of God

On the day set aside for worship, Jesus went to teach in the synagogue – a Jewish place of worship. While Jesus was there, He healed a woman who had been ill for many years. This made the person in charge very angry, because to him, rules were more important than people.

Jesus asked, "What is the kingdom of God like? It is like a mustard seed, which a man took and planted in his garden. It grew and became a large tree in which birds made their nests.

The kingdom is also like yeast that a woman mixed into a large amount of flour until it worked through the dough and made it rise."

What is the kingdom of God?

What does a bit of yeast and a tiny mustard seed have in common? Although neither seems like much, in the right place, both grow bigger and bigger!

When Jesus started His ministry, the kingdom of God was like a small seed. Then the disciples joined Him, and soon others believed and became part of God's kingdom. The kingdom spread from town to town, and from country to country as more and more people heard about Jesus and believed. But what is the kingdom of God – and where is this kingdom?

A kingdom is all the land and the people over which a king rules. As Lord of all, the kingdom of God is everywhere He rules. He has a heavenly kingdom and an earthly kingdom. God rules in heaven where His perfect will is done (2 Timothy 4:18). And if the Lord is King of your life, His kingdom is also inside you.

OCTOBER 5

VERSE FOR TODAY

The Lord has established his throne in heaven, and his kingdom rules over all.
PSALM 103:19

The great feast

While Jesus was having a meal at the home of a Pharisee, He told one of the guests this story: "There was once a man who invited many guests to a great feast. When everything was ready, he sent his servants out to tell the guests, 'Come to the banquet. Everything is ready.' But one after the other started making excuses.

The first man said that he had just bought a field and needed to go look at it. The second man said he had bought some oxen, which he needed to try out. The next man said he had just got married and couldn't come.

So the servants went back and told their master that no one would come. The owner of the house was angry and said to his servants, 'Go out quickly into the streets and country roads of the town and bring in the poor, the crippled, the blind and the lame.'"

Why would someone not want to go to a feast?

If you were invited to a friend's party, would you think up a silly excuse not to go? Yet many people come up with all sorts of excuses for not accepting God's invitation to the greatest celebration ever – in heaven!

Some don't believe in God or in heaven (so they don't believe that there is going to be a feast).

Some are just too busy. One man had bought some property; another was busy (at work) wanting to try out his new oxen.

Some are afraid of upsetting their family and friends. One man had just married and didn't want to risk a disagreement.

Invitations to the great feast in heaven have been sent out, and your name is on one of them. When it is time, will you be there?

VERSE FOR TODAY

"Blessed are those who are invited to the wedding supper of the Lamb!"
REVELATION 19:9

The Father's love

One day, some tax collectors and outcasts came to listen to Jesus. The Pharisees and teachers of the Law started complaining, "This man [Jesus] welcomes dishonest crooks and even eats with them."

Then Jesus told them this story to show how much God loves sinners. "There was once a man who had two sons. The younger son said to his father, 'Give me my share of the inheritance now.' So the father sold a part of his property and gave the money to his son.

The son left home and went to a country far away where he wasted all his money. Then a famine spread across the country and he was left with absolutely nothing. So he went to work on a farm where he looked after smelly pigs. He was so hungry that even the pigs' food started to look tasty.

At last the son came to his senses and said, 'I will get up and return to my father.' While he was still a long way from home, his father saw him and ran out to meet him. The father hugged his son and welcomed him home. Then he held a big party to celebrate because his son had come back."

Does God's love for us ever change?

When we have sinned and gone our own way, it may not feel as if God loves us because our guilt and shame makes us feel far from Him. The son who left home could not feel his father's love while he was far away, but that didn't mean that his father had stopped loving him. The son only felt his father's love the day he returned home.

God's love for us will never change, even when we rebel and go our own way. But when we come back, He is overjoyed, no matter how far we have gone or what we have done.

VERSE FOR TODAY

"In the same way, I tell you, there is rejoicing in the presence of the angels of God over one sinner who repents."
LUKE 15:10

OCTOBER 7

JESUS

Luke 17:11-19

The man who came back

OCTOBER 8

On His way to Jerusalem, Jesus entered a village and met ten men who had a dreaded skin disease called leprosy. The men stood at a distance and shouted, "Jesus, Master! Have pity on us."

When Jesus saw them, He said, "Go show yourselves to the priests." (In those days only the priests could declare someone free of leprosy and give them permission to live among the people of the town again.)

On their way, the ten men were healed of their disease.

One of them, when he saw that he was healed, praised God in a loud voice and went back to thank Jesus.

Jesus said to him, "There were ten of you; where are the others? Are you the only one who came back to give thanks? Go your way; your faith has made you well."

Doesn't God get bored when we thank Him for everything?

If you had to think of a hundred things to thank God for, it probably wouldn't take you long to make a list. For a start, just look around you.

We can thank God for big things as well as for small, everyday things. But instead of going through a long list every day, why not get into the habit of thanking God for things as they happen, or as you see them.

For example, you can thank Him for a warm bed on a cold winter's night, or for delicious food. You can thank Him for eyes that see the beauty of a sunrise or for the love of a friend when you're feeling down.

God loves it when we thank Him because it shows that we notice His goodness and see the details of His creation.

VERSE FOR TODAY
Sing and make music in your heart to the Lord,
always giving thanks to God the Father for everything.
Ephesians 5:19-20

Mark 10:13-16

JESUS

Jesus blesses children

While Jesus was teaching a group of people, some mothers brought their children to Him so that He would bless them and pray for them. But the disciples told the mothers to take their children away.

When Jesus noticed this, He was upset and said to His disciples, "Let the children come to Me, and do not stop them because the kingdom of God belongs to them."

"I tell you this: anyone who does not receive the kingdom of God like a child will never enter it."

Then Jesus took the children in His arms, placed His hands on each of them and blessed them.

OCTOBER 9

Are kids as important to God as adults?

Adults seem to have so many privileges like going to bed when they want, making up rules in the home, and buying whatever they want at the store. Adults are also able to do many things that kids can't do. At times, it may even feel as if church is mainly for grown-ups, and this could make you think that God is actually more interested in adults than in kids.

Although adults do have more privileges and are able to do more than children can, they also have more responsibilities. But in God's eyes, that doesn't make adults more important than kids.

We are important to God because He created us!

When it comes to getting God's attention, you don't have to wait at the back of a queue while God sorts out important things with the adults. Jesus told His disciples never to stop children from coming to Him, because the kingdom of God belongs to those who are like children.

VERSE FOR TODAY
From the lips of children and infants you have ordained praise.
PSALM 8:2

ZACCHAEUS

A tax collector in a tree?

As Jesus was passing through the town of Jericho, a large number of people lined the streets to see Him. In the same town lived a tax collector named Zacchaeus who had cheated many people. He stood right at the back somewhere, and because he was short, he couldn't see Jesus. So he ran on ahead and climbed up a tree.

When Jesus passed by, He stopped, looked up into the tree and said, "Zacchaeus, come down, because I must come and stay with you today!"

Zacchaeus hurried down and welcomed Jesus with great joy. Then he said to Jesus, "I will give half of what I own to the poor, and if I have cheated anyone, I will pay him back four times as much!"

Would Zacchaeus have met Jesus if there hadn't been a tree?

Do you think Zacchaeus' life would have changed if that tree had not been next to the road?

While Jesus was on earth, He could only be in one place at one time. Even so, He changed the lives of many people by going out of His way to meet those who were searching for truth. Now that He is in heaven, He makes Himself known to all who truly search for Him.

God said, "You will seek Me and find Me when you seek Me with all your heart" (Jeremiah 29:13). He is watching for those whose hearts long to find Him. Whenever someone, like Zacchaeus, wants to meet Jesus, God in His power can make it happen. God can work things out for that person to be in the right place at the right time to hear about Jesus and invite Him into his heart.

VERSE FOR TODAY

For the eyes of the LORD range throughout the earth to strengthen those whose hearts are fully committed to him.

2 CHRONICLES 16:9

John 12:1-8

The sweet smell of perfume

It was the time of the year when Jewish people celebrate the Passover, so Jesus and the disciples made their way from Jericho to Jerusalem. On their way, they stayed over in Bethany.

Martha served the dinner, which had been prepared in honor of Jesus. While they were eating, Mary took a jar of very expensive perfume and poured it on Jesus' feet. Then she wiped His feet with her hair. The sweet smell of the perfume filled the whole house.

Judas, one of the disciples, sneered, "We could have sold this perfume and given the money to the poor!"

But Jesus replied, "Leave her alone! She has done a beautiful thing to Me. The poor will always be around, and you can help them whenever you want, but you will not always have Me."

Why did Mary pour perfume on Jesus' feet?

In those days, it was a custom to offer a guest a jar of water to wash his hands and feet when he entered the house. Mary did much more.

Although it wasn't her house, she went across to Jesus and poured her precious perfume over His feet. The perfume – which cost as much as some people earn in a year – was Mary's gift of love. It was the most precious thing she owned. By pouring it over the feet of Jesus, Mary showed that she no longer had anything that was more precious to her than Jesus.

Yet Mary felt that even this gift was only suitable for washing the feet of her Lord. So Mary gave more: she gave herself by bowing down at the feet of Jesus and drying his feet with her hair.

OCTOBER 11

VERSE FOR TODAY
May my prayer be set before you like incense;
may the lifting up of my hands be like the evening sacrifice.
Psalm 141:2

JESUS

"The Lord needs it"

On their way to Jerusalem, where Jesus and His disciples were headed, they came to the village of Bethpage. Jesus sent two of the disciples on ahead, saying, "Go to the village over there and you will find a donkey tied up with her colt next to her. Untie them and bring them to Me. If anyone says anything to you, say that the Lord needs them, and he will let you take them."

The two disciples went and did what Jesus told them. They fetched the donkey and the colt and threw their cloaks over them for Jesus to ride on.

Should I allow others to use my things?

Someone leans over and taps you on the shoulder. "Could I use your pencil for a minute?" After school, someone wants to borrow one of your books to take home. That afternoon, a friend wants to know whether he can borrow your bike to go for a ride.

If someone has asked to borrow something and you were to follow the example of the man who owned the donkey, how would you know whether to say yes, or no?

We may want to do the right thing by being kind and helpful, yet we also need to be responsible about lending things to others.

For a start, there are some things that are personal – like your toothbrush. Don't let others use your personal things!

There are certain things that are valuable, which you should not lend to others without first checking with your mom or dad.

But there are things you can let others use in order to help them out. Remember; sharing builds friendships.

VERSE FOR TODAY
"Give to the one who asks you, and do not turn
away from the one who wants to borrow from you."
MATTHEW 5:42

Jesus enters Jerusalem

The disciples brought a donkey and its colt to Jesus as He had asked them to. As Jesus rode on the donkey, a large crowd spread their garments on the road like a carpet, while others cut palm branches from nearby trees and spread them on the road.

There were people walking ahead and people following behind, all shouting, "Hosanna! Blessed is He who comes in the name of the Lord."

When Jesus entered Jerusalem, the whole city was in chaos. Some asked, "Who is this?"

"This is Jesus, the prophet from Nazareth," the crowd answered.

Then Jesus went to the Temple and chased out the people who were doing business there, saying, "My House will be called a house of prayer, but you have turned it into a den of thieves." Then He healed the sick; and all the children shouted, "Hosanna to the Son of David!"

What does "hosanna" mean?

A large crowd had gathered for the Passover feast. Jerusalem (called the city of David) was buzzing with activity as people from all over the country came for the yearly celebration. By this time, many people had either met Jesus or heard of Him. When they saw Him riding into the city, they started shouting "Hosanna!" meaning "save us."

The Romans, who had conquered the country, were making life difficult for the Jewish people. Jesus had shown His power by doing amazing miracles, and some thought that He was the One who would set them free from the Romans. But Jesus had come for more than that: Jesus came to set the *whole world* free.

OCTOBER 13

VERSE FOR TODAY
Shout, Daughter of Jerusalem! See, your king comes to you,
righteous and having salvation, gentle and riding on a donkey,
on a colt, the foal of a donkey.
ZECHARIAH 9:9

JESUS

Should we pay taxes?

The Pharisees were very unhappy that Jesus had dared to drive traders from the Temple area while allowing children to shout praises to Him as He healed the blind and lame.

So the Pharisees tried to think of a way to trap Jesus by getting Him to say something against the Romans (who ruled at that time). Then they'd be able to accuse Him of something for which the Romans would punish Him. They came up with a plan and asked Jesus, "Is it against our Law to pay taxes to the Roman Emperor, or not?"

Jesus asked them to show Him a coin for paying taxes and said, "Whose name and face is on the coin?"

"The Roman Emperor's," they answered.

"Well, then, pay to the Emperor what belongs to the Emperor, and to God, what belongs to God."

What are taxes?

There are many things that a government – those in charge of a country – must do for its citizens; like building roads and hospitals and schools, and making sure that people obey the law. The government needs money to do all these things, and one way of raising money is by getting everyone to pay a portion of what they earn. The money that is paid is called tax.

Paying part of one's hard-earned money for tax is no fun and some people try all sorts of ways to get out of paying what they should. But Jesus clearly showed that paying tax to those in authority is the right thing to do.

Be a person of honor by giving to each one what you owe them – whether it is respect at home and at school, or paying taxes one day.

VERSE FOR TODAY

Give everyone what you owe him: If you owe taxes, pay taxes; if revenue, then revenue; if respect, then respect; if honor, then honor.
ROMANS 13:7

Mark 12:41-44

JESUS

She gave all she had

As Jesus was sitting near the Temple offering-box, He watched people come to put their money in it. Some rich people put in lots of money.

Then a poor woman came along and put in two small coins, which were not worth much.

Jesus called His disciples together and said to them, "Let Me tell you this. That poor widow over there has put more into the offering-box than all the others. The rich only put in some of their spare cash, but the widow put in all she had – every last bit she had to live on."

How can a little be more than a lot?

If you were to tell your friends that the few copper coins in your hand are worth more than a fat bundle of banknotes, they would probably look at you strangely. Imagine the looks on the disciples' faces when Jesus told them that the poor woman had put more into the offering-box than all the money the rich people had put in. It didn't make sense!

The actual value of the money the rich had given may have been more than the widow's coins, but let's look at it the way Jesus saw it. Pretend that you and a friend decide to give your teacher some chocolates. Your friend gives the teacher three chocolates from a big packet she brought to school. You decide to give the one small chocolate your mom put in your lunchbox. Who gave more? You gave more because your friend only gave a little from the big packet she had, while you gave everything you had. "Everything" is more than "a little!"

Jesus doesn't look at how much you give, but how much you have left. Do you put some of your pocket money into the offering?

OCTOBER 15

VERSE FOR TODAY

Each man should give what he has decided in his heart to give, not reluctantly or under compulsion, for God loves a cheerful giver.
2 CORINTHIANS 9:7

JESUS

Luke 22:7-20

The Passover meal

OCTOBER 16

Jesus sent Peter and John ahead to prepare a room for the Passover meal. He told them that they would meet a man carrying a water jar who would lead them to a house with a large room, which they could use.

When everything was ready, Jesus and the disciples made themselves comfortable around the table.

Then Jesus said, "I have looked forward to sharing this Passover meal with you before I suffer. For I won't eat it again until the Passover is given its full meaning."

Jesus took the bread and gave thanks for it. Then He broke off pieces and gave it to them, saying, "This is My body which is given to you. Do this to remember Me."

After supper, Jesus gave them a cup of wine to share, saying, "This cup is the sign of God's new agreement to save you – a lasting covenant sealed with My blood."

How does the bread and wine remind us of Jesus?

Although Jesus had told His disciples that He would suffer and die, they didn't understand what He meant.

At the Passover supper, Jesus used the bread and wine to explain to the disciples what was about to happen and leave them with a practical way to remember His death.

As Jesus broke the bread, He was showing how His body would be broken. He would be whipped and beaten and nailed to a cross the next day.

Then Jesus took the wine and used it to show them how His blood would flow as He hung on the cross.

VERSE FOR TODAY

For whenever you eat this bread and drink this cup,
you proclaim the Lord's death until he comes.
1 CORINTHIANS 11:26

PETER

Peter has his feet washed

While Jesus and the disciples were celebrating the Passover meal in an upstairs room, Jesus got up and wrapped a towel around His waist. He poured water into a bowl and went from one disciple to the next, washing their feet and drying them with the towel.

When it was Peter's turn to have his feet washed, he said, "Lord, are You going to wash my feet too?"

"You do not understand what I am doing," Jesus replied, "but later on, you will understand."

"No!" Peter said, "I won't let You wash my feet."

Jesus answered, "Unless I wash you, you cannot be a part of what I am doing."

"Then wash my hands and my head as well," Peter exclaimed.

Jesus answered, "A person who has had a bath only needs to wash his feet, and you are clean; though not all of you are," because He knew that one of them would betray Him.

Why did Jesus wash Peter's feet?

Peter couldn't bear the thought of His Master doing a servant's job like washing his dirty feet. It made him feel awkward. But when Jesus explained why He needed to do this, Peter wanted Jesus to wash him all over.

Why, then, did Jesus wash Peter's *feet*? Jesus had brought about a change in Peter's life: he had already been made clean by becoming a follower of Jesus. Yet, Peter was not perfect.

Peter still needed to understand that to become the leader Jesus wanted him to be, he had to learn to humbly serve others.

VERSE FOR TODAY

"I have set you an example that you should do as I have done for you."
JOHN 13:15

PETER

John 13:21-26, 33, 36-38

"I will die for You!"

After Jesus had washed the disciples' feet, He said that one of them was planning to betray Him (hand Him over to His enemies). The disciples stared at each other all confused. Who would do such a thing?

John, who was next to Jesus, asked, "Lord, who is it?"

Jesus answered, "It is the one to whom I give this piece of bread after I have dipped it in the sauce."

Then Jesus took a piece of bread, dipped it in the sauce and gave it to Judas. Immediately, Judas got up, went out and headed into the darkness. Jesus said, "Where I am going you cannot follow Me."

Peter asked, "Where are You going, Lord?"

"You cannot follow Me now, but you will follow Me later on," Jesus replied.

"Lord, why can't I follow You now?" Peter asked. "I am ready to die for You!"

Jesus replied, "Before the rooster crows tomorrow morning, three times you will say that you don't know Me."

What is the test of real love?

Both Judas and Peter had been chosen by Jesus. Both had followed Jesus. They had seen many miracles and faced many hardships. Now, both disciples faced an important test: a test of their love and loyalty.

Judas was planning to throw away everything he had been through and betray Jesus for a handful of silver.

Peter was willing to die, if that's what it would cost to stay close to His Lord. Although Jesus knew that Peter would fail this test, He knew that, one day, Peter would prove the full extent of his love.

VERSE FOR TODAY
"Greater love has no one than this, that he lay down his life for his friends."
JOHN 15:13

OCTOBER 18

JESUS

Jesus prays in the garden

Jesus and the disciples left the house and went to the Mount of Olives, a hill east of Jerusalem. When they arrived at their usual spot, Jesus said to His disciples, "Pray that you will not be overcome by temptation."

Then Jesus walked on a little way and knelt down to pray. "Father," He said, "if You are willing, please take away this cup of suffering so that I don't have to drink it. But I want to do Your will, not Mine."

An angel from heaven came to Jesus and strengthened Him, for He was in such agony that His sweat dripped onto the ground like drops of blood. And He prayed even more earnestly. Then Jesus got up and went back to the disciples. He found them asleep, worn out by their sadness. "Why are you sleeping," He said. "Get up and pray that you won't fall into sin when you are tempted."

OCTOBER 19

Did Jesus have to die?

Jesus knew that the time had come for Him to take away the sin of the world. He had prepared His disciples for what lay ahead. Late that night, there in the garden, Jesus prayed to His Father.

Was there still time for Him to flee instead of staying where Judas and the others were sure to find Him? Could God have taken Jesus straight back to heaven so He wouldn't have to suffer? Could Jesus have called down thousands of angels to defend Him? (Matthew 26:53).

Yes, Jesus could have chosen not to die for us. Perhaps His Father could come up with another way to save the world. But, there was no other way! And because Jesus loves us so very much, He was willing to become the Passover Lamb for all of us and give His life to set us free (John 10:17-18).

VERSE FOR TODAY

"But the world must learn that I love the Father and that I do exactly what my Father has commanded me."

John 14:31

JESUS

Jesus is arrested

As Jesus was speaking to His disciples in the garden, a crowd arrived led by Judas. It was night, and Judas came right up to Jesus and kissed Him. Jesus said to Judas, "Are you betraying the Son of Man with a kiss?"

When the disciples realized that the group of people had come to arrest Jesus, they said, "Lord, should we use our swords?" But before Jesus could answer, Peter swung his sword at the servant and cut off his ear.

But Jesus said, "Stop this and put away your sword." Then He touched the man's ear and healed him.

Jesus then said to the chief priests, the elders, and the officers of the Temple, "Why have you come with swords and clubs as though I am a criminal? I was with you in the Temple every day. Why didn't you arrest Me there? But now that it is dark, this is your time to act."

So they arrested Jesus and took Him to the High Priest's house. And Peter followed at a distance.

Does God plan the exact time for things to happen?

God does nothing without a plan. For a plan to work, it is important for things to happen at the right time.

- God's timing. This was not the first time people had tried to kill Jesus (Luke 4:28-30).
- Peter's timing. Peter asked, but he didn't wait for an answer. He wanted to do the right thing by bravely defending Jesus, but it was the wrong time. In Ecclesiastes 3:1,3 it says that there is a time and a season for everything.
- The devil's timing. The devil had his plans too. But his plans always have to fall in with God's will and timing.

VERSE FOR TODAY

My times are in your hands.
PSALM 31:15

PETER

A rooster crows

The soldiers that arrested Jesus in the garden took Him to the High Priest's house. A fire had been lit in the courtyard, and Peter – wanting to be near Jesus – joined those sitting around the fire. In the flickering light, one of the servant girls recognized Peter, and said, "This man was with Jesus too!"

But Peter said, "I don't even know Jesus!"

Later, one of the men said, "You are also one of them."

But Peter replied angrily, "I am not!"

About an hour later, someone else said, "This man is definitely one of them. He comes from Galilee."

Peter replied, "I don't know what you're talking about!"

As Peter was still speaking, a rooster crowed. Jesus turned and looked at Peter. At once, Peter remembered that the Lord had said, "Before the rooster crows, you will deny Me three times." Then Peter wept bitterly.

Can someone who has denied Jesus still go to heaven?

We don't get to heaven by what we do (or by what we don't do). All our good deeds put together cannot get rid of our sin; and no one who has a sinful heart may enter heaven.

You can only be saved from sin when you ask Jesus to forgive you and allow Him to change your life. Once you are born again, you are born into God's family and become His child. From that day on, you will always be His child, even when you do something bad or say something wrong like Peter did. If you are sorry for what you did, Jesus will forgive you!

While you are on earth you will never be perfect. However, you should always do your best to please the Lord.

VERSE FOR TODAY
Be on your guard; stand firm in the faith ... be strong.
1 Corinthians 16:13

JESUS

Pilate must decide

OCTOBER 22

The religious leaders took Jesus to Pilate, the Roman governor. They lied about Jesus and accused Him of misleading the people.

So Pilate asked Jesus, "Are you the King of the Jews?"

"Yes, it is as you say," Jesus replied.

Then Pilate spoke to the chief priests and to the crowd, saying, "I find no reason to condemn this man." When Pilate found out that Jesus came from the region ruled by Herod, he sent Jesus to Herod (who happened to be in Jerusalem at that time). But Herod could also find no fault with Jesus and sent Him back to Pilate.

Again, Pilate could not find Jesus guilty of a single crime. So he took a bowl of water and washed his hands in front of the crowd. Then he had Jesus beaten and handed Him over to the people to be crucified.

Why did Pilate wash his hands?

By washing his hands in front of the crowd, Pilate was trying to prove that his hands were clean; that there was no "blood on his hands" from sentencing an innocent person to death.

Yet, by not using his power and position to make a fair judgment, Pilate chose to side with the unjust. Although he knew that the religious leaders were jealous of Jesus, Pilate was too scared to take a stand against them. He even tried to pass the responsibility for the decision on to Herod, hoping that he would make a decision about Jesus.

Every person has to make the decision Pilate had to make. Jesus said, "He who is not with Me is against Me" (Matthew 12:30). Because Pilate was afraid to decide for Jesus, he went along with the crowd's decision.

VERSE FOR TODAY

Jesus answered, "You would have no power
over me if it were not given to you from above."
JOHN 19:11

The darkest day

Although Pilate could find no fault with Jesus, he let his soldiers take Jesus to be crucified. The soldiers made Jesus carry a heavy wooden cross. A large crowd followed them to a hill outside the city.

When they came to a place, which was known as 'The Skull,' the soldiers nailed Jesus to the wooden beams and lifted the cross upright. They also crucified two criminals: one on His right and one on His left.

Then Jesus said, "Forgive them, Father, for they do not know what they are doing."

The soldiers divided His clothes among themselves, throwing dice to decide who would get each piece.

At midday the sun stopped shining and darkness covered the country for three hours. Suddenly, the thick curtain that hung in the Temple was torn in two. Then Jesus cried out, "Father, into Your hands I commit My spirit." And with those words, He died.

OCTOBER 23

Why did the Temple curtain tear?

There was a special curtain in the Temple that separated the part where the priests could go from the Most Holy Place behind the curtain (Exodus 26:33). Only the high priest could enter the Most Holy Place – once a year. Sin kept people from meeting with God in the Most Holy Place.

When Jesus died, He took our sin and guilt on Himself and opened a way for us to draw near to God. God Himself tore the curtain from top to bottom to show that everyone is welcome in His presence now. If we ask Jesus to forgive us, He takes away our sin and makes us absolutely pure so that we can go meet with God.

VERSE FOR TODAY

Since we have confidence to enter the Most Holy Place by
the blood of Jesus, by a new and living way opened for us
through the curtain, that is, his body, ... let us draw near to God.
HEBREWS 10:19-20

JOSEPH OF ARIMATHEA

A stranger's tomb

By mid-afternoon, Jesus had died. Because it was a special Sabbath day the next day, the Jews did not want to leave someone hanging on a cross. So the soldiers broke the legs of the men on either side of Jesus so that they would die quickly. But when they came to Jesus and saw that He was already dead, they did not break His legs. However, one of the soldiers pierced His side with a spear, causing blood and water to flow from it.

After this, Joseph of Arimathea, who had been a secret disciple, went to ask Pilate for permission to take the body of Jesus down from the cross. Then Joseph and Nicodemus wrapped the body of Jesus in a long linen cloth with the spices used for burial.

There was a big garden near the hill where Jesus was crucified. It so happened that Joseph owned an unused tomb in the garden, so they laid the body of Jesus in the tomb and rolled a large stone in front of the entrance.

How do we know that Jesus is the promised Messiah?

"Messiah" is a Hebrew word meaning the Anointed One. Hundreds of years before Jesus came, Old Testament prophets and writers spoke about things that would help people recognize Jesus when He came.

Although it may seem obvious that they were speaking about Jesus, the Jews living at that time saw Jesus as a normal man.

Here are three of the many prophecies that came true when Jesus died:
- They divide My garments among them and cast lots for My clothing (Psalm 22:18).
- He protects all His bones, not one of them will be broken (Psalm 34:20).
- "They will look on Me, the one they have pierced" (Zechariah 12:10).

VERSE FOR TODAY
"We have found the Messiah" (that is, the Christ).
JOHN 1:41

MARY MAGDALENE

The empty tomb

The day after the Sabbath, before the sun came up, Mary Magdalene and the other Mary went to Jesus' tomb. It was Sunday morning, the third day after Jesus had been crucified.

Suddenly, there was a great earthquake and an angel of the Lord rolled away the stone from the entrance of the tomb. The angel was as bright as lightning, and his clothes were dazzling white. The soldiers who were guarding the tomb were so afraid that they fell to the ground.

When the two women arrived at the tomb, the angel said to them, "Don't be afraid! You are looking for Jesus who was crucified, but He is not here. He is risen, just as He said. Come and see the place where He lay. Now, go quickly and tell the disciples that He is alive!"

So the women left the tomb, afraid, yet filled with joy.

Did Jesus raise Himself from the dead?

Jesus had brought a young girl back to life (Luke 8:53-54). He also raised His friend Lazarus, who had been dead for four days (John 11:43-44). And now, Jesus Himself was dead. He had been beaten, nailed to a cross and pierced in the side. His friends wrapped Him tightly in strips of cloth and laid Him in a tomb. They had even rolled a heavy stone in front of the entrance.

The Bible tells us that God raised Jesus from the dead. By raising Him, God showed that the death of His Son was enough to pay for the sin of all mankind. Even though Jesus took the whole world's sin on Himself, He remained sinless. And so Jesus became the first sinless man to rise from the dead. And when we put our faith in Him, He also makes us sinless; and God will raise us to eternal life with the same power that raised Jesus.

OCTOBER 25

VERSE FOR TODAY

By his power God raised the Lord from the dead, and he will raise us also.
1 CORINTHIANS 6:14

JESUS

Jesus is alive!

OCTOBER 26

When the women told the disciples that an angel had appeared to them saying that Jesus had risen, the disciples didn't believe them. But Peter and John ran to the tomb and found it empty.

The same day, two of Jesus' followers were walking back to their home-town after the Passover celebration in Jerusalem. They had seen Jesus be-ing crucified, and as they walked along the road to Emmaus, they were very sad. Suddenly, Jesus started walking next to them and joined in their conversation, but they didn't recognize Him.

Even though Jesus explained what the prophets had said about the Messiah who was to suffer and be glorified, they didn't realize that it was Jesus talking to them.

When they arrived at Emmaus, they invited Him to stay with them. At supper, Jesus gave thanks and broke the bread; and as He gave it to them, it was as though their eyes were opened and they recognized Him.

Why did Jesus not show Himself to everyone?

There was no need for Jesus to appear to those who didn't believe in Him. If they had not believed in Him at first, they would not believe in Him now. Even if someone had come back from the dead to warn them, they would not have believed (Luke 16:31).

Yet Jesus showed Himself to the two followers walking along the road. Then He appeared to the disciples, and later, to other followers. Jesus want-ed them to be eyewitnesses: to see that He truly was alive. Although the disciples had not believed the women, when they saw Jesus they needed no further proof.

VERSE FOR TODAY
"Now is your time of grief, but I will see you again
and you will rejoice, and no one will take away your joy."
JOHN 16:22

JESUS

Jesus appears to the disciples

The two who had met Jesus on their way home, ran all the way back to the city to tell the disciples that Jesus had risen from the dead. When they got to Jerusalem, they found the disciples together in a room and told them that Jesus had appeared to them.

While they were still speaking, Jesus appeared in the room and said, "Peace be with you."

The disciples were terrified, thinking that they were seeing a ghost. But Jesus said, "Why are you doubting? Look at My hands and My feet, and feel Me. A ghost does not have a body like this."

The disciples were amazed and filled with joy.

Then Jesus asked, "Do you have anything to eat?"

So the disciples gave Jesus a piece of cooked fish, which He took and ate right there in front of them.

Did Jesus have a real body after He rose from the dead?

If you have stubbed your toes in the dark or walked in to a closed door, you will know that your body cannot go through a solid object.

You may wonder how Jesus got into a room with a locked door (John 20:19). The disciples were terrified that the Jewish leaders would do to them what they had done to Jesus. So they made sure no one could get in. But even a solid wall and a locked door couldn't stop Jesus.

Jesus was able to walk through anything, yet He was also able to eat, speak, and hold things. He even had marks on His hands and feet from the nails used on the cross. After Jesus had risen from the dead, He had a glorified body (John 12:16).

VERSE FOR TODAY

The Lord Jesus Christ ... will transform our lowly
bodies so that they will be like his glorious body.
PHILIPPIANS 3:21

THOMAS

Thomas believes

Thomas, one of the disciples, had not been there when Jesus appeared to the others. When they told him that they had seen Jesus, he said, "Unless I see the scars from the nails in His hands and feel the hole in His side, I will not believe."

A week later, the disciples were together in the same room. This time, Thomas was with them. Although the doors were locked, Jesus appeared to them again and said, "Peace be with you." Then He said to Thomas, "Put your finger here and see My hands. Reach out your hand and feel My side. Stop doubting, and believe!"

Thomas replied, "My Lord and my God!"

Then Jesus said, "Happy and blessed are those who have not seen Me, yet believe."

Should I believe everything I hear about Jesus?

If a stranger gave you a little book and told you that it's even better than the Bible, would you believe every word in the book? If you heard someone talking on the radio about different religions having the same God, could you trust everything that person said?

Do you believe everything your friends say just because it sounds like the truth? Thomas didn't believe everything he was told by his friends. The problem was not so much that he doubted what his fellow disciples told him, but that he didn't believe what Jesus Himself had said (Luke 9:22).

Everything God wants us to know about Him has been written in the Bible – and God's Word can never be changed! He has given us the Holy Spirit to help us understand the meaning of what is written (1 Corinthians 2:12).

VERSE FOR TODAY
Dear friends, do not believe every spirit,
but test the spirits to see whether they are from God.
1 John 4:1

PETER

At the Sea of Galilee

After Jesus had shown Himself to the disciples, they left the house where they were staying and went to Galilee. Jesus had told them that He would go on ahead and meet them there.

While some of the disciples were at the Sea of Galilee (Tiberias), Peter said, "I'm going out to fish."

The others replied, "We'll go with you." So they went out in a boat; but that night, they caught nothing!

As the sun rose, Jesus stood on the shore and called out to them, "Friends, have you caught any fish?"

"No," they answered. The disciples didn't realize that it was Jesus standing on the shore.

"Throw your net on the right side of the boat and you will catch some," Jesus called.

So they threw out their net. This time, they couldn't pull it in because of the many fish they had caught. John said to Peter, "It is the Lord."

OCTOBER 29

What important lessons had the disciples learned?

From the time Jesus first called Peter and the others to follow Him, they had learned much from the things He taught them and from the example He set. This experience taught them that:
- When we are not doing what Jesus wants us to do, even our best efforts are wasted.
- Faith is the key that unlocks God's power.
- God can, and will, supply all our needs!
  When we help each other, we all share in the blessing.

VERSE FOR TODAY
Nothing is too hard for you.
JEREMIAH 32:17

PETER

Jesus speaks to Peter

After the disciples had managed to drag their heavy net ashore, they noticed a small coal fire. Jesus had prepared some fish and bread for breakfast.

When they had eaten, Jesus said to Simon Peter, "Simon, do you truly love Me more than these here?"

Peter answered, "Yes, Lord, You know I love You."

Again Jesus asked, "Simon, do you really love Me?

"Yes, Lord," Peter answered, "You know that I love You."

Then Jesus asked Peter the third time. "Simon, do you love Me?"

Peter was very sad because Jesus had asked Him a third time. He answered, "Lord, You know all things. You know that I love You."

Why did Jesus ask Peter the same question three times?

Jesus didn't ask questions in order to find out things; He asked questions to make people stop and think.

Peter had denied Jesus three times by saying that he didn't know Him. Peter was obviously feeling very ashamed about what he had said.

Jesus knew that Peter still loved Him and wanted to give him a chance to say so.

The first two times Peter said "I love you" he didn't have the courage to use words that describe a deep, loyal love. But when Jesus asked a third time, "Do you love Me?" Peter replied sadly, "Lord, You know all things. You know that I love You."

If ever you feel ashamed and guilty about something you've done, and the words 'I'm sorry' seem shallow, you can say, "Lord, look into my heart and You will see that I truly love You."

VERSE FOR TODAY
"I have prayed for you ... that your faith may not fail.
And when you have turned back, strengthen your brothers."
Luke 22:32

Jesus goes back to heaven

Jesus and the disciples were back in Jerusalem. Forty days had passed since Jesus had been crucified, and the time had come for Him to return to His Father in heaven.

Jesus led His disciples out of the city to the town of Bethany, where He raised His hands and blessed them.

Then He said to them, "When the Holy Spirit comes upon you, you will be filled with power, and you will be witnesses for Me in Jerusalem, in Judea and Samaria and to the farthest places on earth."

After saying this, Jesus was taken up to heaven and hidden by a cloud.

While the disciples were still looking up, two men dressed in white appeared beside them and said, "Why are you standing here looking up at the sky? This Jesus, who was taken from you into heaven, will come back in the same way as you have seen Him go to heaven."

Where is heaven?

The Bible tells us that heaven is up above us. But in a world that is round, which way is up? Astronauts have gone into outer space, circled the earth, and come back saying that they didn't see heaven up there. So, is heaven really up in the sky somewhere?

Like the sky above, heaven may be very near, or it may be further than the furthest star.

But we should also remember that we cannot see heaven with the eyes we have now. That doesn't mean that heaven isn't real. When we die, or if Jesus comes back before then, our bodies will be transformed (made new). With our new bodies we will see just how real and beautiful heaven really is.

OCTOBER 31

VERSE FOR TODAY

I lift up my eyes to you, to you whose throne is in heaven.
PSALM 123:1

November

PETER

The Holy Spirit comes down

The disciples, now called apostles, were gathered together in a house on the day of Pentecost (a Jewish feast to celebrate the beginning of the harvest season).

Suddenly, the rushing noise of a strong wind filled the house, and what seemed like tongues of fire came to rest on each of them. All those in the house were filled with the Holy Spirit and spoke in other languages.

Many godly Jews had come from far-off countries to gather for the celebrations in Jerusalem. When they heard the strange sound of wind above the house, they came running to see what was happening. They were even more amazed when they heard the apostles speaking in their language.

"How do these men know our language?" they exclaimed, "They are all from Galilee!" But others mocked them saying that they were probably drunk.

Did the Holy Spirit fill people in Old Testament times?

In Old Testament times, there were a number of people who had a special blessing of God's Spirit on them for a time, to do a special task. For example, the Spirit of the Lord came on Samson and gave him power to tackle and kill a lion with his bare hands (Judges 14:6). Others were given the Spirit to lead God's people, for example, when David was anointed as king of Israel.

When Jesus went back to heaven, He sent the Holy Spirit to live in *all* who followed Him (John 16:7). Now the Holy Spirit lives in *every* believer! When someone becomes a follower of Jesus by believing in Him, the Holy Spirit comes to live (and stay) in that person from that moment on (1 Corinthians 6:19).

VERSE FOR TODAY
In the last days, God says, I will pour out my Spirit on all people.
Your sons and daughters will prophesy, your young men
will see visions, your old men will dream dreams.
Acts 2:17

PETER

Acts 2:14, 37-47

The Church is born

A large crowd had gathered around the house where the Holy Spirit had come down in an amazing way and filled the apostles with power.

Peter, who was filled with the Holy Spirit, boldly started preaching to the crowd, telling them what the prophet Joel had said: "God will pour out His Spirit on everyone."

When the people heard Peter's words, they felt guilty about their sin and asked, "What should we do?"

Peter replied, "Turn away from sin and be baptized in the name of Jesus. Then God will forgive you and fill you with the Holy Spirit."

Many believed and were baptized, and about three thousand people were added to the Church that day. They met often; shared their belongings, and worshiped in the Temple area every day.

NOVEMBER 2

How and when did the Church begin?

While the disciples were crowded together in a room, it was as though the Lord was busy forming the Church; preparing it to be born.

On the day the Holy Spirit came down, the disciples burst into the streets with the message of Jesus. And so the Church was born as thousands came to know Jesus:

- They met for worship, prayer, and breaking of bread (communion).
- They eagerly listened to the apostles' teaching.
- They shared what they owned and gave money to the poor.
- They used their spiritual gifts, and miracles happened.

As they preached the Word of God, many turned from their sin and were saved. Those who were saved joined the believers, and the Church grew.

VERSE FOR TODAY

"And I tell you that you are Peter, and on this rock I will build my church, and the gates of Hades will not overcome it."
Matthew 16:18

PETER

A new day for a beggar

One afternoon, Peter and John were on their way to a prayer meeting when they saw a crippled man sitting at the Temple gate. When the man saw Peter and John, he asked them for money.

Peter stopped and said to the beggar, "Look at us." The man looked up expecting some money.

Instead, Peter said to him, "We do not have silver or gold, but what we do have we will give to you. In the name of Jesus of Nazareth, walk!"

Taking him by the hand, Peter helped him up. Immediately the man's feet and ankles became strong. Then he went into the temple area with them, walking and jumping, and praising God.

When the people saw the man walking and realized that he was the cripple who sat at the gate every day, they were utterly amazed.

Has everyone got the gift of healing?

God has chosen certain people to have the gift of healing. The Holy Spirit gives them power to heal the sick and the disabled in miraculous ways. Do you wish you could help sick people? Maybe your mom has been sick and you felt helpless as you stood next to her bed. God has not given everyone the gift (ability) to heal someone, but that doesn't mean we can't pray for the sick. God will always hear and answer a prayer of faith! (James 5:15-16).

Paul tells us that there is something more important than having the gift of healing – and that is, having love. You could help a sick person feel better just by showing that you care! Why not pick some flowers, write a cheerful note, draw a funny picture, or do odd jobs for someone who is sick.

NOVEMBER 3

VERSE FOR TODAY

Do all have gifts of healing? Do all speak in tongues?
Do all interpret? But eagerly desire the greater gifts.
1 CORINTHIANS 12:30-31

PETER

God is glorified

The cripple who had been healed was holding on to Peter and John with joy. People rushed from all sides of the Temple porch to see the beggar who had been healed.

When Peter saw the people, he said to them, "Men of Israel, why are you so surprised? Why are you staring at us as if we made this man walk by our own power? It is the God of Abraham, Isaac, and Jacob, who has glorified His servant Jesus. You handed Him over to be killed, but God raised Him from the dead. The man you see here was made strong by faith in the name of Jesus. It is in the name of Jesus that this man was healed."

How can I glorify God?

When we think of God, we think of Him as being awesome and majestic – and He is! One would think that the only way to glorify such a great God is by doing something impressive. Yet, if that were true, those who are not very talented and don't have much to give wouldn't be able to glorify Him. But God notices the small things we do for Him. It is often the things that no one else notices that please God most.

If ever there was a person who had absolutely nothing to give, it was John the Baptist. Yet, he glorified Jesus by saying, "He must become greater; I must become less" (John 3:30).

Whenever you are obedient and allow God to use you, you magnify Him – you make Him greater in the eyes of others. Peter says that we should live such good lives that even unbelievers will see our good deeds and glorify God (1 Peter 2:12). Every time we glorify the Lord by our actions, our words and our songs, we let God and others know that He is truly the Greatest!

NOVEMBER 4

VERSE FOR TODAY
I will praise you, O Lord my God, with all
my heart; I will glorify your name forever.
PSALM 86:12

PETER

Peter and John are threatened

While Peter and John spoke to the crowd that had gathered around them, some Temple officials came to arrest them and put them in jail. Meanwhile, many of those who had heard Peter's message put their trust in Jesus, and the number of believers grew to about five thousand.

The next day, leaders and teachers of the Law gathered in Jerusalem and had Peter and John brought to them. The council of leaders asked Peter and John many questions. "With what kind of power or in whose name did you heal this cripple?" they wanted to know.

Then Peter told them about Jesus whom they had rejected and crucified. The leaders were surprised by the boldness of Peter and John and were amazed when they found out that they were just ordinary men with little education.

How did Peter, the fisherman, suddenly know so much?

Would you feel nervous if you had to stand in front of everyone at school and speak to them?

Peter wasn't used to speaking to large crowds. In the past, Jesus had done all the teaching and preaching. But now, Jesus wasn't there anymore. In a way, Peter was on his own; yet in another way, Jesus was right there with him. Jesus had promised to send the Holy Spirit to teach them what to say (John 16:12-14).

The Holy Spirit was guiding Peter's thoughts as he spoke – and people were absolutely amazed!

You can also speak out for Jesus like Peter did. By reading the Bible and asking the Holy Spirit to guide your thoughts, you will know what to say.

NOVEMBER 5

VERSE FOR TODAY
"The Holy Spirit will teach you at that time what you should say."
LUKE 12:12

PETER

The believers' prayer

When the priests and elders realized that they couldn't really punish Peter and John for healing a lame man, they warned them never to speak about Jesus again.

But Peter answered, "We cannot stop speaking about what we have seen and heard."

After being warned again, Peter and John were released and returned to the group of believers. When the believers heard about the chief priests' threats, they joined together to pray to God.

"Creator of heaven, earth and sea," they said. "Hear the threats that have been made against us. Let us speak Your message with boldness! Reach down and heal people, we ask, and may there be many wonders and miracles. We pray this in the name of Jesus. Amen."

Why do we say 'in Jesus' name' when we pray?

When we pray in Jesus' name, we pray to God the Father with the support and blessing of His Son. So when we use Jesus' name to end a prayer, we must be sure that Jesus agrees with what we have prayed. We should pray with a pure heart that listens to God's Spirit. "Pray in the Spirit on all occasions with all kinds of prayers and requests" (Ephesians 6:18).

When a king instructs his servant to do something, the servant acts with the king's power and authority. Although he is only a servant, his words are a direct instruction from the king and must be obeyed.

The name of Jesus is the most powerful name in the universe: it is greater than every other name (Philippians 2:9). By praying in the name of Jesus, we – His servants – pray with the power and authority of the King of kings.

VERSE FOR TODAY

"I tell you the truth, my Father will give you whatever you ask in my name. Until now you have not asked for anything in my name. Ask and you will receive ..."
JOHN 16:23-24

THE BELIEVERS

The believers are one

All those who had put their faith in Jesus were united – they believed one message and had one purpose. They shared everything because they realized that what they owned had been given to them by God.

The apostles' message spread all over Jerusalem. They taught the truths they had learned from Jesus.

Because the believers cared for one another, no one in their group had any needs. Some believers even sold their houses and land, giving the money to the apostles so they could help the needy.

Why is unity in the Church so important?

The believers were one in heart and mind (verse 32): they had the same faith in their hearts, and the same belief in their minds.

When Jesus was with His disciples, He prayed to the Father, saying, "I will no longer remain in the world, but they are still in the world … protect them by the power of Your name, the name You gave Me, so that they may be one as We are one" (John 17:11).

So God sent the Holy Spirit to unite believers. The Holy Spirit brings us together and makes us one in Jesus; and it is only when we are one through our love for Him and each other that we can:

- It is only when we are one through our love that we can:
- Help each other grow in our faith (1 Corinthians 14:26)
- Worship and glorify God with one heart (Romans 15:5-6)
- Pray with power (Matthew 18:19)
- Give an offering that is pleasing to God (Matthew 5:23-24)
- Witness for Jesus with the right attitude (Philippians 1:15).

NOVEMBER 7

VERSE FOR TODAY

Make every effort to keep the unity of the Spirit through the bond of peace.

EPHESIANS 4:3

PETER

Acts 5:1-4

The lie

NOVEMBER 8

Some new believers were so keen to help the poor that they decided to sell their houses and land and give the money to help the needy.

Ananias and his wife Sapphira also sold some property but decided to keep some of the money for themselves. Ananias went to the apostles and put the money at their feet.

Then Peter said to him, "Ananias, why have you let Satan take control of you? You have lied to the Holy Spirit by keeping some of the money. Before you sold the property it belonged to you, and even after you sold it, the money was yours. You have not lied to men – you have lied to God."

Is it wrong to pretend?

Do you sometimes play a game where you have to pretend something? God doesn't mind when children (or adults) use their imaginations to pretend things in a fun way. However, it is wrong when you allow people to believe a lie – when you mislead them by keeping quiet or by hiding something from them.

Ananias went to put the money at the apostles' feet – as others had done – pretending that it was all the money he got from selling his land. He could have kept all the money for himself, or put just some of it in the offering. But instead, he came to the apostles as if he were giving everything, and acted out a lie.

Giving to God is an act of worship. God is holy, and He wants us to worship Him in spirit and in truth (see John 4:24). Ananias dared to lie to the Holy Spirit who is the Spirit of truth. The Lord wants us to be honest in *everything* we do; especially in the way we worship Him.

VERSE FOR TODAY

No one who practices deceit will dwell in my house;
no one who speaks falsely will stand in my presence.
Psalm 101:7

PETER

The unstoppable Church

The apostles met in the Temple area and did many miracles. As more and more people became believers, the high priest and others became very jealous. They arrested the apostles and put them in jail.

But during the night, an angel of the Lord came and opened the jail door. He led the apostles out and told them to go and preach the message of a new life in Christ.

When the chief priests heard that Peter and the apostles were preaching in the Temple area, they arrested them again and wanted to kill them. But Gamaliel, one of the religious teachers said, "Don't take action against these men. Remember the two leaders, Theudas and Judas, who had crowds of people following them? Both these men were killed and the crowds that followed them scattered. If what these 'Jesus-followers' believe is not from God, they will scatter too; however, if it is from God, not even you will be able to stop them!"

Can people stop the Church of Jesus from growing?

Gamaliel used examples of two groups whose members had scattered when their leaders were killed. Jesus had also been killed, but He rose again! His small group of followers was growing by the day.

Since then, the enemies of Jesus (and even some religious people) have tried to stop the Good News from spreading. They have tried to stop people believing in Jesus by killing them and burning their Bibles. Yet, the Church just keeps growing as more and more people get to know Jesus.

Isn't it exciting to be part of this Church that has spread all over the world? It just keeps growing, and it will never come to an end!

NOVEMBER 9

VERSE FOR TODAY

Jesus said, "… I will build my church,
and the gates of Hades will not overcome it."
MATTHEW 16:18

THE BELIEVERS

Acts 6:1-7

Staying focused

The believers were kind to the poor and needy. Every day they handed out food to widows who didn't have enough to live on. Everything was going well until some widows from one group complained that they were not getting food like the others were. So the apostles got together to see how they could sort out this problem.

"It wouldn't be right for us to get involved in checking that each widow gets her fair share," they said. "If we did that, we wouldn't have time to preach. We should rather choose seven wise men that are filled with the Holy Spirit and give them the task of handing out food. Then the rest of us can get on with praying and with preaching the Word of God."

Everyone was happy with the idea. So they chose seven men and prayed for them as they started their work among the poor.

NOVEMBER 10

What is the most important job of the Church?

It would be silly if a team of hockey players got so involved with choosing team colors, displaying trophies, and raising funds, that they didn't have time to practice or play a match.

In the same way, there are many activities happening in the Church. Most of these are good, and – like the feeding program – are blessed by God. However, the apostles realized that they shouldn't get so caught up that they wouldn't have time to do what they were supposed to.

The last thing Jesus said to them was, "Go all over the world and make disciples; teaching them all that I have told you" (Matthew 28:19-20). Telling others about Jesus is still the most important task of the Church.

VERSE FOR TODAY
"… You will be my witnesses in Jerusalem, and in all Judea and Samaria, and to the ends of the earth."
ACTS 1:8

PETER

"Surely not, Lord!"

One day, while the midday meal was being prepared in the home where Peter was staying, he went upstairs onto the flat roof of the house to pray. While he was praying, he had a vision – a picture-message from God.

A large sheet came down from the sky. On the sheet were all sorts of animals, reptiles and birds, which Jews are not allowed to eat. Then he heard a voice say, "Get up, Peter. Kill and eat!"

"Surely not, Lord!" Peter replied. "I have never eaten anything unclean like this."

The voice spoke to him again: "Do not call anything unclean that God has made clean." This happened three times, and then the sheet was taken back to heaven.

While Peter was wondering what this could mean, some men arrived at the house. They had been sent by Cornelius, a Roman army officer. Immediately, the Spirit said to Peter, "Go with these men, for I have sent them."

Can our religious beliefs keep us from pleasing God?

God wanted Peter to go speak to Cornelius (who wasn't Jewish like Peter was). But Peter had allowed his Jewish belief to shape his thinking and block his understanding of God's plan.

Religious traditions aren't wrong if they remind us of a truth or help us understand a Bible truth better. However, we should be careful of ideas and traditions that keep us from pleasing God.

If you are unsure about which beliefs are from the Bible and which are simply traditions, ask someone to show you the part in the Bible that brings out the true meaning of the belief.

VERSE FOR TODAY

See to it that no one takes you captive through hollow and deceptive philosophy, which depends on human tradition and the basic principles of this world rather than on Christ.

COLOSSIANS 2:8

PETER

No favorites in the Church!

The day before Peter's vision, Cornelius, a Roman official, had also seen a vision. In his vision an angel appeared to him and told him to send men to find Peter.

When the men arrived in Joppa, they found Peter and told him that Cornelius wanted to see him. So the next day, Peter and the men left for Caesarea. When they arrived, they found Cornelius and his family and friends waiting patiently.

Then Peter spoke to those who had gathered, saying, "Our Jewish custom does not allow us to enter the house of a Gentile (a person who isn't a Jew). But through a vision, God showed me that He accepts all those who do what is right, no matter what race they belong to."

NOVEMBER 12

Does God have favorites?

The Good News of Jesus is for everyone – every person from every race, every class, every belief, and every culture. Yes, God loves every person on this earth (John 3:16). But just because He loves so many millions of people, don't think that He doesn't notice you in the crowd.

Because God made you special, He knows you and loves you in a special way, and He has a special purpose for your life. God loves you with a love that is just for you – as though you were the only person in the universe. Yet God loves every other person that way too, and because He has no favorites, it means that you will never be less important than someone else! God's love is so great that He can love all His children as though each of them was His favorite child.

VERSE FOR TODAY

My brothers, as believers in our glorious
Lord Jesus Christ, don't show favoritism.
JAMES 2:1

PETER

Powerful prayers

While Peter was speaking to those who had gathered in the home of Cornelius, the Holy Spirit came on them. Everyone believed the Word of God and was baptized.

However, as the message of Jesus spread, King Herod started arresting the believers in order to keep the Jews happy. He had Peter arrested and put him in prison with sixteen soldiers to guard him. Meanwhile the other believers gathered to pray for Peter's safety.

During the night, while Peter was sleeping between two guards, suddenly, an angel of the Lord appeared next to him. The angel shook Peter and woke him up. "Hurry! Put on your shoes and coat and follow me!" the angel said.

So Peter followed the angel out of the prison cell, past the guards, and up to the huge iron gate leading into the city. Then the iron gate opened by itself. Peter thought he was seeing a vision, but after they had walked down the road, the angel disappeared and Peter knew he was free.

Why is it so important to pray with others?

When the believers got together to pray, God did a mighty miracle. Did everyone expect a miracle? (see Acts 12:12-15). Sometimes, when we pray on our own, our faith seems small. Yet, if God can use faith the size of a little seed, imagine what He can do when a whole lot of believers pray together.

We are the body of Christ. He wants us to be joined together in all we do – in worship, in serving Him and in prayer.

When we pray in a group, Jesus is right there with us, listening to every word (Matthew 18:20).

NOVEMBER 13

VERSE FOR TODAY

"Again, I tell you that if two of you on earth agree about anything you ask for, it will be done for you by my Father in heaven."
MATTHEW 18:19

PHILIP

"Go to the desert!"

One day, an angel of the Lord said to Philip, "Go to the road that goes down from Jerusalem to Gaza."

So Philip went there and saw someone riding along in a chariot (a horse-drawn cart). It was the treasurer of Ethiopia! He had gone to worship in Jerusalem and was on his way home. The Spirit told Philip to go up to the chariot and stay close to it. As he did, he heard the man reading aloud from the book of Isaiah.

"Do you understand what you are reading?" Philip asked.

The Ethiopian invited Philip onto his chariot and said, "How can I understand when there is no one to explain it?" He had been reading this passage in Isaiah: "He was led like a sheep to the slaughter, and as a lamb is silent before the shearers, so He did not open His mouth."

And so, Philip used that passage to tell him the good news.

How can I reach my friends for Jesus?

Philip had gone to preach in Samaria, where many were turning to God. Even though Philip was being used there in a wonderful way, the Spirit told him to leave the area and go to the desert. This shows how important it is to God to reach the heart of a single person who is ready to receive Him. Here are just some ways God can use you to reach someone:

- Let your life be an example of what it is like to follow Jesus.
- Use the Bible (Philip used Isaiah 53:7). You could use verses like these: Sin – Romans 3:23; God's love – John 3:16; Believing in Jesus – Romans 10:9; Forgiveness – 1 John 1:9.
- Pray that the Spirit will work in the hearts of your friends.

VERSE FOR TODAY

Jesus answered, "I am the way and the truth and the life.
No one comes to the Father except through Me."
JOHN 14:6

NOVEMBER 14

PHILIP

This is the best news!

As Philip and the Ethiopian traveled along the desert road in a chariot, Philip explained the whole message of Jesus to him, starting with God's promise to send us a Savior. Then Philip told him that God had fulfilled this promise by sending Jesus to die in our place. He also told him how Jesus had risen again and commanded His followers to make disciples and baptize them.

As they traveled, they came to a place where there was water. The Ethiopian said to Philip, "Here is water! What is keeping me from being baptized right here?"

The Ethiopian official ordered the chariot to stop. Then he and Philip went down into the water, and Philip baptized him. When they came up out of the water, the Spirit of the Lord took Philip away, and the Ethiopian went on his way with great joy.

Why do people get baptized?

The Ethiopian wanted to be baptized because he believed in Jesus. Philip had told him the Good News of Jesus; about becoming a disciple, being baptized and learning all that Jesus commanded (see Matthew 28:19-20).

Baptism is an outward sign of an inward change. It shows that the person's life of sin has died, and a new life has risen with Jesus. "Having been buried with him in baptism and raised with him through your faith in the power of God, who raised Him from the dead" (Colossians 2:12).

Baptism is a command. Jesus instructed His disciples to tell everyone about Him, to make new disciples (followers), and baptize them in the name of the Father, the Son and the Holy Spirit.

NOVEMBER 15

VERSE FOR TODAY

You are all sons of God through faith in Christ Jesus, for all of you who were baptized into Christ have clothed yourselves with Christ.
GALATIANS 3:26-27

BARNABAS

Acts 4:36, 11:19-24

Son of Encouragement

Barnabas, one of the Levites who served in the Temple, had become a believer. He was from Cyprus, a large island in the Mediterranean Sea. His real name was Joseph, but the disciples named him Barnabas, which means Son of Encouragement.

The Jewish leaders in Jerusalem, hated the believers and persecuted them more and more. Some believers fled to distant cities, spreading the Good News of Jesus wherever they went. Many who heard their message believed and were saved.

When news of this reached the Church in Jerusalem, they sent Barnabas to encourage the believers in the city of Antioch. Barnabas was overjoyed to see the wonderful things God was doing in Antioch and encouraged the believers to stay faithful to the Lord.

How important is the gift of encouragement?

If there's one thing everyone needs, it is encouragement. Life is tough! We all get discouraged and need someone to help us see past the difficult situation we're in; someone who helps us think positive, helpful thoughts.

Many of the new believers had to change their way of life because they were used to serving heathen gods. Some were rejected by their families and friends, and some lost their jobs. The believers, who were insulted and mistreated, needed someone like Barnabas to renew their hope.

The Spirit has given us different gifts: some prophesy, some enjoy serving, some are able to teach and some have been given the gift of encouragement (see Romans 12:6-8). If you are a positive person who loves to cheer up those who are downhearted, you are an encourager!

VERSE FOR TODAY

Therefore encourage one another and build each other up,
just as in fact you are doing.
1 Thessalonians 5:11

NOVEMBER 16

Acts 7:54-60, 11:25-26

STEPHEN

Christians in Antioch

Stephen, a faithful believer, was one of the men chosen to help give out food to poor widows in Jerusalem. In the same city there were jealous leaders who hated those who followed the Way of Jesus, but Stephen boldly told them about Jesus. That made them so mad that they dragged him out of the city and killed him.

When the other believers saw what the leaders had done to Stephen, they fled for their lives. Many went to live in far-off places like the city of Antioch where Barnabas was encouraging the Church and teaching them the truths of the Gospel.

It was in Antioch that believers were first called Christians.

How do I become a Christian?

If your parents were born in China and speak Chinese, you could think of yourself as being Chinese. If you were born in Spain, you would be Spanish. If you are born in a Christian country and your parents go to Church, would that make you a Christian?

The believers in Antioch were not born in a Christian country; they were not born in to a Christian family, yet they were Christians. The people there called them Christians because they believed in Christ and followed in His Way.

You become a Christian when you believe in Jesus – when you tell Him you are sorry for your sins and ask Him to forgive you. Jesus then makes your heart new and sends the Holy Spirit to live in you and help you do what is right. This is God's firm promise: that you are His child forever (Ephesians 1:13-14).

NOVEMBER 17

VERSE FOR TODAY
For it is with your heart that you believe and are justified,
and it is with your mouth that you confess and are saved.
ROMANS 10:10

PAUL (SAUL)

Acts 9:1-9

A voice from heaven

As more and more people heard the message of Jesus and believed, Saul (who hated Christians) asked the high priest for letters to make it easier for him to arrest the Christians in Damascus.

While Saul was on his way to Damascus, a bright light flashed from the sky. Saul fell to the ground and heard a voice say, "Saul, Saul. Why are you persecuting Me?"

"Who are You, Lord?" Saul asked.

"I am Jesus, whom you are persecuting," the voice replied. "Go to the city where you will be shown what to do."

Saul got up from the ground, but he couldn't see a thing. He was completely blind. So the men who were with Saul took him by the hand and led him to the city of Damascus.

NOVEMBER 18

Why do some people hate Christians?

Do you think it would matter to a stranger living in another town that you read your Bible and believe in Jesus?

Why did Saul spend so much time and energy hurting Christians who were just minding their own business? In fact, they were helping poor people, healing the sick, and spreading the Good News of God's love.

These Christians were taking the Light of Jesus into the dark (sinful) parts of the world. Saul's problem was that their message of Light was also showing up the sin and wrong motives in *his* heart. Jesus said, "Everyone who does evil hates the light, and will not come into the light for fear that his deeds will be exposed" (John 3:20).

VERSE FOR TODAY

Jesus said, "No servant is greater than his master.
If they persecuted me, they will persecute you also."
JOHN 15:20

Acts 9:10-19

PAUL (SAUL)

Saul – a changed man

Ananias, a believer in Damascus, had a vision in which the Lord said, "Ananias! Get ready and go to Straight Street, to the house of Judas and ask for Saul. In a vision, he saw you placing your hands on him to heal him of his blindness."

Ananias answered, "Lord, many people have told me about this man and about the terrible things he has done to your people in Jerusalem. He is coming to Damascus to arrest all those who worship You."

The Lord said to Ananias, "Go, because I have chosen him to serve Me."

So Ananias went to the house where Saul was staying and said to him, "The Lord sent me to you so that you will see again and be filled with the Holy Spirit."

Ananias placed his hands on Saul, and at once he was able to see again. Then Saul got up and was baptized.

How can you tell if someone is a Christian?

Ananias was afraid of Saul – but God had changed Saul's heart. The Bible gives us number of ways that show when someone is a child of God.

Someone who is born again:
- believes that Jesus is the Son of God and the Savior (1 John 4:15, 5:1)
- obeys the commandments of God (1 John 2:3)
- follows the example of Jesus (1 John 2:5)
- does not deliberately keep on sinning (1 John 3:9, 5:18-19)
- shows love in practical ways (1 John 3:18-19, 3:14)
- has the Spirit of God living in him (1 John 3:24, 4:13).

VERSE FOR TODAY

"Likewise every good tree bears good fruit, but a bad tree bears bad fruit. Thus, by their fruit you will recognize them."
MATTHEW 7:17, 20

PAUL

Acts 13:1-3, 14:21-28

Paul's first missionary trip

One day, while the believers in Antioch were worshiping and fasting, the Holy Spirit said to them, "Set aside Barnabas and Saul for a special job I have for them."

So the believers placed their hands on them and prayed for them. Then Barnabas and Saul (who became known as Paul) went on their way and took John Mark as their helper. The Holy Spirit guided them as they went from place to place. Paul, and his faithful companion Barnabas, preached the message of Jesus, and many were saved.

On their way back, they visited the new believers and encouraged them to stay true to Jesus. They also chose leaders in the new churches and prayed for them.

What is discipleship?

NOVEMBER 20

A seed that has not been planted is dead. But when it is buried in the ground and watered, suddenly, there is life! A person who doesn't know Jesus is like a dead seed. But when he allows Jesus to bury his old life of sin (Romans 6:4) and receives the life-giving water of the Holy Spirit (John 4:13), a new life appears – completely different from before.

Once a seed has sprung to life, it needs to be watered. In the same way, new believers need to be discipled. They need special care until their faith has taken root. As Paul preached the Word, he visited the believers to strengthen their faith.

Evangelism is telling people the good news of the Gospel (Mark 16:15).
Discipleship is caring for new believers (Matthew 28:19-20).
Do you have friends whose faith is not that strong yet? Pray for them.

VERSE FOR TODAY
The man who plants and the man who waters
have one purpose, and each will be rewarded ...
1 Corinthians 3:8

A disagreement

Some time after Paul's first missionary trip, he said to Barnabas, "Let's go back to the towns where we preached, and find out how the new believers are getting along."

Barnabas wanted to take John Mark with them, as they had done on their first missionary trip. But Paul felt it wouldn't be right to take him because he had left them to go back home during their first mission trip.

Paul and Barnabas had a big disagreement about this, so each went their own way. Barnabas took John Mark and sailed to Cyprus, while Paul chose Silas to go with him and headed for Syria.

Should Christians always agree about everything?

Paul and Barnabas were best friends who were passionate about serving God. Yet, it was probably their enthusiasm that made them feel so strongly. The problem was that on their first missionary trip John Mark had decided that this was not for him (see Acts 13:13).

Paul didn't want a half-hearted quitter tagging along. His goal was to serve the Lord! Paul wanted a helper who was dedicated to the Lord – not someone who would get him sidetracked.

Barnabas, on the other hand, always looked for the best in others. He was the one who helped Paul get started, and had seen the potential in John Mark. Now John Mark was willing to try again, and Barnabas was willing to give him another chance.

God uses our different gifts and personalities to serve Him in different ways. Paul's firm strength kept him focused, while Barnabas' friendship brought out the best in others.

NOVEMBER 21

VERSE FOR TODAY
And whatever you do, whether in word or deed,
do it all in the name of the Lord Jesus …
COLOSSIANS 3:17

PAUL

Paul's second missionary trip

Paul and Silas set out on their second missionary trip to visit the churches that they had started up on their first trip.

But as they traveled through the province of Asia, the Holy Spirit kept them from preaching there. At one stage, they tried to go into the area of Bithynia, but the Spirit of Jesus stopped them again. So they carried on traveling across the province of Mysia, to the coastal city of Troas.

During the night, Paul had a vision of a man from Macedonia begging him to come and help them. After Paul had seen the vision, he got ready at once to leave for Macedonia and boarded a ship going to Philippi.

Should I wait for God to guide me before I do good?

NOVEMBER 22

Is it okay to do good and speak out for Jesus at any time, or should I wait for Him to show me what to do?

God has made us in His image and given us the ability to reason – to respond to the feeling that inspires us; use what we've learned; check with what we believe and then make a decision. Sometimes Jesus speaks to us directly by putting His thoughts in our minds. We have the mind of Christ (1 Corinthians 2:16). When we are in tune with His Spirit and follow Bible principles, most of what we do should be exactly what God wants.

A ship that isn't moving cannot be steered. Paul didn't sit around waiting for God to point him in the right direction. It was as he went out to preach that the Spirit showed him where to go.

It is better to go out and do things that please God than do nothing while you wait for "special instructions".

VERSE FOR TODAY

Therefore, as we have opportunity, let us do good to all people, especially to those who belong to the family of believers.
GALATIANS 6:10

PAUL

Paul and Silas in prison

When Paul and Silas were in Philippi, they set a slave girl free from an evil spirit that lived in her. The girl's owners were furious because she had made money for them by telling people what would happen in the future. So they dragged Paul and Silas to the marketplace and had them stripped and beaten. Then they took Paul and Silas and threw them in jail. The jailer who would be sentenced to death if he let them escape, locked them in the inner dungeon and put their feet in wooden clamps.

At about midnight, while Paul and Silas were praying and singing praises, there was a great earthquake! The prison doors swung open and the prisoners' chains fell off. The jailer – who had been sleeping – was so afraid that he was about to kill himself with his sword. But Paul yelled, "Don't do it! We are all here."

Will praising God change my difficult situation?

From what happened to Paul and Silas, it seems that when we praise God in difficult circumstances, He sets us free from our horrible situation.

Paul and Silas probably had no idea that their praise songs were like a key to their prison cell. The fact that they didn't try to escape shows that they were quite happy to stay in the cell – if that's where God wanted them to be. Their praise songs were bringing glory to God; blessing the other prisoners and helping them to feel the peace and joy of the Lord.

Praising the Lord in faith may well bring a change to your situation because He is such an awesome and powerful God. But even if you are not set free from your troubles straight away, singing praise songs to God will set your *heart* free.

NOVEMBER 23

VERSE FOR TODAY
I have learned the secret of being content in any and every situation.
PHILIPPIANS 4:12

PAUL

Paul in Athens

When the earthquake struck the prison where Paul and Silas were prisoners, the terrified jailer asked them what he should do to be saved.

"Believe in the Lord Jesus, and you will be saved, and your family too," they said. Then Paul and Silas told them about Jesus, and they all believed.

Paul and Silas were released from prison and left Philippi. They traveled to Thessalonica, and on to Berea, preaching in the synagogues. Some listened to them eagerly, while others were jealous and caused so much trouble for them that the believers feared for Paul's life and sent him to Athens. While Paul was waiting for Silas and Timothy to join him, he told the people of Athens about the only true God. Some, who liked discussing new ideas, invited Paul to tell them more.

"I see that you people are very religious," Paul said. "As I walked through your city, I saw the places where you worship, and found an altar with the words, 'To an Unknown God' written on it. Well, I know this God: He is the One who made the world and everything in it."

Do all religions worship the same God?

You might have heard someone say, "It doesn't really matter what you believe because all religions worship the same God."

Well, that's what the people in Athens thought. In fact, they weren't quite sure who God is, so they made idols and altars for many different gods. And, just in case they missed one, they even had an altar dedicated to an 'Unknown God'. This gave Paul a chance to tell them about the God they didn't know. "Your imaginary gods are dead," he told them. "There is only one God, the Creator of heaven and earth."

NOVEMBER 24

VERSE FOR TODAY
For there is one God and one mediator
between God and men, the man Christ Jesus.
1 TIMOTHY 2:5

PAUL

Paul in Corinth

After preaching in Athens, Paul went to the city of Corinth. There he stayed with Aquila and Priscilla, who were also tentmakers like Paul.

One night, the Lord spoke to Paul in a vision. "Do not be afraid," He said. "Keep on speaking about Me, for I am with you. No one will attack you or harm you in any way." So Paul stayed in Corinth for a year and a half, teaching people the Word of God.

When Gallio became the new governor, a group of Jews arrested Paul and took him to Gallio to be judged. They accused Paul of getting people to worship God in a way that was against their law. But Gallio became impatient with the Jews and said, "This man has not committed a crime. Sort out your own religious problems!"

And with that, Paul was set free. God had kept His promise!

How do I know which promises in the Bible are for me?

The Bible is filled with the promises of God: some were made to the Israelites of the Old Testament, some are for born-again believers and some promises are for everyone.

There are also personal promises, like the promise God made to Paul, to keep him from being harmed. And as we know, God did keep Paul safe while he was in Corinth. Does this mean that the promise God made to Paul has no meaning or value for us?

God's written Word is also His living Word. He uses the Bible to speak to us personally, even though our situation may be quite different from the one in the Bible. That is the way God guides us – and that is what makes the Bibles so useful and exciting.

VERSE FOR TODAY
For the word of God is living and active.
HEBREWS 4:12

PAUL

Acts 21:27-36, 25:9-12

Paul is arrested

From Corinth, Paul sailed across the sea, visiting some of the churches he had started. His long journey ended at the seaside city of Caesarea from where he traveled on land back to Jerusalem.

As usual, Paul went to the Temple, and it wasn't long before some of the Jews from the province of Asia noticed Paul and dragged him out of the Temple. They even tried to kill him, but the Roman soldiers stopped the riot and took Paul to the fort.

About forty Jews met secretly and planned to kill Paul, so the commander of the Roman soldiers sent Paul, guarded by a troop of soldiers, to Felix the governor in Caesarea. There, Paul was put in prison until Felix died two years later and Festus became the new commander. Festus wanted to send Paul back to Jerusalem to be tried by the Jews, but Paul – being a Roman citizen – asked to be tried by the Emperor of Rome instead.

How can I be sure of my faith?

How could Paul have been so sure of what he believed when people kept telling him that he was wrong?

Jesus was so real to Paul that it didn't matter to him what others believed. When you are around others who don't believe in Jesus and you wonder if their ideas could be true, remember these few points:

Talking to Jesus is as real as talking to one of your friends – whom you can't see – on the phone. Ask the Holy Spirit to let you feel the closeness of Jesus.

Read the Bible, which is the Book of Truth (John 17:17). The more we read the Bible, the stronger our faith becomes.

NOVEMBER 26

VERSE FOR TODAY
Consequently, faith comes from hearing the message,
and the message is heard through the word of Christ.
ROMANS 10:17

PAUL

A storm at sea

Paul was handed over to an officer and put on a ship sailing to Rome where he was to be tried (judged) by the Emperor.

A strong wind was blowing out at sea, which made sailing slow and pretty rough. Eventually they got to a harbor called Fair Havens where they stayed for some time. The captain and crew didn't want to spend winter at that harbor and were ready to sail out a few days later. But Paul warned them: "Men, it will be dangerous for us to keep sailing. We must stay here!"

But when the wind died down, the captain decided to set sail and head out to sea. However, once they were out at sea, the strong wind started to blow again, so the sailors had to throw cargo overboard to keep the ship from sinking. They lowered the sail and let the wind and waves drive the ship along for two whole weeks.

Will the Holy Spirit warn me of danger?

Paul was guided by the Holy Spirit (not by the wind). He had learned to pray about things and be sensitive to what the Lord was saying to him.

Some people rely on the advice of experts; others look for signs to guide them. Then there are those who simply react to circumstances. In this case, the captain of the ship was the expert – he knew the sea. The signs were good – the wind had died down. The circumstances weren't great – no one wanted to spend winter in that dump of a harbor.

It isn't wrong to ask others for their opinion to help you make a sensible decision. However, when you pray before you make the decision, the Holy Spirit can warn you of danger.

VERSE FOR TODAY
The way of a fool seems right to him, but a wise man listens to advice.
PROVERBS 12:15

PAUL

The shipwreck

One night, while on the ship, an angel of the Lord appeared to Paul and said, "Don't be afraid, Paul! You will appear before the Emperor of Rome. And because of God's goodness to you, He will also spare the lives of those with you."

The next day, Paul spoke to the men on the ship. "You should have listened to me and stayed in the harbor," he said. "But take heart, although the ship and everything on it will sink, not one of you will drown."

Then everyone had something to eat; then they threw the rest of the food into the sea to lighten the ship.

When daylight came, they saw an island in the distance so they hoisted the sail and headed for the beach. But the ship struck a sandbank and started to break up. Everyone jumped overboard into the rough sea. Some swam ashore while others clung to pieces of wood, until finally, everyone reached the shore, cold and exhausted.

Is it wrong to feel like giving up?

Do you think Paul ever felt like giving up? Do you think it is wrong to feel discouraged? This wasn't the first shipwreck Paul had survived. It didn't seem fair that Paul, who served God with such eagerness, should face so much hardship.

Feelings are real. We wouldn't be human if we didn't get discouraged. What is important, however, is that we don't allow the feeling of discouragement to control our actions, because then we would probably quit.

Paul realized that having a goal – and being determined to reach that goal – made the decision to keep going much easier (Philippians 3:14).

VERSE FOR TODAY
Let us not become weary in doing good, for at the proper
time we will reap a harvest if we do not give up.
GALATIANS 6:9

PAUL

In Rome at last

The people living on the island of Malta – where Paul had been shipwrecked – were kind and helpful. They made a fire on the beach where the survivors could warm themselves, and they also gave them food. After three months, those who had been shipwrecked boarded a ship heading for Rome.

When Paul arrived in Rome, he was allowed to live in a house with a soldier guarding him. Paul lived in the house for two years and welcomed all those who came to see him. Although he was not allowed to leave the house, he was able to preach about the kingdom of God and teach those who came to hear more about Jesus.

Did God really want Paul to spend years in prison?

Although the house where Paul lived for two years was guarded day and night, it was a lot better than the other prisons he had been in. Paul had spent many years in prison, not because he had done something wrong, but because he told others about Jesus.

You might think that Paul could have reached many more people if he hadn't 'wasted' all those years sitting in jail. But Paul saw it differently, and this is what he said; "Because of my chains, most of the brothers in the Lord have been encouraged to speak the word of God more courageously and fearlessly" (Philippians 1:14). Now it was no longer just Paul preaching. Because of his courage and faith, many others started speaking out for Jesus.

And while Paul was in prison, he wasn't just sitting there doing nothing. Because he couldn't get around to visit the churches, he wrote letters to them and to his friends. These letters have become part of the Bible; and now, everyone can read the words of Paul and be blessed by them.

NOVEMBER 29

VERSE FOR TODAY

(Paul said), "And pray for us, too, that God may open a door for our message, so that we may proclaim the mystery of Christ, for which I am in chains."
COLOSSIANS 4:3

PAUL

Paul's letter to the Romans

While Paul was in Corinth, he wrote a letter to the people in Rome. Paul was longing to go to Rome but hadn't been able to get there, so he wrote a letter to the Romans telling them of God's plan to save them from sin.

Paul wrote: Sin came into the world because of Adam's disobedience. Because of one man, Adam, sin and death spread all over the world; but through another man, Jesus, there is forgiveness for everyone.

The Lord gave us laws to help us realize that we can never be perfect, and so, we must turn to Him for forgiveness and help. The more sin there is, the more we realize just how willing God is to accept us. Does that mean we should keep on sinning so that God will keep on showing His kindness? Of course not! How can we keep on sinning if our old sin-nature has died? With our new life in Jesus, God has given us power over sin – the same power that raised Jesus from the dead.

Is a person who keeps the Ten Commandments sinless?

Have you ever tried to pick yourself up by your shoelaces? Everyone knows that would be silly because the force of gravity is pulling you down.

Just as our bodies are affected by the law of gravity, our spirits are affected by the law of sin. From the day we are born, both these forces pull at us – that is why we fall, and that is why we sin (Romans 7:23).

God gave us rules to show us that, on our own, we can never be good enough to meet His standard of holiness. There is only one way to be sinless, and that is by allowing Jesus to fill us with His goodness (Romans 8:1).

VERSE FOR TODAY

"There is no one righteous, not even one."
ROMANS 3:10

December

PAUL

A living sacrifice

Paul's letter to the Romans continued as he wrote: "Dear brothers, because God has been so merciful to us, give yourselves as a living sacrifice to Him by being completely dedicated to Him and wanting to please Him. This is the kind of worship you should offer to God.

Don't copy the behavior of godless people, but be a new and different person on the inside by thinking thoughts that are good and pure. Then you will know exactly what God wants you to do; what is good and what pleases Him.

Don't think of yourselves more highly than you should, but be honest and humble in the way you see yourself. Rather measure yourself by the amount of faith God has given you."

Do we still need to offer sacrifices to God?

In Old Testament times (before Jesus came), God allowed people to kill an animal and put it on an altar as a sacrifice for their sin. The sacrifice had to be perfect – without a single spot or fault. But this sacrifice was only a sign pointing to the day when Jesus would give His life as the real Sacrifice. When Jesus died on the cross and rose again from the dead, His sacrifice was enough to pay for the sins of the whole world. This means that people no longer need to offer animals for their sins.

However, there is an offering that we should bring to God every day: a sacrifice of praise for His mercy. By allowing God to be in charge of our lives, we are offering ourselves to Him as a living sacrifice! Although we are not perfect (as a sacrifice should be), God is pleased to accept us because Jesus has made us spotless!

DECEMBER 1

VERSE FOR TODAY

Through Jesus, therefore, let us continually offer to God a sacrifice of praise – the fruit of lips that confess his name.
HEBREWS 13:15

Real freedom

The believers in Corinth were surrounded by people who lived in sin and did as they pleased. Paul wrote this letter to help them understand that their freedom in Christ did not mean they could do everything they wished.

"Although people may say that it's okay to do anything you want – not everything is good and helpful," Paul said. "Think of those who may fall into sin because of something you are doing. For example, God made all sorts of food for us to enjoy, yet there are those who feel that it is wrong to eat meat that has been offered to idols. You may ask, 'Why should I have less freedom because of what other people believe?'

But let me tell you this: whatever you do, whether you eat or drink, do everything for God's glory."

Am I free to do anything?

When Jesus died for us, He bought us with His blood and freed us from being slaves of the devil. And because the devil is no longer our master, he no longer controls us!

Instead, we now willingly serve the Lord because we love Him with the love He put in our hearts. We, who belong to Christ, need not fear punishment for our sin, because through Jesus Christ, the Spirit of life has set us free from sin and death (Romans 8:1-2). Now we don't keep God's rules only because we're afraid of being punished, but we do what is right because the Holy Spirit shows us what pleases Him.

Jesus did not set us free to carry on sinning and do as we like; but rather, He has given us real freedom – freedom from sin, freedom from guilt, and freedom to enjoy life fully.

DECEMBER 2

VERSE FOR TODAY
It is for freedom that Christ has set us free.
GALATIANS 5:1

PAUL

One body

In his first letter, Paul told the Corinthians that they are all part of the Body of Jesus Christ (verse 27). "Our bodies are made up of many parts. When the parts are put together, they become one body. That is how it is with the body of Christ: each of us is a part of it. The Holy Spirit has fitted us together even though we are different and come from different backgrounds.

One part of the body cannot say to another, 'I don't need you!' If the whole body were and eye, how could you hear? And if it were an ear, how could you smell? God, in His wisdom, has put ever part of the body where He wants it to be and has given it a special task.

If one part of the body suffers, the other parts suffer with it. If one part is praised, all the other parts are glad as well."

How do I know which part of the body I am?

Jesus Christ is the Head of the church, and the church is the body of Christ (Colossians 1:18). If Jesus rules in your heart, you have become part of the body. Without you there would be an important part missing! Every person, whether a child or an adult, can be a blessing to the other parts by letting the fruit of the Spirit show in their lives.

As you grow, God will show you the special tasks He wants you to do for Him. He has given you spiritual gifts to help you do your part well – whatever it may be. As you faithfully serve the Lord and help others, you will discover what spiritual gifts you've been given. Some of the gifts of the Holy Spirit are listed in 1 Corinthians 12:8-10 and Romans 12:6-8.

VERSE FOR TODAY

From him the whole body, joined and held together by every supporting ligament, grows and builds itself up in love, as each part does its work.
EPHESIANS 4:16

All about love

After explaining to the Corinthians that we are all part of the body of Christ, Paul went on to write about the kind of love that keeps the body together and working properly.

He said to them, "If I had the gift of speaking in a heavenly language but didn't love others, I would just be making a noise. If I had the gift of preaching and was wise enough to know every secret; or if I had enough faith to move a mountain, but I didn't have love, I would be nothing. If I gave away everything I own and were willing to die for someone, but didn't have love, it wouldn't mean a thing.

Love is patient and kind; never jealous or proud; never selfish or irritable. Love does not want to remember wrongs. Love is not happy with evil, but is happy with the truth. Love never gives up! It always trusts and it always hopes."

How can I show love when I don't feel like it?

When things go well, it's easy to love our family and friends. But what about the times when we feel miserable? And what about showing love to people we don't like and who irritate us?

Jesus knows that your heart doesn't bubble over with nice feelings all the time. He doesn't expect you to like every single person. Yet He did say that we should love everyone – just as He loves us (John 13:34). Love is measured by your kind-hearted actions, not by your feelings. And because love doesn't depend on how you feel, you can be kind to everyone – even when you don't feel loving!

DECEMBER 4

VERSE FOR TODAY
Dear friends, let us love one another, for love comes from God.
1 John 4:7

PAUL

Living in a tent

In his second letter to the Corinthians, Paul encouraged the believers to look forward to what God has prepared.

He wrote: "We know that when this earthly tent we live in now is taken down (when we die), God will give us new bodies – homes in heaven that will last forever. That is why we look forward to the new bodies we will have in heaven, which God will put on us like new clothes. Then our fragile bodies, which are like flimsy tents, will be made new and completely perfect.

It is God who has made us and prepared us for this change. He has sent the Holy Spirit to live in us as a promise of what lies ahead; and so we believe these things even though we cannot see them. That is why it is our goal to please God."

In what way is our body like a tent?

Have you ever spent a whole night in a small tent? It is fun when the weather is fine. But when the wind is howling and it is pouring with rain, a flapping, shaky tent no longer seems the best place to be. In the same way, our bodies are fragile in a world that is often unfriendly and unsafe. Yet, just as you can stay dry inside a tent, even in a storm, so your spirit will be kept safe inside your body until God gives your spirit a new home – a body that will last forever!

When we get our new bodies in heaven, we will be perfect. We won't just be like invisible spirits or angels, we will have real bodies! And the best part is that our new bodies will never feel pain, embarrass us, or make us feel that we're not good enough. We will be totally happy forever.

DECEMBER 5

VERSE FOR TODAY

But our citizenship is in heaven. And we eagerly await a Savior from there, the Lord Jesus Christ, who ... will transform our lowly bodies so that they will be like his glorious body.
PHILIPPIANS 3:20-21

Light and darkness

Paul wrote and told the believers in Corinth not to become partners with those whose values and beliefs do not honor God. "Right and wrong cannot be partners, just as light and darkness cannot live together," he said. "Jesus Christ and the devil can never agree; neither will a Christian and an unbeliever have the same purpose in life."

God said, "I will make My home with My people and live among them; I will be their God and they will be My people. You must leave them and be separate from them. Have nothing to do with the sinfulness of the world, and I will accept you."

How can I keep myself separate from the world?

What does it mean to be separate from the world? We know that Paul isn't saying that we should leave this world, because God put us on this earth for a purpose. What Paul means is that we should stay away from things (and people) that draw us away from God.

Jesus, the holy Son of God, also came to this sinful earth – and even He was tempted. The devil tried to make all sorts of deals with Jesus by offering Him things that would get Him to agree to his plan. But Jesus did not sin. So the devil started using the people to trap Him (Matthew 22:15).

We live in a sinful world with sinful people. We cannot leave this world to escape sin, nor can we avoid ungodly people. But we should be careful not to make close friends or be partners with those who are in the habit of doing bad things. If we do, we will soon be tempted to do the wrong things they do. Then others won't be able to see that we are different from those who don't love God.

DECEMBER 6

VERSE FOR TODAY

Do not conform any longer to the pattern of this world,
but be transformed by the renewing of your mind.
ROMANS 12:2

PAUL

The painful thorn

Paul tells us a bit about himself and how that an ongoing problem helped him not to become proud.

He wrote, "If I boasted about myself it wouldn't just be foolish talk – I would be telling the truth. But I don't want anyone to think that I am great because of the things they have seen me do or heard me say. In fact, to keep me from becoming full of myself, I was given a problem that has been like a painful thorn. It reminds me of my weakness and keeps me from becoming proud.

I asked the Lord three times to take this problem away. But every time He said, 'My grace is all you need. When you are weak, My power shows up best in you.'

So, now I am glad that I have this weakness, because it helps me to rely even more on God's power and protection. For when I feel weak, I am actually strong because of God's power in me."

Can any good come from the things that frustrate me?

If you have stood on a thorn or had a sharp stone in your shoe, you would know that every step hurts until you stop and take it out. Paul tells us of a thorn that kept bothering him. We know that it wasn't an actual thorn, but a problem that pricked and irritated him all the time. Yet Paul's problem didn't keep him from doing God's work; it actually helped him depend more on God's grace and power. He could have been proud of who he was (see 2 Corinthians 11:21-28), but instead his thorny problem helped him to humbly trust God for strength and wisdom every day.

DECEMBER 7

VERSE FOR TODAY

In all these things we are more than conquerors through him who loved us.
ROMANS 8:37

PAUL

Live by the Spirit

Paul wrote a letter to the Christians in Galatia to remind them of the simple message of being saved by faith and living by the Spirit – not by a set of rules.

"Christ set us free to enjoy perfect freedom in Him. Be careful that you don't get yourselves tied up in the chains of slavery again. By faith you were freed from the chains that kept you tied to a set of rules and customs. What counts now is a faith that comes from your love for God.

You were doing so well. Who made you stop walking in the way of Truth? It certainly wasn't the Lord: He called you to a life of freedom! Don't use your freedom to do wrong. Rather use it to love and serve others. For God's rules are based on one command: Love others as you love yourself."

How does the Spirit make the Christian life exciting?

Do you go to church only because you're expected to go? Do you read your Bible only because you feel guilty if you don't? When we don't have a relationship with Jesus that is real, we could easily slip into a routine of 'religious duties' that become a heavy burden of boring rules.

Obviously it isn't wrong for us to obey the rules God has given us in the Bible. But the Lord doesn't want us to be trapped by the rules we have added to ease our conscience. When you allow Jesus to be your best friend, the Spirit sets your heart free.

So, for example, if you have always said the same prayer when giving thanks for a meal, remember that the Spirit has set you free to use your own words of thanks.

Let love, not rules, be the reason for everything you do!

DECEMBER 8

VERSE FOR TODAY

This is love for God: to obey his commands.
And his commands are not burdensome.
1 John 5:3

PAUL

Galatians 5:16-23

The fruit of the Spirit

"Let the Holy Spirit control your lives!" Paul said in his letter to the Galatians. "When the Spirit is in control of your thoughts, you won't want to do all the wrong things your human nature wants you to do.

For our sinful nature wants to do the exact opposite of what the Holy Spirit tells us to do.

What our human nature wants is quite obvious. It shows itself by impure thoughts, hatred, fighting, jealousy, anger, selfishness and complaining.

But when the Holy Spirit controls our lives, a special kind of fruit starts showing – the fruit of the Spirit. The good things that start to grow in our lives are; love, joy, peace, patience, kindness, goodness, faithfulness, gentleness and self-control."

How can I bear fruit?

Have you ever walked through an orchard or picked fruit from a fruit tree? It's a real miracle how God makes colorful, juicy fruit grow on woody branches. When the Holy Spirit comes to live in you, He does a miracle too! He makes you new and then lets the fruit of the Spirit show in your life!

An apple tree doesn't have to try hard to make apples grow from its branches. It just soaks up sunlight from above and moisture from the soil. In the same way, when you are rooted in Christ (Colossians 2:6-7), you will soak up the fresh newness of the Spirit. By living in the sunshine of God's love you will produce the kind of goodness that pleases the Lord. Then, as you grow in Him, He will work through the struggles in your life to trim back the branches that aren't growing right. Then you will bear even more fruit!

DECEMBER 9

VERSE FOR TODAY
Live as children of light (for the fruit of the light consists in all goodness, righteousness and truth).
Ephesians 5:8-9

PAUL

All about relationships

Paul wrote this letter to the churches in and around the Greek city of Ephesus. He gives them practical advice on how to act in their relationships:

"Children, obey your parents, for this is the right thing to do. Respect your father and mother. This commandment comes with a promise of a life filled with God's blessing.

Parents, don't treat your children in a way that will discourage them and make them resentful. Rather, bring them up with a loving discipline that pleases the Lord.

Workers, obey the person in charge and be eager to do your very best as if you were serving Christ. Don't only work when someone is watching, but work gladly and honestly as if you were doing it for the Lord.

Masters, treat your workers fairly. Do not threaten them, since you also have a Master and Lord in heaven who has no favorites."

Why is obedience so important?

Have you noticed how fair God is? God has given everyone rules and responsibilities, including parents, teachers and bosses. It isn't only children who have to obey and do things for others.

Your mom and dad have many things to care about. They may work for a grumpy boss, have difficult people working for them, and then come home to do all the things that parents need to do.

It isn't easy to have the right attitude toward everyone all the time. But when you realize that by obeying your parents you actually make their task easier, it isn't all that hard to please them – or even surprise them by doing more than they expect.

DECEMBER 10

VERSE FOR TODAY
Do everything without complaining or arguing, so that you may become blameless and pure, children of God.
PHILIPPIANS 2:14-15

PAUL

Ephesians 6:10-17

The Armor of God

Paul ends his letter to the Ephesians with practical example to help believers in their battle against their enemy, the devil.

Be strong by relying on the Lord's strength in you. Put on the full armor of God so that you will be able to stand up against the enemy's tricks. For we are not fighting against people, but against the spiritual forces of evil.

Use every part of the armor God has given you. Don't let the devil push you down, but keep standing firm when he tempts you.

To do this, you will need the belt of truth around your waist and the breastplate of holy goodness to cover your heart. Wear shoes that will help you spread the Good News of God's peace. You need faith as your shield to stop the burning arrows which the devil aims at you. God's gift of salvation is your helmet, and your sword is God's Word, the Bible.

Why do we need armor?

Our God – the God of peace – has an enemy who wants to destroy all that is good and all that belongs to Him! The devil – who was thrown out of heaven when he rebelled – hates goodness.

One of the ways the devil tries to get back at God is by tempting us to sin. When we sin, we are wounded by the sin, and the Lord is dishonored. But God hasn't left us to struggle against the enemy without any help. He has given us strong armor to stop evil. We have armor that shields and protects us, and we have a sword (the Bible) to defend ourselves.

The Armor of God gives us power to stop sinning. This is how the God of peace gives you victory (see Romans 16:20).

DECEMBER 11

VERSE FOR TODAY
The night is nearly over; the day is almost here. So let us put aside the deeds of darkness and put on the armor of light.
ROMANS 13:12

PAUL

Being like Jesus

Philippians is a letter Paul wrote to the church he started in Philippi. In this letter, Paul shows them how true joy can only come from following Jesus.

He writes: "If you are encouraged from being brought together by Christ, if you are comforted by His love and enjoy His closeness, if your hearts are tender and caring, then make me truly happy by working together toward one goal. Don't be selfish and don't try to make a good impression on others, but be humble and think of others as being better than yourselves.

Your attitude should be the same as that of Jesus Christ, who, having the nature of God, did not demand to be equal with God, but left His glory to become a servant here on earth. He was obedient to His Father and gave His life for us on the cross. Because He was willing to do this, God raised Him up to be above all and gave Him a name that is greater than any other name."

Can I really be like Jesus?

Does Paul really mean that we should have the same attitude that Jesus had? How can we be as caring and forgiving as Jesus is, and how can we be completely humble and obedient all the time?

Well, the Bible wouldn't tell us to do something if it were impossible. Read Philippians 2:2 again and you will see that the one thing that helps us have the right attitude is *love*. Jesus' love for God and His love for us is the reason His attitude pleases God completely.

Ask the Spirit to pour His love into your heart.

DECEMBER 12

VERSE FOR TODAY

God has poured out his love into our hearts
by the Holy Spirit, whom he has given us.
ROMANS 5:5

PAUL

Completely satisfied

In Paul's letter to the Philippians, he tells them how they can be truly happy in Jesus.

He says, "Be really happy in the Lord! Let your gentleness be seen by all. The Lord is coming soon! Do not worry about anything, but in every situation tell God what you need, and remember to thank Him for His answers. God's peace – which is more wonderful than we can understand – will keep your hearts and your thoughts safe in Jesus.

And now, I remind you to keep your thoughts on things that are true, good, right, pure, lovely, and honorable.

I am glad that you could show your care for me (even though I have not felt uncared for). For I have learnt to be satisfied with what I have. I know what it is like to be in need, and what it is like to have enough. I have learnt to be content, whether I have enough or whether I don't."

Is it wrong to complain to God in our prayers?

Remember how the Israelites kept grumbling and complaining on their way to the Promised Land? God became angry about their constant moaning because they weren't satisfied with the way He provided for them. On the other hand, David often told God exactly how he felt when Saul was chasing him all over the countryside. "I pour out my complaint before Him; before Him I tell my trouble" (Psalm 142:2).

God doesn't mind when we talk to Him about how we feel, or when we tell Him about our problems. But we shouldn't just complain to Him and not trust Him for an answer. By faith, we must believe that He is able to change our situation, if and when He chooses.

DECEMBER 13

VERSE FOR TODAY

Do not be anxious about anything, but in everything, by prayer and petition, with thanksgiving, present your requests to God.
PHILIPPIANS 4:6

I can do all things

Paul ends his letter to the Philippians by telling them what a blessing the gift they sent him had been.

He writes to them saying, "I can do anything through the power that Jesus Christ gives me!

It was so good of you to help me in my troubles. In the early days of my preaching, you were the only ones to help me. When I was in Thessalonica, you helped me more than once. What pleased me more than receiving your gifts was to know that God would bless you for giving it.

My God will give you all you need from His storehouse of riches and blessings. To God our Father be all the glory for ever and ever! Amen."

Can I do the impossible?

Did Paul say that he could do *many* things through Christ's strength? (see verse 13). Did Paul say he could do *most* things? No, Paul said that he can do ALL things through the power of Jesus that works in his life.

Does that mean Paul was able to do anything and everything he wanted to? Could Paul have jumped over the moon? No! Paul knew that Jesus would give him strength to do the things God wanted him to do.

Paul also had the strength to face his problems because he had learnt to be content (at peace) in whatever situation he found himself. Despite Paul's hardships, he kept going because he knew that God was in control all the time.

God promises to give us everything we need in order to do the things that please Him – and that may well include the "impossible"!

DECEMBER 14

VERSE FOR TODAY
"Everything is possible for him who believes."
MARK 9:23

PAUL

Jesus Christ, the Creator

While Paul was in prison in Rome, he wrote a letter to the Colossians telling them about Jesus, the Ruler of all.

Paul wrote that "Jesus is the exact image of the unseen God. He existed before anything in creation. Through Him, God created everything in all of creation – the things we can see and the things we can't: spiritual powers, rulers and kings. All were created by Him and for His glory. He existed before anything was created and He holds all of creation together perfectly.

Jesus was also the first to conquer eternal death by rising from the grave. He has become the first in all things. For God wanted all of creation to come back to Him through His Son who brought peace by His death on the cross."

Who created the earth?

In Genesis 1:1 it says, "In the beginning God created the heavens and the earth."

Then, in John 1:1-3 it says, "In the beginning was the Word (Jesus), and the Word was with God, and the Word was God. He was with God in the beginning. Through Him all things were made; without Him nothing was made that has been made."

We know that Jesus and God are one (John 10:30).

We know that the Holy Spirit was also there, when the earth was still shapeless and empty (see Genesis 1:2). God, Jesus, and the Holy Spirit do everything together because they are one. So when we think of God creating the world, we know that He created everything through Jesus so that His Son would reign over all creation (1 Corinthians 15:27-28).

DECEMBER 15

VERSE FOR TODAY

"I am the LORD, who has made all things, who alone stretched out the heavens, who spread out the earth by myself."

ISAIAH 44:24

PAUL

Let peace and love rule

Paul wrote that Christ is all, and is in all. There is nothing that makes one person more special than another because He lives in each one.

He then writes: "Since God has chosen you to live a life of holiness, you should be caring, kind, humble, and gentle. Be patient and understanding with each other; forgiving those who have hurt and upset you.

Let your love be the kind that everyone can see, for love will help you do all these things with the right attitude.

You were chosen to be part of the body of believers; so let the peace of Christ rule in your hearts. And remember to be thankful.

Let the words of Christ be alive and meaningful in your life as you talk to each other about His truths, and sing songs of praise and gratitude to God. So, whatever you do and say, let it bring glory to God."

How can I keep wrong feelings from my heart?

Because we are imperfect and we live in an imperfect world, others hurt us, and we hurt them. When anger, jealousy and guilt fills our hearts, we often take it out on others by our sulky and irritable moods.

There is a way to guard against letting those kinds of emotions rule your heart: by wearing the love of Jesus like a coat around you. Read Colossians 3:14 again. Love will help you be in control of your emotions. When you love others, you can conquer irritability by being patient; pride by humbly helping others; and bitterness by forgiving. When love fills your heart, there won't be room for bad feelings that can lead to sin.

DECEMBER 16

VERSE FOR TODAY

Pursue righteousness, faith, love and peace, along with those who call on the Lord out of a pure heart.
2 TIMOTHY 2:22

PAUL

Jesus is coming in the clouds

Paul wrote this letter to strengthen the Thessalonians in their faith and tell them that Jesus is coming back.

He said, "Fellow Christians, we want you to know what happens to believers who have died so that you won't be sad like those who have no hope. For the Lord will come down from heaven with a loud shout and with the sound of God's trumpet.

The believers who have died will be the first to rise. After that, we who are alive will rise to meet Jesus in the clouds. Then we will be with the Lord forever! So encourage each other with this hope.

This day will come without warning, like a thief in the night. Yet, because you don't live in the darkness of sin, this glorious day – when Jesus comes again – won't take you by surprise."

What happens if I'm sleeping when Jesus comes?

The Christians in Paul's time were looking forward to Jesus coming back in their lifetime. But, as time went by, some believers died. The others became discouraged and wondered whether those who had died would miss out on the great day when Jesus would come back (see Acts 1:11).

Although those who have died are in the Lord's presence right now (Luke 23:43), all believers will be given a special new body on the day that Jesus comes back.

If you have missed out on some big event in the past, you may be afraid of missing out again. But you needn't worry at all! Wherever you are and whatever you are doing; if you love Jesus, you will be taken up in your new body to be with Him forever.

DECEMBER 17

VERSE FOR TODAY

You also must be ready, because the Son of Man will come at an hour when you do not expect him.
Luke 12:40

Sitting and waiting

Paul wrote a second letter to the Christians in Thessalonica to tell them that they shouldn't just sit around waiting for Jesus to come back, but keep working.

He said, "Fellow believers, we command you to stay away from those who are lazy and refuse to work. You should follow the example we set while we were with you. We paid for our food and worked hard day and night to make a living.

If a person doesn't work, he shouldn't eat! We say this because we hear that there are some among you who live lazy lives. As for you who are faithful and obedient, never get tired of doing what is right and good."

What is the difference between resting and being lazy?

The Bible tells us that it is good to rest. In fact, God even commands us to rest! (Exodus 20:9-11). So, if it is good to take it easy, is there really a difference between resting and laziness?

Laziness is when we don't do what's expected of us. For example:
- Leaving work unfinished and doing things half-heartedly.
- Putting things off that should have been done right away.
- Letting others do our share and never offering to help.

Resting is giving our minds and bodies a break. For example;
- We rest by taking a break from our daily activities to sleep.
- We rest in the Lord by spending time with Him.
- We can have fun by spending our free time doing things we really enjoy. Work hard and do your best, then you will enjoy a well-deserved rest!

DECEMBER 18

VERSE FOR TODAY

We do not want you to become lazy, but to imitate those who through faith and patience inherit what has been promised.

HEBREWS 6:12

PAUL

Set an example

Paul wrote a personal letter to his friend Timothy, to encourage him and give him advice about leading a church.

This is what Paul said: "Don't let others look down on you because you are young, but be an example to them by the way you live and speak. Let them see your love, faith and purity. Spend your time preaching and teaching the Word of God.

And don't forget about the spiritual gift you were given when the elders laid their hands on you. Use the abilities God has given you so that others will see how well you are doing.

If you stay true to what is right, God will bless you and make you a blessing to others."

Can a young person be an example to an older person?

Can a child lead a blind man? Yes, it is easy for someone who can see to lead a person who can't. Some people can see with their eyes, but their hearts are blind to the truth of the Gospel. Maybe their hearts have become so hard toward God that even the words of an adult can no longer change their stubborn attitude.

Yet, there is something about a child that can make the heart of an older person soften. Maybe it is the honest and trusting nature of a child. Maybe it is the joy and freedom that shows in a child's face that makes older people long for God's peace.

Jesus once used a little child to teach His disciples about God's kingdom. "Unless you become like little children," He said, "you can never enter the kingdom of God" (Matthew 18:3).

DECEMBER 19

VERSE FOR TODAY
To this you were called, because Christ suffered for you,
leaving you an example, that you should follow in his steps.
1 PETER 2:21

PAUL

Be brave

Paul wrote a second letter to his friend Timothy. Paul wanted to prepare him for the difficult days ahead:

He told Timothy, "Be strong by relying on the grace and power of Jesus Christ. Don't be scared to stand up for Jesus even though you may suffer for doing so.

Be courageous like a loyal soldier. A good soldier wants to please his commander and doesn't get sidetracked by the pleasures of the world.

An athlete running a race cannot hope to win a medal if he doesn't keep the rules of the race.

A farmer, who has worked hard by plowing and sowing, should be the first to enjoy a share of the harvest."

Is the Christian life always going to be tough?

A soldier doesn't have an easy life. He has to be brave and obey every instruction his commander gives him. An athlete has to train hard every single day so that he'll be fit to run his race. The farmer has to work hard in his field to grow his crop.

You could be thinking that if the Christian life is anything like this, it sure sounds like a lot of hard work.

Although the Christian life is hard, we are not alone. Jesus, who understands our struggles and hardships, is with us to help us all the time.

Always remember: the soldier is on the winning side and his battle will be over some day (1 Corinthians 15:57). The athlete will win a prize when he has finished the race (Philippians 3:14). A day will come when the farmer can rest and enjoy the harvest (James 3:18).

DECEMBER 20

VERSE FOR TODAY
He will keep you strong to the end, so that you will
be blameless on the day of our Lord Jesus Christ.
1 Corinthians 1:8

Doing what is good

Titus was a pastor who served the church on the island of Crete. Paul wrote this letter to advise him about running his church, and what to teach:

"Remind your people to respect and obey their leaders. They should not say bad things about others, but be peaceful and friendly, having a gentle attitude. For we ourselves were once foolish and disobedient.

But when God showed us His kindness and love, He saved us – not because of any good we may have done – but because of His kindness. He saved us by washing away our sins and making us new through the Holy Spirit. And having been made completely good in God's eyes, we can share in the riches of eternal life."

What happens to our sin when God forgives us?

Some think that when they no longer feel guilty about a sin, they don't have to do anything about it because it has somehow faded away. Although you probably know that you should always say sorry when you've done wrong, you may not realize that when you ask God to forgive you, He actually has to do something with your sin to get rid of it.

When Jesus died on the cross, God put all our sins on Jesus. Every time we ask God to forgive us, Jesus' blood washes our sin away and makes us clean. Micah the prophet talks about God actually taking our sin and throwing it in the deepest part of the sea (Micah 7:19). God takes our sin so far away that no one will ever see it again, and even God won't think about it ever again!

DECEMBER 21

VERSE FOR TODAY

As far as the east is from the west, so far
has he removed our transgressions from us.
PSALM 103:12

Be merciful

Paul wrote this short note to his friend Philemon asking him to forgive a slave of his who had run away:

"To Philemon, a dear friend and fellow-worker,

I ask you to please show kindness to Onesimus (O-nesi-mus), who became like a son to me when he came to know the Lord while I was in prison.

Onesimus has not been of much use to you in the past, but now he has become useful both to you and to me. I am sending him back to you; and in a way, I am sad because I would have liked to keep him here with me.

Maybe Onesimus left you for a short while so that you could have him back, not as a slave, but as a brother. Please welcome him back as if you were welcoming me."

Why should we be merciful to others?

In Paul's time there were laws that gave the master of a slave complete power over him.

Philemon had every right to have his slave Onesimus killed for running away. However, he now had to choose whether to use his right to punish Onesimus, or listen to Paul and be merciful. What would you have done?

Jesus said, "Blessed are the merciful, for they will be shown mercy" (Matthew 5:7). Every one of us has run away from God and deserves His punishment (Isaiah 53:6). But Jesus has been merciful by forgiving us and taking us back, not as slaves or servants, but as friends (John 15:15). That is true mercy!

Will you use an opportunity to get even with someone who wronged you, or be merciful?

DECEMBER 22

VERSE FOR TODAY
So you are no longer a slave, but a son; and since
you are a son, God has made you also an heir.
GALATIANS 4:7

JAMES

Looking in a mirror

James, the brother of Jesus and a leader in the church at Jerusalem, wrote this letter to Christians in far-off places:

"My dear brothers,

Remember this: It is best to listen much, speak little and not become angry. For anger does not bring out the goodness in us that God is looking for.

So, get rid of sin and bad habits in your life and be glad that God's Word has been planted in your hearts.

Don't only listen to the Word, but do what it says. Someone who hears the Word and doesn't do what it says is like a person who looks at his face in a mirror, then goes away and forgets what he looks like. But the one who keeps looking into God's Word, remembers it, and does what it says, will be blessed by God in everything he does."

How often should I read the Bible?

Would it be okay if I only read the Bible once a week?

If you didn't use a mirror, how would you know whether your hair is a mess or whether your face is dirty? The Bible is even better than a mirror because it can show the spots of sin in your life. When you read your Bible, you will start seeing yourself as God sees you on the inside.

You wouldn't look at someone else to find out if your face is dirty. In the same way you shouldn't compare yourself with others to find out if your life is clean and pleasing to the Lord. Keep looking into God's "Mirror" by reading the Bible every single day. Once you have read it, do what it says and you will be blessed!

DECEMBER 23

VERSE FOR TODAY
I have hidden your word in my heart that I might not sin against you.
PSALM 119:11

JAMES

Asking for things

"How do quarrels and fights start?" James asks in his letter to believers.

He answers them by saying, "They come from wanting pleasures and earthly things so much that it upsets you on the inside. You keep longing for these things until you can't think of anything else, and when you can't get what you want, you become angry.

The reason you don't have the things you want is that you don't ask God for them; and when you do ask, God doesn't give them to you because you are selfish and greedy.

God stands against those who are proud, but His underserved blessing is on those who are humble."

Is it wrong to ask God for things we don't really need?

Is James saying that we shouldn't ask God for any of the fun things we would like to have?

James is talking here about things that draw us away from God: not only sinful pleasures, but also things that fill up our hearts, our thoughts and our time. These are things that keep us from thinking about God and caring about others.

How dull life would be if we couldn't look forward to receiving gifts, or celebrating the wonderful things God has done for us. God wants us to enjoy life and have good things, but He will never give us something that will harm us (Luke 11:11-13).

It isn't wrong to ask God for things we'd really like, but we should patiently wait for Him to answer and be happy with whatever He allows us to have. Then our hearts will be at peace and our faith in Him will grow.

DECEMBER 24

VERSE FOR TODAY

Command those who are rich in this present world not to be arrogant nor to put their hope in wealth, which is so uncertain, but to put their hope in God, who richly provides us with everything for our enjoyment.
1 Timothy 6:17

JOHN

A light to the world

The apostle John (one of the disciples of Jesus) had become an old man. He wrote this letter to the believers while he was in Ephesus:

"Christ was alive from the very beginning, yet I myself have heard Him speak. I have seen Him with my eyes and touched Him with my hands. He is God's message of Life.

When He came to earth, we saw Him and can tell you with certainty that He came down from His Father in heaven.

This is the message we heard from Him: God is light and there is no darkness in Him at all.

If we say that we really know Him but carry on living in spiritual darkness, we are only fooling ourselves. But if we live in the light as He is in the light, we enjoy a wonderful friendship with each other."

How does a bright star remind us of Jesus?

Jesus came as a light to our world, which has been darkened by sin and death. He brought the Good News of God's love; sending out bright beams of hope in a dark, scary world.

The apostle Peter put it this way: "And we have the word of the prophets made more certain, and you will do well to pay attention to it, as to a light shining in a dark place, until the day dawns and the morning star rises in your hearts" (2 Peter 1:19).

As you think about the birth of Jesus and why He came to earth, let the light of His love bring you hope and peace, and let the light of His holiness make you pure.

DECEMBER 25

VERSE FOR TODAY

"I have come into the world as a light, so that no one who believes in me should stay in darkness."
JOHN 12:46

God is love

"This is how God showed His great love for us," John wrote to the believers. "He sent His one and only Son to earth that we might have eternal life through His death."

John continued, "This is love: not the kind of love we have for God, but the love He showed us by sending Jesus to take the punishment for our sin.

God is love. Whoever lives a life of love lives in God and God lives in Him. In this way our love is made perfect and we will not be ashamed when we stand before Him on the day of judgment.

We do not need to fear someone who loves us perfectly, because fear has to do with punishment. A person who is afraid of being punished does not know or understand the love of God."

What does it mean "to fear God"?

How do you feel when you've done something wrong and know you'll be punished for it? How do you feel when someone is angry with you and shouts at you?

Sometimes we feel guilty, and even afraid of God, when we've done something we shouldn't have. Because we feel guilty, it is hard for us to imagine how God would still love us just the same. And because we doubt God's love we become afraid of Him. We may even imagine that God will take something away from us, or make us sick, or punish us in some way.

When the Bible talks about fearing God, it doesn't mean we should be scared of Him, but that we should respect His awesome holiness.

If God sent His only Son to die so that you could be forgiven, why would He punish you if you've asked Him to forgive you?

DECEMBER 26

VERSE FOR TODAY
But the eyes of the Lord are on those who fear him,
on those whose hope is in his unfailing love.
PSALM 33:18

JOHN

"We know ..."

John ends his letter by assuring Christians that they can be certain of their relationship with God.

He wrote: "I am writing this to you who believe in Jesus that you may know that you have eternal life.

We know that we are God's children when we don't want to keep on sinning against Him. For Jesus will keep us from being drawn away by the evil one.

We know that Jesus has come so that we can know the true God. We now live in God and in His Son, Jesus Christ."

How can I know that I am saved?

Have you ever wondered how you can be absolutely sure you will go to heaven? There are many things that can cause you to doubt. It could be something you heard someone say; it could be that you don't feel close to God; or it may be that you keep slipping up and doing wrong.

God doesn't expect to never do anything wrong. When we put our faith in Him, He makes us perfect by the blood of Jesus. We are sinners saved by God's grace. "For it is by grace you have been saved, through faith – it is the gift of God" (Ephesians 2:8).

Feelings cannot affect your salvation. If you have given your life to God by faith, you are born into His family and you will always be His child – even when it doesn't feel like it (John 10:28). During the times when you don't feel close to God, your faith has a chance to grow stronger. Remember to keep reading the Bible, because faith comes by hearing, and hearing by the Word of God (Romans 10:17).

DECEMBER 27

VERSE FOR TODAY
We know that we live in him and he in us,
because he has given us of his Spirit.
1 JOHN 4:13

JOHN

The Glory of the Lord

John wrote this letter to the seven churches in Asia (and to all believers) while he was on the Island of Patmos.

This is what he wrote: "It was Sunday and I was praying and worshiping as the Spirit led me. Suddenly I heard a loud voice behind me saying. 'I am the First and the Last. Write down what you see and send it to the seven churches.'"

When John turned around, he saw seven golden lampstands, and there among them was someone like Jesus. His face was as bright as the midday sun. When John saw Him, he fell down at His feet as though he were dead.

When John had received a message for each of the seven churches, he looked up and before him was a door standing open in heaven. A loud voice said, "Come up here and I will show you what must happen after this."

At once, John was in the spirit and right before him, was a throne with someone sitting on it. His face gleamed with the beautiful colors of precious stones and there was a green glow like a rainbow around the throne.

Will I be able to look into the face of God?

Imagine looking straight into the sun (don't ever do this because you will damage your eyes). Think what it would be like to look at a light that is far brighter than the sun.

In the Old Testament we read that God had to shield His face to hide His glory from Moses, otherwise Moses – being sinful – would have died (Exodus 33:22-23). No one can see the face of God and live. Even John, who was not in his body when he saw Jesus, fell down before Him as dead.

In our new bodies we will be holy and made pure by the blood of Jesus.

DECEMBER 28

VERSE FOR TODAY

But we know that when he appears, we shall
be like him, for we shall see him as he is.

1 JOHN 3:2

JOHN

The Judgment

DECEMBER 29

John wrote down everything God allowed him to see – things in heaven and on earth that would happen at the end of time, when God judges the earth.

John said, "Then I saw God sitting on His great white throne, and everything fled from His presence. I saw those who had died – great and small – standing before the throne. The book of life was opened, and the dead were judged for what they had done."

Will I also be judged?

Are you afraid of standing before God to be judged for every wrong thing you have done? You have nothing to fear if you have asked Jesus to forgive you and let Him be Lord of your life.

God, who is fair and holy, will judge those who have not followed Jesus or listened to Him. Because God is holy He must deal with sin; and those who have not asked Jesus to take their sin away must answer to God for every wrong they have done. The punishment for sin is eternal death. It's a spiritual death far away from the goodness of God.

Christians will be judged too. However, we will be judged for the good we have done – not for our sins. Our judgement is more like a prize giving to test our motives and to reward us for the things we did that brought glory to God (1 Corinthians 3:12-15).

Believers need not fear God's judgement because Jesus has already taken our punishment. What a wonderful God we serve!

VERSE FOR TODAY

For we must all appear before the judgment seat of Christ,
that each one may receive what is due him.
2 CORINTHIANS 5:10

Revelation 21:1-7, 22:3-5

Everything is new

After the final judgment, John saw a new heaven and a new earth. He saw the Holy City coming down from above – prepared and ready – like a bride, ready to meet her husband. Now God will live with His people and be their God. He will wipe away every tear and there will be no more death or sadness, crying or pain. The old things have disappeared!

Then God said, "See, I make all things new. Those who keep on going till the end will have the right to freely drink living water from the spring of Life."

The throne of God and the throne of Jesus the Lamb will be in the city. His servants will worship and serve Him there and His name will be written on their brows.

What will heaven be like?

Do you sometimes wonder what it will be like in heaven one day? It is hard for us to imagine how beautiful heaven is because we can only see and experience things with our physical bodies. What John saw was so wonderful that he couldn't describe it in words. The best he could do was to compare it to things here on earth.

What we do know is that God will make everything new. There will be no bad memories or regrets, and the devil will no longer be able to tempt us or make our lives miserable. There will be no more tears or sadness.

There will be so much to do in Heaven that you won't be bored for a single moment. You won't even need to go to bed because there will be no night. In heaven there will be unimaginable joy as we serve and worship our wonderful God for ever and ever.

DECEMBER 30

VERSE FOR TODAY

"I am going there to prepare a place for you. And if I go and prepare a place for you, I will come back and take you to be with me that you also may be where I am."

John 14:2-3

JOHN

"I am coming soon!"

John ends his letter to the churches with a message of hope and an invitation from Jesus Himself:

"'See, I am coming soon, and I bring My reward with Me to give to everyone according to the deeds he has done. I am the First and the Last, the Beginning and the End.'

The Holy Spirit and the bride of Christ say, 'Come!'

Whoever is thirsty, let him come; and whoever wants, let him drink of the water of life.

He [Jesus] who has said all this, declares: 'Yes, I am coming soon.'

The grace of the Lord Jesus be with you all. Amen."

Can anyone come to Jesus?

Jesus invites all those who are thirsty for Living Water to come to Him. This is the same invitation He gave to the woman at the well (John 4:13). The Living Water is the Holy Spirit (John 7:38-39), whom Jesus gives to everyone who comes to Him.

The invitation is to every single person on earth. That is why Jesus simply said, 'whoever', which is another way of saying, anyone and everyone. It is the same word used in John 3:16. "For God so loved the world that He gave His one and only Son, that whoever believes in Him shall not perish but have eternal life."

Have you asked Jesus to be your Savior?

DECEMBER 31

VERSE FOR TODAY
May the grace of the Lord Jesus Christ, and the love of God, and the fellowship of the Holy Spirit be with you all.
2 CORINTHIANS 13:14

Topical Index

Giving
Mar 11, Jul 4, Sep 2, Oct 11, Oct 12, Oct 15, Nov 8

God leads us
Apr 22, Apr 25, Apr 26, Apr 27, Nov 22, Nov 27

God provides
Jan 25, Feb 29, Mar 1, Apr 17

God's greatness
Feb 19, Mar 5, Mar 22, Apr 23, Jun 16, Nov 4, Dec 15, Dec 28

God's love
May 29, Jun 8, Jun 30, Jul 18, Jul 28, Aug 14, Sep 8, Sep 10, Sep 15, Oct 7, Nov 12, Dec 26

God's plan
Jan 16, Jan 17, Jan 20, Jan 27, Jan 29, Feb 3, Feb 19, Feb 22, Mar 13, Mar 19, Apr 2, Apr 5, Apr 28, May 15, Jul 12, Jul 23, Aug 19, Oct 20, Nov 29

God's power
Jan 11, Apr 3, Apr 12, May 6, May 9, Dec 15

God's presence
Mar 12, Jul 27, Aug 22, Sep 5, Oct 23

God's promises
Jan 15, Jan 22, Feb 14, Mar 23, Nov 25, Dec 14

God's protection
Feb 3, Feb 25, Mar 19, May 9, Jun 28, Jul 26, Jul 27, Aug 8, Dec 11

God's rules
Mar 4, Mar 6, Nov 15, Nov 30

Growing as a Christian
Jun 27, Aug 2, Aug 3, Sep 4, Sep 19

Heaven
Jun 14, Jun 18, Jul 6, Aug 31, Oct 6, Oct 21, Oct 31, Dec 30

Holiness
Feb 18, Mar 3, Mar 7, Mar 9, Jun 6, Jun 26, Jul 6, Nov 30, Dec 5

Holy Spirit
Mar 1, Mar 12, Apr 22, May 2, Jun 16, Jun 19, Jul 2, Jul 29, Sep 11, Oct 28, Nov 1, Nov 2, Nov 5, Nov 7, Nov 27, Dec 8, Dec 9

Honesty
Jan 19, Feb 6, Apr 9, Aug 16, Nov 8

Hope
Jul 11, Aug 15, Aug 26, Sep 1, Dec 25

Jesus
Apr 19, May 3, May 21, May 27, May 29, Jul 13, Jul 14, Aug 23, Aug 27, Aug 29, Aug 30, Aug 31, Sep 3, Sep 4, Sep 29, Sep 30, Oct 13, Oct 16, Oct 24, Oct 25, Oct 26, Oct 27, Dec 25, Dec 30

Judging
Jan 13, Aug 16, Aug 18

Kindness
Jan 26, Feb 2, Feb 12, Feb 16, Mar 18,
Jul 4, Aug 9, Sep 16

Kingdom of God
Sep 17, Oct 5, Oct 9, Oct 13, Dec 19

Knowing God
Jan 2, Jan 3, Jan 8, Mar 5, Apr 21,
Jun 4, Jun 10, Jul 6, Jul 18, Aug 4,
Aug 20, Sep 21, Oct 4, Oct 10, Oct 28

Leaders
Feb 16, Feb 22, Mar 2, Apr 25,
May 3, May 12, May 15, May 18,
May 25, Jun 12, Jul 16, Aug 7,
Aug 13, Oct 17

Living like Jesus
Feb 18, Mar 9, Mar 20, Apr 1, Apr 23,
May 1, May 7, May 12, May 17,
May 26, Jun 17, Jun 19, Jun 29, Jul 9,
Jul 15, Jul 21, Aug 3, Sep 7, Sep 19,
Oct 2, Oct 29, Nov 19, Nov 20,
Dec 12

Loneliness
Jan 21, Apr 6

Loving others
Jan 9, May 20, Jun 20, Jun 22,
Aug 9, Oct 1, Oct 3, Nov 3, Nov 12,
Dec 4, Dec 16

Miracles
Feb 28, Mar 1, Mar 28, Jun 19, Sep 8,
Sep 14, Sep 15, Oct 25, Nov 3, Dec 14

Money and possessions
Jan 19, Feb 10, Jun 2, Jun 13, Sep 27,
Oct 4, Oct 14, Nov 8, Dec 24

Nature
Jan 12, Jan 13, Jan 15, Feb 28, Mar 1,
Mar 16, Mar 28, Sep 5

Obedience
Jan 10, Jan 15, Jan 16, Jan 24, Jan 25,
Feb 9, Feb 20, Feb 21, Mar 4, Mar 6,
Mar 17, Mar 24, May 1, May 28,
May 30, Jul 1, Jul 11, Aug 5,
Sep 6, Oct 14, Dec 6, Dec 10

Peace
Feb 25, Apr 15, May 28, Sep 3,
Sep 18, Sep 25, Dec 25

Prayer
Feb 26, Mar 23, Apr 26, May 31,
Jun 25, Jul 30, Aug 1, Aug 7, Aug 8,
Aug 22, Aug 25, Aug 26, Sep 21,
Oct 8, Nov 6, Nov 13, Dec 24

Punishment
Jan 13, Jan 14, Mar 16, Mar 25, Jul 8,
Jul 22, Aug 21, Dec 26, Dec 29

Sacrifice
Jan 25, Jul 13, Aug 27, Oct 16, Oct 19

Salvation
Feb 17, Feb 23, Feb 24, Feb 29,
Mar 7, Mar 22, Apr 24, May 4,
May 21, May 26, Jun 30, Jul 2,
Jul 8, Jul 13, Jul 14, Aug 24,
Aug 27, Aug 29, Aug 31, Sep 9,
Sep 10, Sep 15, Sep 17, Oct 6,
Oct 16, Oct 19, Oct 21, Oct 22,

Oct 25, Nov 15, Nov 17, Dec 21,
Dec 27, Dec 31

Saying sorry
Feb 1, Apr 14, Apr 27, Jul 7, Jul 28,
Oct 30

Second Coming
Jun 18, Jul 11, Dec 17, Dec 28

Serving God
Jan 24, Jan 30, Feb 5, Feb 8, Feb 9,
Feb 12, Feb 20, Mar 2, Mar 10,
Mar 11, Mar 29, Mar 31, Apr 7,
Apr 11, Apr 14, May 2, May 8,
May 19, Jun 13, Jun 15, Jun 17,
Jun 22, Jun 27, Jul 10, Jul 19, Jul 24,
Aug 5, Aug 11, Aug 15, Sep 7,
Sep 26, Oct 1, Oct 2, Oct 17, Oct 18,
Nov 4, Nov 5, Nov 21, Dec 2

Sickness and health
Jun 8, Jun 24, Jul 24, Sep 13, Sep 15,
Oct 3, Nov 3

Sin
Jan 4, Jan 5, Jan 6, Jan 9, Jan 10,
Jan 14, Jan 17, Jan 23, Jan 28,
Feb 18, Mar 8, Mar 15, Mar 16,
Mar 25, Mar 26, Apr 9, Apr 13,
Apr 24, May 6, May 9, May 16,
May 27, May 28, Jun 7, Jun 26,
Jul 20, Jul 1, Aug 12, Aug 16,
Sep 17, Sep 20, Sep 22, Oct 7,
Oct 17, Nov 8, Dec 6

Solving problems
Jan 20, Jan 31, Feb 7, Mar 24,
Apr 15, Apr 20, May 10, Jun 11,
Jul 12, Nov 23

Trusting God
Jan 18, Feb 8, Feb 20, Feb 21, Feb 28,
Mar 14, Apr 4, Apr 26, Apr 29, May 8,
May 13, May 25, Jun 11, Jun 23,
Aug 6, Sep 1, Sep 14, Dec 7

Wisdom
Jun 1, Jun 3, Jun 4, Jun 5

Witnessing
Jan 23, Jan 26, Feb 20, Mar 21,
Mar 30, Jun 29, Jul 10, Jul 30, Aug 1,
Sep 7, Oct 5, Oct 10, Nov 9, Nov 10,
Nov 11, Nov 14, Nov 18, Nov 24

Work
Jan 30, Feb 5, Apr 17, May 19,
May 30, Aug 4, Aug 10, Dec 18

Worship
Jan 8, Feb 27, Mar 3, Mar 7, Mar 12,
Apr 29, May 5, May 23, Jul 5, Jul 19,
Jul 25, Aug 3, Aug 17, Aug 28,
Sep 12, Oct 8, Oct 11, Nov 4, Nov 23,
Dec 1, Dec 19

You are special
Jan 1, Feb 4, Feb 9, Feb 15, Mar 10,
Mar 31, Oct 9, Nov 12, Dec 19